Teaching Creativity – Creativity in Teaching

Teaching Creativity – Creativity in Teaching

First published in 2010 by Libri Publishing

Copyright © Libri Publishing

ISBN 978 1 907471 17 9

Authors retain copyright of individual chapters.

The right of Claus Nygaard, Nigel Courtney and Clive Holtham to be identified as the editors of this work has been asserted in accordance with the Copyright, Designs and Patents Act, 1988.

A CIP catalogue record for this book is available from The British Library

Cover design by Helen Taylor

Design by Carnegie Publishing

Printed in the UK by Short Run Press Ltd

Libri Publishing
Brunel House
Volunteer Way
Faringdon
Oxfordshire
SN7 7YR

Tel: +44 (0)845 873 3837

www.libripublishing.co.uk

Contents

About the Editors

Claus Nygaard is Professor in Management Education and Director of Research at CBS Learning Lab, Copenhagen Business School, Denmark. Originally trained in business economics and administration, where he holds a PhD, he first became Associate Professor in Economic Sociology at Department of Organization and Copenhagen Business School. In 2000 he changed position to CBS Learning Lab, and began to work with Quality Enhancement of Higher Education. He was a driving force behind the formulation and implementation of the "Learning Strategy" for Copenhagen Business School in 2005. He has received distinguished research awards from Allied Academies, outstanding paper awards from Students in Free Enterprise, and he was voted "best teacher" at Copenhagen Business School in 2001. His research has resulted in several anthologies, and he has published in leading journals such as *Higher Education, International Studies of Management & Organization, International Journal of Public Sector Management*, and *Assessment & Evaluation in Higher Education*.

Clive Holtham is Professor of Information Management and Director of the Learning Laboratory at Cass Business School, London, UK. After taking a Masters degree in management, he trained as an accountant and was Young Accountant of the Year in 1976. Following six years as a Director of Finance and IT, he moved to the Business School in 1988. His research is into the strategic exploitation of information systems, knowledge management and management learning. He has been an adviser to the European Parliament on educational technology, and led a major EU project on measurement and reporting of intangibles as well as the highly rated QuBE project into quality enhancement in business schools. In 2003 he was awarded a UK National Teaching Fellowship, and is a board member of the Non-Profit E-learning Network (2008–2011), a major initiative to promote management education through informal online learning. He is author of a large number of publications, and lectures, broadcasts and consults in the UK and internationally. He was a founding member of the Worshipful Company of Information Technologists, the City of London's 100th livery company.

Nigel Courtney is an Honorary Senior Visiting Fellow at Cass Business School, City University London, UK, where he took the MBA and gained his PhD. He is a chartered engineer, a certified management consultant and a certified IT professional, with extensive experience in project and general management. His firm, Courtney Consulting, has served the European Commission, Transport for London, London Underground, the Higher Education Academy and the National Endowment for Science, Technology and the Arts. At Cass he teaches Business Information Management on the Executive MBA. He manages a longitudinal research project by a six university consortium on quality in business education (qube.ac.uk) and has been a Visiting Research Fellow at the Australian Graduate School of Management, Sydney. His research interests include innovation in management education, support for part-time teachers, and the effective use of teaching room technologies.

Claus and Clive are the founders of LIHE, an international academic association for the enhancement of Learning in Higher Education. http://www.lihe. wordpress.com

Foreword

The world needs people who can combine and integrate their knowledge, skills and capabilities in creative and adventurous ways to work with complexity, create wealth and prosperity and enrich enterprises, societies and cultures. The problem with higher education is that it pays far too little attention to students' creative development: individual creativity is taken for granted and subsumed within the traditional cognitive skills that are valued. Creativity as an outcome of higher education, at least in the UK, is often more by accident then design. All too often our curricular designs and assessment requirements at best ignore and at worse inhibit students' creative development and self-expression. Higher education is full of creative people yet our ability to design a curriculum that nurtures students' creative spirit and development seems to be hindered by a paradigm that stifles our imagination. In the spirit of trying to create a new perspective I recently offered a series of propositions for a curriculum that offered more affordances for students' creative development (Jackson, 2010).

I argue that education that is dominated by the mastery of content and cognitive performance in abstract situations – a necessary part of the development of specialist knowledge and critical thinking/problem solving capacities – is not enough for a world that is becoming increasingly complex. To prepare students for the complexities of their lives we need to pay much more attention to the development of their capability for dealing with real world situations:

capability that includes their creativity. Stephen Covey's (2004:4) expression of human agency is both relevant and inspiring: *"Between stimulus and response there is a space. In the space lies our freedom and power to choose our response. In those choices lie our growth and our happiness"*.

This freedom to choose space is rich in affordances. It represents the decision space at the heart of every situation we participate in – the fundamental building block of daily life. But it also represents the decision space that relates to who we are and who we want to become. Both concepts are relevant and central to our individual creativity.

Our will to be creative usually stems from a deep intrinsic motivation inspired by the personal choices we are able to make in our life. We talk a lot about student-centred learning but if we respected the learner as the designer of their own life experience, which includes higher education as part of that experience, we would have more chance of embracing, supporting and recognising their capability to deal with real world situations and the creative acts embodied in such capability.

My proposition is that we can move towards this situation by honouring students' creative spirit and encouraging them to fulfil their creative potential for dealing with situations in the real world by adopting and practising a lifewide concept of higher education. *"The desire to do something because you find it deeply satisfying and personally challenging inspires the highest levels of creativity, whether it's in the arts, sciences or business"* (Amabile, 2008:3).

On Teaching Creativity

John Dewey, whom I admire greatly, is reputed to have said: *"I believe that education… is a process of living and not a preparation for future living"*. My thesis is that it is both of these things.

"If the purpose of higher education is to help students develop their potential as fully as possible, then enabling students to develop and use their creative potential, should be an explicit and valued part of their higher education experience. This is clearly not the case" (Jackson, 2008). I wrote this in 2008 at the start of a paper which framed the development of students' creativity in higher education as part of the wicked problem (Rittel & Webber, 1973) of how we prepare students for a lifetime of working, learning and living in uncertain and unpredictable worlds.

Wicked problems emerge from the technical, informational, social, economic, political and cultural complexity that we are immersed in. The 'Credit Crunch' and ensuing recession is a good example. Such problems cannot be solved through rational, linear thinking because the problem definition and our understanding of it evolve as new possible solutions are invented and implemented. We are trying to prepare students for jobs that don't yet exist (or in the current recession that no longer exist!), using technologies that have not yet been invented, in order to solve problems that we don't know are problems yet. It may sound dramatic but the reality is that the majority of our students will have many careers, they will have to change organisations, roles and identities many times and be part of new organisations that they help to create or existing organisations that they help to transform. Many will have to invent their own ways of earning an income and or create and juggle a portfolio of jobs requiring them to maintain several identities simultaneously.

Jackson & Shaw (2006) reveal that academics associate a number of features with creativity regardless of disciplinary, pedagogic, problem or work context. For example:

+ Being imaginative – generating new ideas, thinking out of the boxes we normally inhabit, looking beyond the obvious, seeing the world in different ways so that it can be explored and understood better.

+ Being original. This embodies: a) the quality of newness for example: inventing and producing new things or doing things no one has done before, b) being inventive with someone else's ideas – recreation, reconstruction, re-contextualization, redefinition, adapting things that have been done before, doing things that have been done before but differently, and c) the idea of significance and value – there are different levels and notions of significance and utility and value are integral to the idea.

+ Being curious with an enquiring disposition – willing to explore, experiment and take risks. i.e. the attitude and motivation to engage in exploration and the ability to search purposefully in appropriate ways in order to find and discover. It is necessary to work in an uncertain world and often requires people to move from the known to the unknown.

+ Being resourceful – using your knowledge, capability, relationships, powers to persuade and influence, and physical resources to overcome whatever challenge or problems are encountered and to exploit opportunities as they arise.

+ Being able to combine, connect, and synthesise complex and incomplete data/situations/ideas/contexts in order to see the world freshly/differently to understand it better.

* Being able to think critically and analytically in order to distinguish useful ideas from those that are not so useful and make good decisions.

* Being able to take value from feedback and use it constructively to improve ideas.

* Being able to represent ideas and communicate them to others – the capacity to create and tell stories, pitch and sell ideas, empathise with others and show people possibilities, opportunities and solutions in ways that make sense to them or capture their imagination.

There seems to be wide acceptance within higher education communities, validated by the many times I have invited audiences to comment on their appropriateness, that these characteristics are generally applicable to most educational contexts.

One of the difficulties we have with the idea of creativity is that we need some way of discriminating between the levels of effects of creativity. We might represent this in a simple way using the ideas of newness/novelty and significance in terms of scale of effect. I believe creativity is an integral part of an individual's will and capability to influence the situations which they encounter or create. For the most part we are dealing with the creative thoughts and acts that affect an individual's immediate zone of influence – the people and situations they personally interact with. We all do this every day but some people are more accomplished than others at doing it. More rarely, we witness creative acts that bring about change in networks of relationships, organisations and fields beyond the individual's immediate zone of influence. In exceptional cases individuals, through their will and agency that includes their creativity, manage to change the world. Education should be about inspiring people to influence and shape the world around them and creativity is a necessary part of an individual's capability to do so.

If we want to support the development of learners as thinkers who can integrate their analytical and creative thinking and action then we need to understand the epistemology that connects learning and practice (using the idea that practice is about people working on purposeful activity to achieve their goals regardless of whether they are working for a degree or working to earn an income).

The main problem with preparing learners for the complexities of the world ahead is that higher education seems to take such a narrow view of what learning and knowledge are. Higher education is pre-occupied with codified knowledge and with its utilisation by learners in abstract hypothetical problem solving. This is not to say that handling complex information in this way is not useful – far from it: it is an essential process for enabling students to learn how to think about and work with complexity.

We are all immersed sequentially and simultaneously in a continuous flow of situations, many of which are connected through the intention or will to achieve a goal that is meaningful and worthwhile to us.

Being able to engage with a situation and then follow through with appropriate actions requires capability, defined by Michael Eraut (2009:6) in terms of *"what individual persons bring to situations that enables them to think, interact and perform"* and *"...it is everything that a person (or group or organisation) can think or do"*. In his research into how professionals learn through work, Eraut identified over 50 dimensions of professional capability which he called learning trajectories. At any point in time professionals are either developing or regressing within a particular trajectory or related group of trajectories depending on the opportunities and experiences they are gaining through their work. This is an important point: we cannot improve our capability for the modern world unless we develop the capability and willingness to learn and keep on learning as our needs and interests demand. Underpinning the idea of learning for a complex world is this capacity and wilfulness to develop ourselves to fulfil the multiplicity of roles and identities we assume in life.

Although creativity is part of our capability to deal with situations we may not be conscious of how it contributes in a particular situation. This is why we often have difficulty in recognising our own creativity – because it is totally integrated into our overall capability.

Richard Greene (2004) provides the most comprehensive view of how creativity might operate within a model of personal capability. His paper 32 Capabilities of Highly Effective People in Any Field shows the complex way in which creativity might manifest itself in the thinking, feelings, actions, behaviours and personal missions of highly effective people (and presumably to lesser extents in people who are less effective). It is instructive to see the rich constructions he creates to represent capability which are so much more powerful in communicating acts of significant change than for example Michael Eraut's learning trajectories.

The complexity of creativity is a confounding issue for teachers who are often deeply perplexed by the whole idea of developing practice to support students' creative development. What exactly is it that they are trying to develop? Most would not argue with the complex capabilities of highly effective people proposed by Greene, but would quite rightly question whether higher education alone could develop such capability. The fact that higher education alone cannot develop such capability then becomes an excuse for not trying.

The individual leaner (you, me, our students, friends and family and everyone else) lies at the heart of the *learning for a complex world* metaphor that has inspired our work at the University of Surrey, and central to this idea is our will to make a difference. Through our will we live the person we want to be and become. I agree with Ron Barnett (2005:15) when he says that *"Will is the most important concept in education. Without the will nothing is possible".* We cannot achieve anything of significance. We cannot make decisions about a situation we find ourselves in, we cannot act in ways that are ethical and appropriate to the situation, we cannot learn how to deal with the situation or learn from the experience and we cannot strive to be creative, without the will to do so.

On a Curriculum for Creativity

A fundamental question for higher education curriculum designers is what forms of experience nurture the spirit that will enable learners to become who they want to become and provide the affordances necessary for them to develop their creativity, as an integral part of their overall capability for a modern world. In a recent paper (Jackson, 2010), I argued for a lifewide concept of higher education and set out a number of propositions that could be fulfilled by such a paradigm.

Firstly, if learners are to motivate themselves to be creative we have to adopt a concept of curriculum that nurtures their spirit and their will to be and become a better more developed person and to create new value in the world around them. Allied to this they must have the freedom to make choices so that they can find deeply satisfying and personally challenging situations that inspire and require their creativity.

Secondly, if we are to prepare learners for the complexities they will undoubtedly encounter in their future lives we must create a curriculum that inspires and enables them to experience and appreciate knowledge and knowing in all its forms and appreciate themselves as knower, maker, player, narrator and enquirer.

Thirdly, we have to enable learners to appreciate the significance of being able to deal with and create situations and develop their capability to deal effectively with situations. Situations are the point at which an individual's creative thinking and their capability to turn new and novel ideas into action and reality are applied. To facilitate students' creative development we therefore need a curriculum that encourages them to create new situations individually and with others, by connecting people and transferring, adapting and integrating ideas, resources and opportunities, in an imaginative, wilful and productive way, to create new value in the world around them.

Such a curriculum must also prepare them for and give them experiences of venturing into uncertain and unfamiliar situations. It must enable them to encounter and learn to deal with situations that do not always result in success and which require resilience and persistence to overcome difficulties and meet the challenge. Within such a curriculum learners should not be penalised for 'mistakes' and the lack of an immediately successful outcome should not be seen as a failure to achieve. Rather, the process of taking risks and trying to achieve in such uncertain and difficult circumstances should be seen as a successful achievement.

A curriculum that would facilitate students' creative development for the modern world would enable them to develop the communication skills and literacies that are necessary to be an effective learner and communicator. Such a curriculum should encourage participation in the social communities that are created around some forms of new media, because knowledge and capability to learn resides in these distributed social structures.

Grappling with complex changing situations requires us to provide students with the conceptual tools to help them think about and understand change and the experiences of dealing with change as they participate in evolving situations over time. A world that requires you to participate in continuous change and to contribute to change must also engender a commitment to personal and cooperative learning. It must promote the continuing development of capability for the demands of any situation and the more strategic development of capability for future learning.

My belief is that a curriculum that is only based on learning within an institutional environment will not prepare learners adequately for the complexity they will encounter. Only a curriculum that also incorporates the opportunity and support to learn from experiencing the world both inside and outside the institutional environment can achieve this goal. Many universities in the UK recognise this (Rickett, 2010) and have developed, or are in the process of developing schemes to value students' informal learning.

But How Can We Turn these Ideas into Reality?

It is one thing to have a creative thought, quite another to bring new educational practices into existence in an environment that is, at best, ambivalent to anything that challenges the status quo.

Our studies of learners at the University of Surrey have encouraged us to see the spaces which students occupy outside the academic curriculum as providing rich opportunities for learning and personal development. Ron Barnett's study (Barnett, 2010) demonstrated that:

- a student's learning often takes place in a number of sites [not just their academic programme]

- a student's formal course of study may constitute a minority of the learning experiences undergone by a student while he or she is registered for that course of study. (In some courses in the humanities and social sciences, after all, 'contact time' may amount to less that ten hours per week)

- much of the learning that a student achieves while at university is currently unaccredited, and involves unaccredited learning that is both within the course of study and unaccredited learning that is outside the course of study (either on or off campus)

- much of the student's learning is personally stretching, whether it is on or off campus, and whether it is part of a formal course of study or not; it may involve situations quite different from anything hitherto experienced (across social class, ethnicity, language, nation, and other forms of social, cultural and economic differentiation)

- much of the student's experiences outside the course of study is highly demanding, and may involve high degrees of responsibility (perhaps for others).

It seems self evident that we are who we are because of the way we have lived our lives and the way we currently live our lives and what and how we learn through our experiences holds the potential to become who we want or need to be. Lifewide learning (Jackson, 2008, 2010) embraces the many sites for being and learning that occur in a learner's life at any point in time. The concept adds value to the well established idea of life-long learning which captures the continuous set of patterns of learning that emerge from personal needs, aspirations, interests and circumstances throughout an individual's life. Lifewide education (Barnett, 2010) is given meaning and material substance through the intentional designs and actions of an institution or educational provider which seeks to encourage, support, recognize and value learning from all parts of a learner's life.

When designing higher educational experiences we typically begin with provider defined purposes and the outcomes, create a design often around the content, encourage learning through prescribed teaching and learning activities, provide some supporting resources (usually text based) and assess learning against strict criteria that reflect the answers we expect. There is no room for outcomes that are not anticipated or outcomes that learners individually recognise as being valuable to them.

But what if we were to begin with the learner and their life, and see the learner as the designer of an integrated meaningful life experience? An experience that incorporates formal education as one component of a much richer set of experiences that embrace all the forms of learning and achievement that are necessary to sustain a meaningful life. Integration suggests the bringing together of separate entities to make a new and more connected whole. We see study, work and play as separate activities because that is the way our culture sees them. But these experiences are integrated into our life along with all the learning that flows from them and we develop as individuals through the unique combination of experiences that compose our lives.

Working backwards from the learner and their life perspective, I proposed the idea of a lifewide curriculum (Jackson, 2008) to address some of the deficiencies of the traditional higher education curriculum, in respect of its ability to nurture students' creative development and spirit. "A lifewide curriculum honours informal/accidental/by-product learning in learner determined situations as well as formal learning in teacher determined situations. It embraces learning in the physical/emotional social spaces that characterise the work/practice environment and it honours formal and informal learning in all other environments that learners chose to be in because of their interests passions and needs. Because of this a lifewide curriculum is likely to provide a better framework for encouraging, supporting, recognising and valuing learners' creativity and self-expression, than a curriculum that is solely based on academic or academic and professional practice experiences".

A lifewide curriculum could facilitate students' creative development in three ways. Firstly in the forms that are necessary to be successful and innovative in the academic disciplinary or interdisciplinary domain. This includes disciplines that are traditionally considered to be creative (e.g. linked to Creative Arts or Design) and those that are not considered to have a creative basis. Secondly in the forms that are necessary to be successful and innovative in any professional/work domain. This includes work enterprises that are traditionally considered to be creative (e.g. linked to Creative Arts or Design) and those that are not considered to have a creative basis. And thirdly in the forms of self-expression that learners chose for themselves in their lives outside the academic and practice curriculum. This domain is particularly rich in affordances and possibility spaces and it is this domain in which it is currently most difficult to honour and recognise learning and creative enterprise.

Since 2008 we have tried at Surrey to turn these ideas and beliefs into new educational practices. The concrete expression of a lifewide curriculum translates into a curriculum map containing three different curricular domains all of which have the potential (should the learner wish) to be integrated into a learner's personalised higher education experience and be valued and recognized: 1) academic curriculum which may by design integrate real world work or community-based experiences, 2) co-curriculum – designed experiences that lie outside the credit-bearing programme which may or may not receive formal recognition for learning, 3) extra-curricular experiences that are determined by the learners themselves.

Progress has been slow in realising our educational vision but in May 2010 we began piloting a Lifewide Learning Award which gives recognition for learning and achievements gained by students in the co- and extra-curricular spaces they choose to live in. It's early days yet but the first accounts of learning to emerge seem to vindicate our beliefs.

I know I am fortunate to have the opportunity and freedom to make choices and create satisfying situations that inspire and require my creativity. Writing as a process involving lots of connected situations is an important part of my life. My capability for doing it involves many things amongst them my creativity for finding things out, seeing connections, creating deeper meanings, making more sense of things that did not make sense to me before, and expressing ideas in words and pictures that convey my ideas and understanding to others in a meaningful way. I know that there is a lot of stuff that is not creative and I find it hard to put my finger on anything that others would think was creative, but somehow the whole comes together in a highly emergent and magical way. The process certainly nurtures my will to try to create new value in the world around me.

Looking back to what I wrote in the final paragraph of my 2008 paper I feel that we are witnessing, with the widespread introduction in the UK of co-curricular and extra-curricular awards, the first step towards a lifewide concept of education through which the aspiration of a higher education system that is more valuing of students' creative development, can be realised. *"Being creative is a matter of choice, a matter of opportunity (often self-created) and a matter of knowing how to be creative in a given situation, or having the confidence to try and learn through the experience of trying. If we want learners to be creative we have to foster their will to be creative and help them develop the confidence, knowledge and capabilities to be creative. Imagine inventing an education system that has [this] as its core value and purpose"* (Jackson, 2008).

This anthology accelerates us significantly closer to the achievement of the goals I espouse. The authors offer a wide range of perspectives from many parts of the world and the editors have done well to ensure that the collection flows and the contributions are integrated and cross-refer. I appreciate greatly the invitation to contribute to this anthology and I commend this book as an important contribution to better understanding of the teaching of creativity and of creativity in teaching and higher education learning.

Norman Jackson, July 2010

About the Author

Norman Jackson is Professor of Higher Education and Director of the University of Surrey Centre for Excellence in Professional Training and Education (SCEPTrE), University of Surrey, England. He can be contacted at this e-mail: norman.jackson@surrey.ac.uk

Chapter One

Creativity – a Review

Claus Nygaard, Nigel Courtney
and Clive Holtham

Why Creativity?

This book presents contemporary research and practice on creativity in higher education. It is collaboratively written by a group of international researchers and practitioners within higher education, who have dealt professionally with creativity in their research and/or educational practice. Stemming from the title of the book *Teaching Creativity – Creativity in Teaching*, two questions are prominent: firstly, "how is creativity taught?" and secondly, "what is creative teaching?" These questions are related in the sense that students' development of creative capacities may stem from creativity in teaching.

To us, there are at least three obvious reasons for writing about creativity in higher education. First of all, following the gradual industrial restructuring of the last thirty years students are graduating into workplaces where creativity has become a key component. Empirical studies of industrial organisation show a large variety in modes of organising and operating within different industries and markets (Kristensen, 1997; Kristensen & Zeitlin 2001; Lane, 1997; Morgan, 1997; Lilja, 1997; Whitley, 1994, 2001). Within the public sector, the doctrine of new public management is reported to change the organisational principles and behaviour too (Laurell & Arellano, 1996; Ahmad & Broussine, 2003; Helgøy & Homme, 2006; Eckel, 2007) as the public sector has become more market driven (Rusaw, 2007). No standard operating procedures will lead to success within the private or public sectors. As such it is the capacity of the workforce to use a variety of modes of organising that leads to competitive advantage of organisations today. In the words of Florida (2005), flexibility, innovation and creativity are highly needed skills. Gibbons *et al.* (2004) expresses a requirement for socially robust knowledge, called "mode 2 knowledge", as a consequence of globalisation, innovation and social change. Mode 2 knowledge is characterised by five aspects: 1) it is generated within a context of application; 2) it is transdisciplinary; 3) it is heterogeneous; 4) it is highly reflexive; and 5) it leads to the emergence of novel forms of quality control. One can argue that creativity is an important component of generating sustainable mode 2 knowledge. Pink (2005:1–2), in a similar vein, writes about the move from the information age to the conceptual age: *"We are moving from an economy and society built on the logical, linear, computerlike capabilities of the Information Age to an economy and a society built on the inventive, empathic, big-picture capabilities of what's rising in its place, the Conceptual Age".* Together this calls for creative capacities in future university graduates.

Secondly, it seems obvious that these changes towards new forms of competition put pressure on higher education institutions, as they are forced to move from a situation with fixed curricula based on deep specialist knowledge to flexible curricula based on transformative learning between different domains. The society at large is not divided into academic disciplines but is indeed multidisciplinary. The demand for flexibility and creativity calls for the development of curricula which use a wide range of disciplines and learning methods. Crucial for graduates are their preparedness to self-produce, self-develop and further contextualise their knowledge (Bennett, 2002; Nygaard & Andersen, 2005; Nygaard *et al.*, 2008). It is crucial, we should argue, for the success of higher education that students learn to learn and further develop transformative skills (Ball, 1986; Bridges, 1993; Harvey & Knight, 1996). Such indeed requires the development of curricula that not only enable students to develop higher-order thinking skills (analyses, synthesis, and reflection) (Lewis & Smith, 1993), but also enable their development of creative capacities that helps them facilitate future challenges and tasks in the job market in alternative ways.

Third, studying general approaches to curriculum development as well as teaching practices in higher education we find that there is a need to inspire key decision makers to move to a learning-centred curriculum (Nygaard & Holtham, 2008) with a strong focus on students' learning outcomes (Nygaard et al., 2009). It seems to us that there is a too long tradition of syllabus-driven didactic teaching (Nygaard et al., 2008), generating a culture of compliance at universities rather than a culture of imaginative co-creation of knowledge between staff and students, and within groups of fellow students. By focusing on teaching creativity and creativity in teaching we hope to inspire changes in this.

A Review of the Debate

With the need for creativity, an obvious question becomes: *"what is creativity"?* There are many definitions of creativity and to choose just one does little justice to the field, or to the different chapters in this volume. Instead, let us take a quick look at the broader research. As a phenomenon, creativity has been researched and defined mainly at three different levels: 1) individual creativity; 2) team creativity; 3) organisational creativity. Let us briefly touch upon these types of creativity and discuss how they relate to higher education.

Individual Creativity

Within broader educational literature since the 1950s, the explicit link to individual creativity originated within the fields of music education (Melby, 1952; Schmidt, 1955; Gray, 1960; Canfield, 1961; Joio et al., 1968) and art education (Bugart, 1961; Raleigh, 1966; Covington, 1967; Russell, 1979, 1981). It has continuously appeared as a phenomenon within these fields (Dineen et al., 2005; Livingston, 2010), and has spread to other fields such as engineering education (Court, 1998; Cropley & Cropley, 2000; Lewis, 2004) and ITC-based education (Clements, 1995; Wheeler et al., 2002).

Early on, creativity was linked to divergent thinking and presented as a fruitful alternative to deductive and convergent thinking. Guilford (1959) emphasised the importance of individual divergent thinking: *"...most investigations have used measures of divergent thinking which have one dimension in common: the ability to produce multiple, unique responses to a single stimulus. Many authors have noted the significance of such ability in creative production and have pointed out the failure of traditional intelligence tests to assess this ability. Indeed, traditional IQ tests appear to concentrate upon the measurement of a convergent thinking: the ability to select a single correct response from a series of alternatives or to deduce it from multiple stimuli"* (cf. Raleigh, 1966:16).

Creativity guru Kao (1996) is clear in linking creativity to knowledge-creation processes, when he argues that creativity is the crucial variable in turning knowledge into value. Perkins (1999:348) on the other hand links creativity to product, writing about creativity: *"By definition, creativity involves producing something that is unexpected but works. If the something were expected, it would not count as creative, and neither would it if it were unexpected but did not work".* Generally speaking creativity may be linked to both process and product, and both perspectives are present in the chapters of this volume. For us a creative process may or may not lead to a creative product, and vice versa.

Creativity has been perceived as personal trait (Stein, 1984; Amabile, 1988; Barron, 1988) and studies of individual creativity (Kirton, 1989; Ford, 1996; Oldham & Cummings, 1996) suggest that individual behavioural preferences account for innovative practices. Ford (1996), in his theory of creative individual action, points at three personal characteristics leading to creativity: sense making, motivation, and knowledge and ability. The argument is that they drive behaviour from convergence to divergence. In that respect creativity is about promoting freedom of thought rather than order (Lewis, 2004). Baltzer (1988) presents six items which are considered components of individual creativity: fluency, flexibility, originality, elaboration, imagination, and independence of thought.

If students need to develop creative capacities, individual creativity is an important concept for teachers, because its conceptualisation has consequences for the way in which we develop curricula in higher education. Can a traditional syllabus-driven didactic lecture help nurture the just mentioned components of individual creativity in students? We seriously doubt so.

Team Creativity

Faced with the challenges of mode 2 knowledge in the Conceptual Age, it is our belief that students in their future careers will work closely together with colleagues in their innovative problem solving activities using new forms of communication and social interaction. Therefore, team creativity becomes important. Studies show different ways to enhance team creativity (Mohrman *et al.*, 1995; Paulus, 2000; Rickards & Moger, 2000). The underlying premise is that teamwork is an important basis for increasing innovation within the workplace. Gino *et al.* (2010:103) studied the role of task experience on team creativity, and found that direct task experience leads to more team creativity and the development of more divergent products. *"By gaining firsthand experience, teams can better understand the task requirements, learn from their mistakes and learn to better coordinate their activities. Direct experience with the task allows individuals to develop a transactive memory system. Further, transactive memory systems transfer from one task to a related one".* If we suppose this positive effect of direct task experience on team creativity and product development, it puts requirements on higher education to develop curricula in which students get more direct task experience, for example through problem oriented project work (Meier & Nygaard, 2008) or problem based learning (Chehore & Scholtz, 2008), where the role of the teacher shifts from a traditional lecturer to an integration of roles as facilitator, coordinator, supervisor and evaluator (Nygaard & Bramming, 2008).

Yang & Chen (2010:216) studied the role of various kinds of embeddedness for the creativity of teams of students working with information system projects, and found that structural embeddedness (teams with many members frequently interacting) had a positive effect on team creativity. *"Students learn the concept of web 2.0 and develop the solutions of project task based on their own knowledge and life experiences. Thus, a project with many members can have rich ideas and suggestions for project problems because of member heterogeneity".* On the other hand they found that positional embeddedness (teams with important members with high centrality) had a negative effect on team creativity. It tells us that hierarchical positions and power relations does not necessarily lead to team creativity. In relation to curriculum development it calls for an egalitarian structure in which students (team members) can freely interact and support each other in their learning processes facilitated by teachers and supervisors.

In another study, Choi & Thompson (2005) compared the creativity of groups that experienced a change in their membership across tasks with groups whose membership was invariant across tasks. They found that more different kinds of ideas were generated in open groups, and that it was the productivity of newcomers that exerted a positive impact on groups and furthermore increased the creativity of oldtimers. In relation to higher education, their study can inspire us in the ways in which we form study groups and have them work together.

Fostering team creativity is in itself a challenge, and Burningham & West (1995) looked at ways in which broader contextual aspects influences team creativity, arriving at the conclusion that creation of innovative teams requires more than aggregating creative individuals. The same argument is presented for organisational creativity as concept. An aspect of importance in relation to team creativity is a culture nurturing collaboration, and tasks of the team that generate intrinsic motivation, the kind of motivation that develops when personal identity, team roles and task at hand are integrated in a way that makes sense to the individual and the team.

Organisational Creativity

According to Woodman *et al.* (1993:293) *"Organizational creativity is the creation of a valuable, useful new product, service, idea, procedure, or process by individuals working together in a complex social system".* It becomes obvious that organisational creativity as concept is an aggregate of creative individuals engaged in teamwork within organisations (complex social systems). In that respect, the underlying thought about individual creativity is not different, but adding the organisational context introduces the role of organisation structure, organisation culture, power relations within organisations, resource allocation procedures, management style, and the like for creative behaviour within organisations. In relation to organisational creativity within education institutions, cultural aspects leading to organisational identity and social collectivity are important. Yamamoto (1975) argued that creativity in the faculty requires more than a collection of solo performers. In his account of how to turn schools into learning organisations, Coppieters (2005:134) argues for the presence of several key components: *"...shared insights or vision; learning based on experience; willingness to change mental models; individual and group motivation; team learning; learning nurtured by new information; increasing the learning capacity to reach a state of continuous change or transformation".* Going all the way back to Leavitt (1962) he argued that an egalitarian organisational structure influences flexibility and creativity in dealing with novel problems. It was also argued that organisational planning and coordination are necessary for the development of both imaginative teachers and learners. So organisational creativity can be argued to stem from a culture of inclusion and change.

For university staff such knowledge of aspects fostering organisational creativity is important as it reminds us that the development of students' creativity and improvement of students' learning outcomes do not come from curriculum development only. Creating an institutional culture with a positive environment for creative thinking, flexible organisational structures, cross-departmental and cross-faculty activities between staff and students becomes key in enhancing organisational creativity. Extra-curricular activities and schemes for students' being involved in research collaboration with faculty members are other activities possibly enhancing organisational creativity.

A Tentative Summary

Having looked at individual, team, and organisational creativity respectively it is clear that they rest on the same foundations of psychological research seeing human beings as intrinsically creative. Roberts (2003:12) puts it this way: *"Creativity involves a person's ability to use imagination or inventiveness to bring something into existence... As a reminder for yourself, believe that students can be creative and they will be creative"*. We believe, however, that universities need to work explicitly with fostering creativity on all levels (individual, team, and organisation). It is not enough to bring exercises for individual creativity into the classroom with one teacher, if the ways in which students form groups and engage in teamwork is governed by methods that are counterproductive for creativity. Meanwhile the university as organisation needs to be open for new ideas from students, being capable of changing curricula according to the creative development of study practices. Such aspects can be related to both teaching creativity and creativity in teaching. In the final part of this chapter, we shall take a closer look at the ways in which the different chapters of this volume contributes to either teaching creativity or creativity in teaching.

Teaching Creativity

The first aspect of creativity in higher education we are dealing with is teaching creativity, which is the fostering of students' creative capacities. In relation to teaching, Derell (1963:69) proposed a warning: *"If teachers are to be creative and foster creativity, they should not draw a road map. One may show methods of determining direction, or may acquaint students with vehicles, or point out conditions that may be faced along the way, but you dare not limit the child by prescribing a route for him in detail"*. Teaching creativity is about developing a curriculum for guidance and inspiration, not about a fixed syllabus. More recently, Csikszentmihalyi (1996:1–2) offered a more upbeat viewpoint: *"...creativity is a central source of meaning in our lives ... most of the things that are interesting, important, and human are the results of creativity... when we are involved in it, we feel that we are living more fully than during the rest of life"*.

Davis (1967:162) mentioned seven general approaches to teaching creative thinking in the classroom:

1. providing a creative atmosphere

2. stimulating thinking

3. encouraging original thinking

4. using the discovery method of thinking and learning

5. changing curricula in the direction of more creative coursework

6. teaching problem solving methods

7. teaching systematic methods for generating new and creative combinations of ideas.

These ideas reach back more than forty years, but are still needed in the development of curricula for teaching creativity, should we believe Livingston (2010:59–60): "*To establish a new experiential paradigm centered on cultivating creativity requires nothing less than an institutional intervention. As long as we cleave only to traditional pedagogies and courses of study and leave little or no room for new experiences, we will not find the time or space necessary for nurturing the act of creativity... we must be willing to honor and live up to the priority of the university as an institution about learning, not teaching*".

There are several key themes about the teaching of creativity, which tend to arise in the teaching of any disciplinary area. The first is that there is some tension between teaching and learning creativity. It is certainly possible for creativity to be learnt, but it can be challenged whether this demands explicit 'teaching', as opposed to creating a climate where student creativity can emerge. In this emergent approach, the academic is much more of a coach or mentor than a traditional teacher. Secondly, much of the everyday thinking about creativity tends to emphasise its divergent dimension, for example in the use of brainstorming. But a creative problem solving process requires both divergent and convergent thinking, and this needs to be taken account of in designing educational processes. Thirdly, a great deal of thought needs to go into designing assessment methods which support the learning of creativity. Assessment methods which have primarily been designed for auditing how far students have accumulated subject matter knowledge are unlikely satisfactorily to underpin the learning of creativity. Finally, it does have to be recognised that some academic disciplines much more explicitly recognise the importance of creativity as a key learning process. Examples include all the fine arts, design, music and creative writing. And architecture and engineering also tend explicitly to value creative problem solving. Other academic disciplines which are only more recently formally addressing the issue of creativity can clearly accelerate their own learning curve by referring to experiences in the classically 'creative' arts and sciences.

Teaching Creativity – Theoretical Viewpoints

Three chapters in this volume present cases about teaching creativity and reflect their cases with theoretical viewpoints. In chapter two, Liezel Frick observes that creativity in doctoral education is multi-dimensional. As a result, supervisors need to understand and integrate the concepts underlying creativity in this context if they are to create learning environments that nurture and value doctoral creativity.

In chapter three, Ann Mitsis and Patrick Foley follow this by investigating the background for students' creative learning preference. In the process they identify the creative learning preference and its possible generation membership culture and personality factors. Ann and Patrick conclude that uncertainty avoidance and task completion were more significant than being 'generation Y'.

In chapter four, Dina Belluigi's chapter focuses on how assessment practices, in the context of fine art, impact on the conditions for creativity and thereby alter students' experiences of learning. She finds that effective conditions can be enabled by altering the assessor's role and feedback and the assessment focus and criteria.

Teaching Creativity – Practical Aspects

Another three chapters present cases about teaching creativity and reflect practical aspects in relation to the challenges. In chapter five, Hanne Kirstine Adriansen sets the tone by inquiring whether it is feasible to teach students creativity in an academic environment in which criticality is highly valued. Her chapter shows that creative and critical thinking are not at odds, but rules and structures can be an impediment to creativity. She recommends that we can teach creativity by teaching creatively.

Chapter six by Patricia Almeida and her co-authors José Joaquim Teixeira-Dias and Jorge Medina shows how students' questions represent a powerful way to establish a relationship between students' questioning and their approaches to creativity. Alongside experimenting, thoughtfulness, attentiveness, environment-setting and resilience they see students' capacity to question as the most significant indicator of creativity. Their study shows the relationship between students' approach to creativity and the type of questions they ask.

In chapter seven, the student voice speaks eloquently in response to the investigation by Anna Reid and Peter Petocz into the range of ways in which participants in the pedagogical process view the notion of creativity. Anne and

Peter conclude that students and teachers with the broadest views of creativity are able to use the widest range of approaches to creative learning or teaching.

Together these six chapters show some interesting aspects that ought to be taken into account when developing a curriculum for teaching creativity. We need to take into consideration that students' and staff's perceptions of creativity are different, linked to their academic background and subject, and matter for the ways in which creativity is taught and learned. We need to acknowledge that the identity projects of students, in their process of becoming future professionals, play an important role for their engagement in learning activities. We need to build into our curricula time for individual reflection. We need to engage students in activities in which they share their personal narratives and experiences.

Creativity in Teaching

The second aspect of creativity we are dealing with in this volume is creativity in teaching. Diakidoy & Kanari (1999:226) writes clearly about the role of the teacher in creative teaching: *"…the facilitation of creativity in the classroom will ultimately depend on the teacher's ability to identify creative potential in students, to recognise creative outcomes, to encourage personal attributes and cognitive processes that have been found to relate to creativity, and, finally, to structure the educational environment in a way that will render it more conducive to creativity"*. A lot of different activities can be included in the curriculum, which enhance creativity in the classroom. Some of the most obvious ones are: *"…brainstorming, visualization, imagination, thought experiments, examination of opposites, mind mapping, lateral thinking, problem reversals, questioning, imitation, metaphorical thinking, assumption smashing, fuzzy thinking, forced relationships, synectics, ideatoons, and storyboarding."* (Gow, 2000:32).

Probably one of the most surprising features of adopting more creativity into teaching is that there can be resistance to such innovation from both academic colleagues and students. The world of academia still deploys processes that were initially forged in the middle ages, and particularly refined during the growth of the "modern" teaching and research university in the nineteenth century. So it is perhaps not too surprising that academics tend to be at least initially sceptical of teaching innovation. In the case of students, there is of course a wide variety of reactions to teaching creatively. But there is little doubt that many are comfortable with conventional, relatively passive methods that emphasise transmission. Less conventional methods may be met with scepticism or worse. The academic considering innovation in teaching and learning is certainly engaged in an activity that is more costly than the conventional alternative, certainly in development costs and perhaps in running costs also. They are also engaged in a riskier activity. They may find, for example, that even the physical auditorium layout of the traditional university is inimical to a more flexible group-based working style. Set against these institutional and personal resistances to change, there is perhaps today one unexpected source of support for more creative teaching. That comes from the needs of employers. Though some employers are seen as embodying the learning needs of yesterday, leading employers are certainly today expecting students to have been exposed to a much wider palette of learning methods.

Creativity in Teaching – Theoretical Viewpoints

Six chapters deal with creativity in teaching. The first three present mainly theoretical viewpoints. In chapter eight, Andrea Raiker's investigation of an education degree discovered that creativity and reflection were not explicitly taught and that tutors' and students' understanding of these terms differed. Andrea identifies that when support to enhance creativity is not given this leads to a potentially adverse effect on achievement.

Chapter nine by Rajendra Chetty looks at the other side of this coin by arguing for a greater engagement with creativity as an outcome of pedagogical work in higher education. He recommends that interdisciplinary, inquiry-based learning, collaboration and critical thinking must be foregrounded to provide a framework for creativity-enhanced learning.

In chapter ten, Brent Meistre and Dina Belluigi investigate one such method, visual metaphoric storytelling, and describe how this allows for pluralistic views of individual students' experiences. Brent and Dina deduce that this approach influences positively on the fostering of creativity.

Creativity in Teaching – Some Cases in Point

The anthology concludes with descriptions of three compelling examples of creativity in teaching. In chapter eleven, Silke Lange writes about learning through creative conversation and her experiences using photographs as a foundation from which to develop these conversations. Noting that important factors are structure and facilitation, she explores the possibilities of using this format in other subject areas, especially those in which no artifacts are produced.

In chapter twelve, Matti Rautiainen and his collagues Tiina Nikkola, Pekka

Räihä, Sakari Saukkonen and Pentti Moilanen consider the subject area of teacher education. They reflect that the Finnish culture for learning creates major challenges and they observe that it is more common for people to oppose than to allow and support change.

One potential remedy is to set up a cross-disciplinary centre in creativity and in chapter thirteen, Clive Holtham describes how his university tackled this issue. A creative approach was used to initiate this multi-university network. Clive reports that holding inaugural meetings in a public place, an art gallery, was exciting and rewarding but raised a range of problems and opportunities about innovative creative events.

Together these six chapters show some interesting aspects that ought to be taken into account when developing a curriculum for creativity in teaching. Interdisciplinarity is a key driver for creativity, and we need to organise our curricula so that teaching and study methods allow for investigations of multiple theoretical backgrounds and disciplines. We also need to open up the classroom to the world around us and actively link teaching and studying to the society at large. Project-based, problem-based, enquiry-based, and case-based teaching count as creative methods that can enhance students' creative capacities. Within the classroom, conversations, questioning, and storytelling are creative methods that foster students' creative capacities, and we therefore need to move from traditional teacher-driven activities, to students-driven activities engaging students as co-creators of knowledge in alternative ways.

How Do We Prepare for Creativity in the Curriculum?

The chapters in this volume show that there are many different understandings and approaches to fostering creativity within higher education both in terms of teaching creativity (teaching students to become creative) and creativity in teaching (practising creative ways of teaching and studying). As it will become apparent when reading the twelve chapters, one major driver for creativity is the willingness to change existing paradigms within higher education. To leave behind the view of higher education as a place where experts (faculty) engage in syllabus-driven didactic teaching to fill students with new knowledge. The alternative is to see higher education as a truly learning-centred activity, where students' learning processes are at the nexus of both curricular and extra-curricular activities. It means that all activities will be defined in relation to student learning. Another major driver for creativity is the formulation of competence profiles for students, where creativity is a key component. Words on paper alone do not change old habits, so developing the curriculum with alignment between competence profiles, pedagogical focus, learning activities, and assessment methods is crucial for nurturing creativity in practice. That means introducing new ways of teaching, new ways of studying, and new ways of assessing students' learning. Such is not done overnight, so yet another major driver for creativity is a change in roles of stakeholders, at least the key stakeholders involved in teaching and learning activities (students, teachers, administrators). Work to blend together the subcultures within these stakeholder groups to form the backbone of a new egalitarian institutional culture, where students, teachers, and administrators are truly interacting and students are given the responsibility to engage in their learning process as academic partners.

It is our belief that higher education institutions that take upon themselves these challenges will over time experience a general improvement in their study programs, in students' creativity, hence their learning outcomes, and in the collaboration between students, teachers, and administrators. That alone is reason enough for us to present to you twelve compelling chapters. We trust you will enjoy and be inspired by this anthology on *Teaching Creativity – Creativity in Teaching*. Happy reading!

About the Authors

Claus Nygaard is Professor in Management Education and Director of Research at CBS Learning Lab, Copenhagen Business School, Denmark. He can be contacted at this e-mail: cn.ll@cbs.dk

Nigel Courtney is Honorary Senior Visiting Fellow at Cass Business School, City of London, UK. He can be contacted at this e-mail: nigel@city.ac.uk

Clive Holtham is Professor of Information Management and Director of the Learning Laboratory at Cass Business School, London, UK. He can be contacted at this e-mail: c.w.holtham@city.ac.uk

Chapter Two

Creativity in Doctoral Education: Conceptualising the Original Contribution

Liezel Frick

Introduction

"In PhD research and beyond, students' work needs to move beyond fact finding, 'busy work', to conceptual, critical and creative levels which problematise, question fixed 'truths', enhance deep learning and contribute to knowledge at a conceptual level" (Wisker & Robinson, 2009:318).

Doctoral study is therefore inherently a creative endeavour through which the student creates a scholarly contribution, extending the knowledge boundaries of a particular discipline. A variety of literature from across the world implies the notion of creativity as a central feature of doctoral education in that the student is expected to create an original, significant and independent knowledge contribution to a discipline (see the definitions of a doctorate as proposed by the Association of American Universities 1998, in Lovitts, 2005; the Australasian Qualifications Framework Advisory Board, 2007, the New Zealand Qualifications Authority, 2001; and the United Kingdom Quality

Assurance Agency for Higher Education, 2008). The United States of America Council of Graduate Schools (1977, as quoted in Bargar & Duncan, 1982:1), goes so far as to proclaim the main purpose of a PhD as a preparation for "...*a lifetime of intellectual inquiry that manifests itself in creative scholarship and research*". However, creativity is not well defined within the context of doctoral education, even though it underlies the notion of doctorateness (as defined by Trafford & Leshem, 2009).

This conceptual conundrum is not new – educational theorists have grappled with possible explanations for the general notion of creativity for some time (Piaget, 1971; Torrance, 1988), and the way in which creativity is encapsulated in the highest degree awarded in higher education raises further unique issues (also see the chapters by Chetty; Raiker; and Reid & Petocz in this volume for related discussions). The suggested framework for this anthology, coupled with MacKinnon's (1970) four elements in creativity, creates the space from which to explore these issues. MacKinnon (1970) identified four elements in creativity: the creative person, the creative situation, the creative process, and the creative product. These elements are useful in guiding a theoretical discourse on the conceptualisation of creativity in terms of doctoral education, doctoral becoming (the creative person), doctoral curriculum (the creative situation), and doctoral outcomes (the creative process and product).

The use of a discourse on creativity in doctoral education in the anthology is twofold. Firstly, an investigation into the nature of doctoral education may facilitate debate on how students are (explicitly) prepared to achieve success. Secondly, the notion of creativity opens the door to a more integrated view on the processes and eventual product(s) associated with doctoral education. The framework for this anthology provides a useful point of departure from which to explore the conceptualisation of creativity in doctoral education, the implications of such conceptualisation for a doctoral curriculum, the facilitation of creativity during doctoral education, and the way these elements translate into eventual doctoral outcomes.

Making a Case for Creativity in Doctoral Education

"*The more I think about creativity the more I realised how little I know about it*" (Parks, 1970:81).

Taylor's (1959, in Torrance, 1988) five levels of creativity add to our understanding of this complex phenomenon:

+ expressive creativity, as a spontaneous and naïve process;

+ productive creativity, during a process where restrictions and freedom are interspersed

+ inventive creativity, where ingenuity in the utilisation of materials, methods and techniques is evident

+ innovative creativity, in which novel conceptualisation leads to improvement through modification

+ emergenative creativity, where an entirely new principle is created that changes schools of thought and movements.

Creativity in doctoral education may lie in any or several of these levels (depending on the discipline and format of the doctoral programme), and therefore Taylor's explanation is only useful up to a point.

Libby (1970) takes a more focused view on creativity in science and describes scientific creativity as discovery through research, and creativity as the purpose of science – regardless of the discipline. He furthermore distinguishes between science and technology: science discovers natural law, while technology applies the discoveries of science. However, this distinction is not always clear in the literature on creativity in the scientific environment, and confirms Lovitts's (2007) argument that conceptualisations – such as creativity – are not operationalised or objectively defined in doctoral education. Barron (1988) adds to this that creative potential is not identified systematically and nurtured responsibly in education preceding the doctorate, and only at this late stage is it explicitly expected as a requirement for independent intellectual work. This lack of conceptualisation and scaffolding between educational levels makes it difficult for students to understand what is expected of them, and complicates the task of the supervisor who needs to guide students on their doctoral journey.

Creativity remains a phenomenon that defies accurate definition and is often used synonymously with terms such as originality. Barron (1995) sees originality as a component of the complex phenomenon of creativity, and the work of Lovitts (2007) positions originality as an eventual outcome of the (creative) doctoral process. While such contributions have greatly enhanced our understanding of doctoral outcomes, the literature focused on creativity as part of the doctoral process seems limited at present. The conceptual distinction MacKinnon (1970) and Sternberg & Lubart (1999) make between the creative process and the creative product may be more useful.

A process view of creativity can be traced back to the Greek word *krainein*, which means to fulfil – it follows that people who fulfil their potential, who express an inherent drive or capacity, can be seen as creative (Evans & Deehan, 1988). This process-oriented view resonates with Pope's (2005:xvi, 11) definition of creativity as *"...the capability to make, do or become something fresh and valuable with respect to others as well as ourselves"*, which involves *"...a grappling deep within the self and within one's relations with others: an attempt to wrest from the complexities and contradictions we have internalised"*. MacKinnon (1970) summarises that the creativity extends from simple problem solving, to the full realisation and expression of a person's potential. In doctoral education, the tasks of identifying and describing a research problem, selecting an appropriate approach to investigate the problem, collecting and analysing data, as well as writing research proposals and papers form part of the creative process (Dewett *et al.*, 2005).

The creative product (according to Sternberg & Lubart, 1999) is an original and appropriate contribution that has value and purpose, and these can be judged according to some external criteria. Creative products result from purposeful behaviour, and often lengthy and arduous processes (Hennesey & Amabile, 1988; MacKinnon, 1970; Sternberg & Lubart, 1999), but which Pope (2005:12) still describes as *"work at play"*. In doctoral education, the creative product may manifest in the doctoral dissertation itself or in refereed journal articles, book chapters, and conference papers.

Pope (2005) challenges definitions that only apply to the creative product as reductionist, and proposes that creativity be seen not only in terms of what it *does*, but also in the socio-historical underlying influences of *who, where, how*. Literature suggests an emphasis on the creative product (Dewett *et al.*, 2005), which Pope (2005) explains as a mid-twentieth century, Western problem-solving response to social and technological changes. Dewett *et al.* (2005:14) therefore describe creativity as *"...a protracted process of creative engagement with many intermediate stops in the journey towards creative products"*. Sternberg & Lubart (1999) argue that creativity extends beyond the generation of novel ideas – it also includes an evaluative component in terms of problem solving as part of the creative process. Creativity may therefore have relevance to the individual and the wider society but it could also have an economic imperative (Sternberg & Lubart, 1999).

How does this conceptualisation of creativity as the interplay between process and product resonate with the significant and original contribution expected of doctoral students? Part of the answer may lie in how we conceptualise doctorateness.

Becoming Doctorate: The Creative Scholar

Doctorateness forms part of a process within which a student becomes a responsible scholar (Barnacle, 2005), who Freire (1970, in Lin & Cranton, 2005:458) describes as a person who *"...has the courage and confidence to take risks, to make mistakes, to invent and reinvent knowledge, and to pursue critical and lifelong inquiries in the world, with the world, and with each other"*. MacKinnon (1970) agrees that courage characterises the creative person – courage to question generally accepted notions, and courage to be destructive in order to create an improved notion of reality – what Jones (1972:61) refers to as *"the dignity of doubt"*.

Nickerson (1999) and Seltzer & Bentley (1999) describe creative learners as those who are able to independently identify new problems, who transfer knowledge between different contexts for the purposes of problem solving and who are willing to take risks, who see learning as an incremental process during which repeated attempts may be necessary for success, and who are able to set and focus on goals (Other work reported in this anthology also broadens our understanding of creative learners - see Almeida on student questioning, Holtham on the need for both divergent and convergent thinking, and a focus on uncertainty avoidance and task completion seeking in Mitsis).

The creative process and product cannot be isolated from the creative person (MacKinnon, 1970), which positions creativity as both an innate and a learned quality. Therefore, creativity requires the interplay between six interrelated person-specific resources: intellectual abilities, knowledge, personality, styles of thinking, motivation and environment (Sternberg & Lubart, 1999). Gardner (1988) translates these as subpersonal, personal, extrapersonal and multipersonal levels of creative analysis.

The relationship between creativity and intelligence has led to controversial findings. Nickerson (1999) provides a balanced view – intelligence is necessary for creativity, but not a sufficient condition in itself. Creativity is inseparable from intellectual (subpersonal) ability, which MacKinnon (1970) describes as a reconciliation of expert knowledge and a childlike perception of fresh ideas. Pope (2005:115) warns of the *"myths"* of right/left brain, and divergent/convergent thinking, which are often associated with creative behaviour. He proposes that we rather think of the creative function in the brain as a complex processing system, with complementary activity. Sternberg (1985) identified three interrelated intellectual abilities central to creativity:

+ synthetic ability (to see problems in new ways and to move beyond the boundaries of conventional thinking), which MacKinnon (1970) also refers to as cognitive flexibility

+ analytic ability (to recognise which ideas are worth pursuing)

+ practical-contextual ability (to know how to persuade others of an idea).

All three abilities are essential for creativity to ensue. For instance, analytic ability only results in critical thinking, but not creativity. Synthetic ability without the other abilities leads to new ideas that are not properly scrutinised (an essential part of academic endeavours). A person with a strongly developed practical-contextual ability may sell ideas, but not necessarily because they are worthwhile or novel.

At a personal level, Dewett *et al.* (2005), Gardner (1993), MacKinnon (1970), Nickerson (1999) and Sternberg & Lubart (1999) emphasise the importance of knowledge and immersion in the field of study in identifying problems and gaps in the field in order to move beyond the existing perspectives and to create something new. Even though domain-specific knowledge is a prerequisite for creativity, such knowledge needs to extend beyond mastering the domain (discipline/field of study). The creative person is driven to transform the domain (see the work of Feldman, 1994 and Gardner, 1993 for more detail) by an experience of asynchrony between what the person thinks and the current boundaries of the domain (Sternberg & Lubart, 1999) – a state that Voltaire (in MacKinnon, 1970:21) calls *"constructive discontent"* and which Graesser & Olde (2003) refer to as cognitive disequilibrium. Creative thinkers thus move beyond the focused, disciplined and constrained elements of critical thinking imposed by a discipline (Nickerson, 1999). Also note Chetty's argument for questioning established notions of knowledge as a form of engagement with creativity in postgraduate education elsewhere in the anthology.

Numerous personality traits seem to influence creativity, most importantly self-efficacy, a willingness to overcome obstacles, to take sensible risks, and to tolerate ambiguity. The person who is willing to move beyond the boundaries of convention and who is prepared to defy custom has the potential for true creativity (Barron, 1988; Hennesey & Amabile, 1988; Sternberg & Lubart, 1999). Davis (1992) concurs and adds awareness of one's own creativity, originality, independence, personal energy, curiosity, humour, attraction to complexity and novelty, artistic sense, open-mindedness, need for privacy, and heightened perception as personality attributes that enhance a person's ability to be creative. These personality traits seem well aligned with the implicit traits students identified in defining creativity in a study conducted by Sternberg (1990). More importantly, these attributes are distinctly different to attributes students used to define intelligence (e.g. practical problem-solving ability, goal orientation and attainment, and fluid thought) and wisdom (e.g. ability to reason, level-headedness, and judgment), which implicates creativity as a distinct component in the learning process.

Creativity is not only determined by the ability to think creatively, but also by choosing to do so – which Sternberg (1988, 1997) refers to as a "*legislative thinking style*". This idea is also supported by Claxton, Edwards & Scale-Constantinou (2006).

Intrinsic, task-focused motivation (extrapersonal level) seems an important prerequisite for creativity (Amabile, 1996; Dewett *et al.*, 2005; Sternberg & Lubart, 1999), even though Dewett *et al.* (2005) found that such motivation had a more significant effect on the eventual research product than the preceding process. External motivators (multipersonal level) may also play a role in creativity (Gardner, 1988). The role of external motivation leads us to consider a supportive and rewarding environment (and integral to this environment, the role of the supervisor) as a necessary stimulus for creativity (Sternberg & Lubart, 1999).

Individual creativity is more than the sum of the above-mentioned resources, but the confluence, interaction and necessary thresholds of these components determine the extent to which creativity (and its development) is possible (Sternberg & Lubart, 1999). Leary (1964, in Taylor, 1988:109) developed a typology for diagnosing creativity according to a diagnostic grid presented in Figure 1.

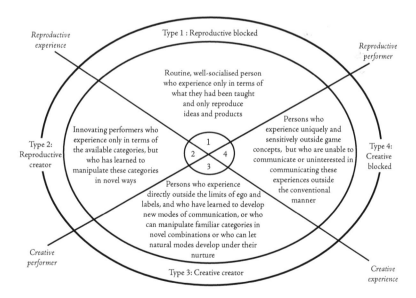

Figure 1: Typology of Creative Persons (adapted from Leary, 1964, in Taylor, 1988:109)

If we were to argue that doctoral students should at least fall within category 2 (reproductive creator), and more preferably in category 3 (creative creator), then it follows that we need to find ways in which to develop these students' creative potential through the doctoral curriculum.

The Doctoral Curriculum: A Situation for Creative Becoming

Curriculum is a formative element in doctoral becoming and may be a catalyst or inhibitor for creativity. Through the curriculum, doctoral students become socialised into the academic community by means of a process that Merton *et al.* (1957:287) describe as the development of a *"...professional self, with its character-istic values, attitudes, knowledge, and skills which govern behaviour in a wide variety of professional (and extraprofessional) situations"*. However, Austin (2009:178) still refers to the doctorate as a *"daunting and often lonely challenge"* while Austin & McDaniels (2006) and Belluigi (2009) found that doctoral curricula lacked systematic and developmentally organised learning experiences that specifically encourage creativity as a learning outcome. Lovitts (2007) points to the lack of explicit expectations and feedback on creativity in doctoral education. Belluigi (2009) and Lizzio & Wilson (2004) argue that outcomes and related underlying processes need to be made explicit, if they are to add value to the development of students' awareness and control over implementing their knowledge crea-tively in an unpredictable professional setting. Doctoral students evidently lack opportunities for guided reflection (Austin, 2002; Belluigi, 2009). These find-ings do not bode well for the development of creativity in doctoral education, and the situation has seemingly not improved over the last five decades. Already in the 1940s, Carl Rogers (in Pope, 2005:21) painted a similar gloomy picture:

"In education, we tend to turn to conformists, stereotypes, individuals whose education is 'completed', rather than freely creative and original thinkers... In the sciences, there is an ample supply of technicians, but the number who can creatively formulate fruitful hypotheses and theories is small indeed. In industry, creation is reserved for the few – the manager, the designer, the head of the research department – whereas for the many life is devoid of original or creative endeavour." The question arises how creativity can be fostered in doctoral curricula through the interac-tion between teaching (more commonly referred to as supervision) and learning.

Arrowsmith (1970:60) calls for *"engaged intellect"* when he critiques the common university structure that rewards and perpetuates specialised research and while applying superficial curricular reform to the detriment of interdisciplinary and applied approaches (with the implication of more permeable disciplinary boundaries) that create scope for more creative research. These impermeable boundaries between disciplines are still evident in current work, for instance the work of Lovitts (2007) who differentiated between disciplines in her work on making doctoral performance expectations explicit. Such disciplinary boundaries bear witness to what Anderson (in Torrance, 1964:126) calls *"closed systems"* of curriculum.

In contrast, *"open systems"* (Anderson, in Torrance, 1964:126) calls for a rethinking of doctoral curriculum. MacKinnon (1970) argues that traditional, surface approaches to learning (e.g. rote learning, learning of unrelated facts, repetitive learning, and precise memorisation) do not foster creativity, and relate to an authoritarian, supervisor-controlled learning environment that may lead to *"destructive friction"* (Vermunt & Verloop, 1999:270). MacKinnon (1970) warns that students immersed in creative processes often act in ways that may make supervision difficult. Creative students are often non-conformists, which may result in tension and adjustment problems (Jones, 1972). Such students often strive for independence, are curious and perceptive, search widely for related information, act intuitively and in non-conformist ways, do not like being confined to pre-determined courses, and need to explore options – even though some options may lead to failure. The ideal learning environment for these students would permit *"constructive friction"* (Vermunt & Verloop, 1999:270).

The effective curriculum aligns assessment, learning and personal development by providing students with choice and opportunities for self-assessment and reflection (Bellugia, 2009). Rethinking doctoral curriculum may require *"…challenging established borderlines and conceptual categories while redefining the spaces of artistic, scientific, and political action"* (Conference on Transgressing Culture: Rethinking creativity in arts, science and politics, as quoted in Pope, 2005:33). Creative spaces are also mentioned in the work of Deleuze & Guattari (1991), who see philosophy, art and literature, and science as three overlapping areas in which creativity can take place. Doctoral education across disciplines relates to all three these spaces, and Manathunga *et al.* (2006) add that an interdisciplinary approach to doctoral education promotes higher-order thinking, an understanding of divergent epistemologies and creative problem-solving behaviour. Creating spaces that support exploration across disciplinary boundaries leads to unique challenges for curricula in which creativity needs to be fostered.

In what way may creativity be facilitated in doctoral curricula? Doctoral curricula need to take various dimensions of the student into account. Sternberg & Lubart (1999) identify a variety of dimensions that influence creative development and that form the foundation on which doctoral students' prior creative learning is founded. These dimensions include:

+ cognitive processes

+ social/emotional processes

+ past and current family aspects

+ formal and informal educational preparation

+ characteristics of the domain and field

+ socio-cultural context

+ historical forces, events and trends.

None of these dimensions is solely responsible for the development of creativity (or a lack thereof), but rather they create the complex context within which creativity is either fostered or hindered.

Csikszentmihalyi (1999) and Kuhn (1962) emphasise that creativity is often not the result of individual endeavour alone, but rather of social systems that judge the merit of individual work. Social systems refer to the cultural domain (such as the academic discipline), and the social field (consisting of competent judges) (Csikszentmihalyi, 1999). The process of creativity can be observed where the individual, domain and field meet, in what Kuhn (1962) describes as "revolutions in science", Feyerabend (1975) calls "epistemological anarchism", and Foucault (1972) refers to as "epistemological breaks". Creativity may result in changes in how reality is viewed within a social system (consisting of the domain and field), or what Taylor (1959, in Torrance, 1988) refers to as "emergenative creativity". Such changes may serve as evidence of doctorateness. Doctoral students should therefore be able and even encouraged to challenge the existing social systems if creativity is to be fostered. However, differences occur in the social systems within which doctoral education takes place (Pope, 2005). Kuhn (1962) notes that creativity may be more difficult in domains where rigid boundaries occur as changes require a redefinition of the permissible problems, concepts and explanations within the discipline and its scientific community.

Creativity results from inquiries that are able to draw lasting support away from competing scientific theories, facts or products, and is sufficiently open-ended to leave an array of problems for the new supporters to resolve (Kuhn, 1962), which Trafford & Leshem (2009:311) refer to as "troublesome knowledge". As such, creativity does not emerge suddenly, but needs to develop and be fostered over time in an atmosphere that allows exploration and expression, regardless of the discipline or programme format (Jones, 1972).

Wallas (1926), MacKinnon (1970) and Torrance (1988) identified five phases in the creative process that we can relate to the ways in which Nickerson (1999) proposes creativity can be enhanced, and the questions asked by McPherson (1964) on facilitating creativity. This explanation of how learning takes place when creativity is called for is useful, as these components align well to the inherent characteristics of the scientific process, and therefore also doctoral learning. Table 1 provides an overview of how this alignment may be conceptualised.

Creative process	Conditions for the enhancement of creativity	Facilitative strategies for the development of creativity	Doctoral research process
Phase 1: Period of preparation during which expertise is gained in order to pose the problem.	Establishing purpose and intention. Building basic skills. Encouraging acquisition of domain-specific knowledge.	Teaching students it is appropriate to strive for creativity. Encouraging students to ask questions. Rewarding questions as an intellectual activity, even/ especially those the supervisor are unable to answer. Trying not to provide all the answers through teaching, but rather the generation of questions that cannot necessarily be answered. Providing examples of long-term problems that defy a quick solution.	Preparation of doctoral proposal, which requires background reading and demarcation of the research question.

Creative process	Conditions for the enhancement of creativity	Facilitative strategies for the development of creativity	Doctoral research process
Phase 2: Period of concentrated effort to solve the problem, which may be frustrating.	Stimulating and rewarding curiosity and exploration. Providing opportunities for choice and discovery. Building motivation, especially internal motivation. Encouraging confidence and a willingness to take risks.	Encouraging students to respect intuition as a genuine thought process, balanced by a thorough knowledge of the field. Providing sufficient materials or models so that students may manipulate materials and experiment.	Refining methodologies and conducting fieldwork (in the case of empirical research), or textual analysis (in the case of more conceptual and philosophical studies), or preparation of artefacts (in creative studies).
Phase 3: Incubation period, often characterised by withdrawal and rejection of the problem, also described as a state of *liminality* (Van Gennep, in Trafford & Leshem, 2009:312).	Providing balance Focusing on mastery and self-completion.	Allowing time for reflective thought in order for creative ideas to emerge. Encouraging students to intersperse different types of work to allow for incubation necessary for the development of creativity. Teaching students that they may find a variety of unique ways that foster creativity within themselves.	Challenging period often experienced by doctoral students when starting to write up their dissertations.

Creative process	Conditions for the enhancement of creativity	Facilitative strategies for the development of creativity	Doctoral research process
Phase 4: Moment of insight.	Developing self-management (metacognitive) skills.	Providing students with data incompatible with conclusions earlier reached, in order to develop the ability to integrate new data. Encouraging students to consider what would happen if their recommendations were implemented. Asking students to combine old ideas in order to develop something new. Asking students for alternative uses and/or explanations for existing theories, findings or products.	Insight gained from aligning the problem posed with a paradigmatic approach used to study the problem, and the eventual result into a coherent whole and an original contribution to knowledge in the field.
Phase 5: Period of verification, evaluation, elaboration, and application of insight.	Promoting supportable beliefs about creativity.	Teaching students that creativity may result in resistance and negative responses. Preparing students for handling critique Rewarding creativity when performance is measured.	Assessment of the doctoral work by peers, followed by scholarly publication to the relevant academic community.

Table 1: An Alignment Between the Processes in Creativity and Doctoral Research

The danger in portraying creativity as part of the scientific process in tabular format is that research may be regarded as a neat, linear process, which is often not the case. Therefore, the boundaries within the table reflect a permeability to indicate that doctoral students may go through the whole process and return to certain aspects throughout their study.

The contributions listed above may be aligned to the doctoral research process itself (as in Table 1), although they may also be used throughout taught components of doctoral programmes. MacKinnon (1970), however, warns that creativity should not be seen as something to be taught, but rather as developed by leading through example. Austin (2009:175) calls this approach *"cognitive apprenticeship"*, as it makes visible experts' thinking processes in understanding and addressing problems. In this way, students are able to develop cognitive and meta-cognitive skills that may enhance their ability to deal with problems creatively. Pope's (2005) notion of creativity as co-becoming, Maslow's (1959) explanation of integrated creativity, and Bohm's (1996) arguments around participatory thought/participatory thinking may be valuable in exploring the role of the postgraduate supervisor as facilitator in creative endeavours. Pope (2005) argues that learning can only be truly creative when all stakeholders' roles in the creative process are acknowledged, while Dewett *et al.* (2005) and Sternberg & Lubart (1999) emphasise the importance of a mentor in the fostering of creativity.

Supervisors need to create nurturing, student-centred learning environments that value divergence and diversity. Exercises that require the transference of knowledge from one area to another, searching for common principles where facts from different areas of knowledge can be related, developing analogies, metaphors and symbolic equivalent experiences, engaging in imaginative play and experimentation, and helping students to step back from facts to gain a greater perspective may foster creativity (Belluigi, 2009; Pope, 2005). Opening discourse through problematising of subjects and the deconstruction of knowledge may encourage what Freeman (2006, in Belluigi, 2009:703) calls *"strong acts of creativity"*. Supervisors may use modelling, coaching and scaffolding, as well as articulation and reflection as strategies to promote a respectful, yet challenging learning environment (Belluigi, 2009; Collins *et al.* 1991, in Austin, 2009). Assessment practices need to ensure positive feedback and diagnostic evaluation (Belluigi, 2009). The best way in which supervisors can facilitate research is to involve students in all the phases of their own research – from conceptualisation and planning to eventual reporting (MacKinnon, 1970).

A curriculum that supports creativity needs to transform students so that aspects of self, knowledge and action interact (Parker, 2003). This implies that doctoral outcomes aimed at supporting creativity should not only be product-oriented, but should also promote process-related outcomes.

Process and Product: Translating Creativity into Doctoral Learning Outcomes

As in the case of creativity, the whole doctoral experience further consists of a process and a product, although doctoral outcomes seem to be focused on the eventual product: *"Dissertations and theses, usually regarded as original contributions, tend to be evaluated in terms of correctness of the methodology rather than in terms of originality, power, and worth of the ideas developed and tested"* (Torrance, 1964:117).

Doctoral outcomes are underscored by ontological, epistemological and methodological development (Frick, 2009). Frick (2009) therefore argues that doctoral outcomes need to be defined on a methodological level, but also an ontological level (in reference to students' understanding of their contribution to their own development as experts in a discipline), and an epistemological level (in relation to students' grasp of the greater body of knowledge in a field of study). Frick's later work (2010) adds the dimension of axiology, referring to the values and ethics inherent to particular disciplines, and into which doctoral students are inducted as part of becoming doctorate. Ontological, epistemological, methodological and axiological positioning is necessary for a doctorate product to merge conceptual, critical and creative elements (Wisker & Robinson, 2009). Epistemological beliefs and methodological approaches become evident in a doctoral dissertation (the product), but ontological and axiological development is much harder to discern.

Dall'Alba & Barnacle (2007) and Paul & Marfu (2001) argue that higher education programmes have favoured epistemological concerns rather than ontological development, while other authors found that more sophisticated epistemological beliefs could be associated with positive learning outcomes (Buehl & Alexander, 2005) and the development of expertise (Barnard-Brak & Lan, 2009). Some authors confirm a strong focus on discipline-based and methodological research outcomes (Lovitts, 2007; Walker *et al.*, 2008). However, Jazvac-Martek (2009) argues that the development of a scholarly identity is just as important as producing knowledge in becoming doctorate, and Belluigi (2009) emphasises that both cognitive and affective skills are necessary for creative thinking. The development of agency, autonomy, confidence and a scholarly voice – ontological elements underlying the courage essential to creativity

– may suffer if only epistemological, axiological or methodological concerns are emphasised and if varying identities are not accepted within a scholarly community. The outcome may be a compliant student, who seemingly performs well, but who hesitates to take the step towards becoming a responsible scholar (Lovitts, 2005). Jones (1972:25) adds that creative growth cannot be forced, only facilitated by giving the student the power and opportunity to take *"creative leap(s)"*, as Arrowsmith (1970:55) points out: *"…you show them what they [the students] are and who they still might be"*.

The idea of creative leaps corresponds to what Kiley (2009), Trafford & Leshem (2009:305) and Wisker & Robinson (2009:317) call *"conceptual thresholds"* along the journey to reaching doctoral outcomes. Kiley (2009) identifies six common threshold concepts in doctoral becoming: argument/thesis, theory, framework, knowledge creation, analysis, and research paradigm. The notion of crossing conceptual thresholds in order to become doctorate implies both process and product, through a process that Kiley (2009) and Trafford & Leshem (2009) describe as transformative. A limited view of creativity only in terms of the eventual product outcome is unfortunate, as it disregards the transformative power of the process on becoming doctorate. The work of Meyer & Land (2005:374) suggests ontological, axiological and epistemological changes as students engage with threshold concepts and therefore lends support to a multi-faceted notion of the doctoral process: *"…as students acquire threshold concepts, and extend their use of language in relation to these concepts, there occurs also a shift in the learner's subjectivity, a repositioning of the self."*

Turner (1979, in Kiley, 2009) suggests that transformation consists of three stages: separation (moving away from what was fixed or known), margin (a state of ambiguous liminality), and aggregation (settling into a new state of being). If students do not reach a state of aggregation when they encounter a threshold concept, they either become stuck or may resort to mimicry – mimicking the language, behaviour and presentation of the perceived desirable understanding or outcome (Kiley, 2009). Although mimicry can be useful in terms of initial socialisation into a domain (Kiley, 2009), long-term use keeps students suspended in a state of uncreative liminality. Students' constant movement through these stages throughout the doctoral process can be described as rites of passage, which enhances an understanding of doctoral becoming.

Sternberg *et al.* (1996) found that when students' efforts were assessed in a way that valued creativity, their eventual academic performance improved. Translating creativity into the doctoral process and eventual outcomes therefore needs to take place on various levels including ontology, axiology, epistemology and methodology.

Conclusion: An Integrated Conceptual Framework for Creativity in Doctoral Research

The anthology provides a useful framework within which to build a discourse on creativity in doctoral education. The key concepts of creativity, curriculum, and teaching/supervision were explored in this chapter in order to develop a framework for translating creativity into doctoral learning outcomes.

The conceptualisation of creativity in doctoral education is multi-dimensional. The work of Beauchamp *et al.* (2009) on Activity Theory in doctoral education provided a useful system that influenced the following interpretation of creativity within the scope of doctoral outcomes (as delineated by Frick, 2009). Figure 2 was developed as a framework for translating creativity into doctoral learning outcomes.

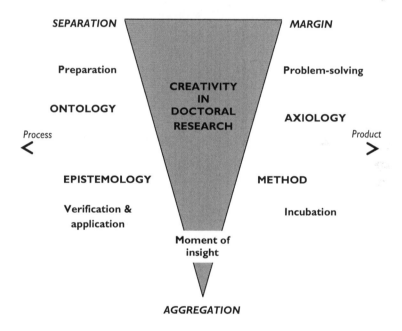

Figure 2: Framework for Translating Creativity into Doctoral Learning Outcomes

According to Figure 2, doctoral learning outcomes may lie on four interrelated levels: ontology, axiology, epistemology and methodology (Frick, 2009, 2010). A conceptualisation of doctoral creativity needs to encompass aspects of both process and product in a transformative manner that takes place on ontological, episte-mological and methodological levels in the various phases of the research process. If these levels overlap, a space is created where doctoral creativity can form part of both the process and product of doctoral education. However, if a student is stimulated or allowed creativity in only some of the levels, and the emphasis is on either teaching or learning, and/or process or product, creativity may suffer.

Integrated into these four levels, doctoral students need to undergo trans-formation in order to be creative. They therefore need to cross conceptual thresholds through the process of separation, margin and aggregation (Turner 1979, in Kiley, 2009).

Doctoral students may experience ontological, epistemological and meth-odological transformation through creatively engaging with the interrelated phases of the doctoral process, consisting of preparation, problem solving, incu-bation, moments of insight, and verification and application (Wallas, 1926). These phases form a cyclical sphere with which doctoral students may recur-sively engage as they become doctorate.

Future debates on doctoral curriculum may have to focus on how such a conceptualisation of creativity in doctoral outcomes plays out in practice, espe-cially since Frick (2009) notes that the meaning of what constitutes academic work continues to be challenged.

If doctoral students are required to ontologically position themselves as scholars, to integrate themselves into the values and ethics underlying the disci-pline (axiology), to negotiate their understanding of and contribution to the discipline (episteme), and to navigate methodological concerns in a dynamic environment, they will need to find ways of crossing their conceptual thresh-olds in creative ways in order to create an original contribution. As supervisors, we need to create environments that motivate students to become creative, to provide the means for them to be creative, and the opportunity to showcase their creativity, since Johnson-Laird (1988:208) claims *"...[c]reativity is like murder – both depend on motive, means, and opportunity"*.

About the Author

Liezel Frick is a lecturer at the Centre for Higher and Adult Education, Faculty of Education, Stellenbosch University, South Africa. She can be contacted at this e-mail: blf@sun.ac.za

Chapter Three

Psychographic Antecedents to the Creative Learning Style Preference

Ann Mitsis and Patrick Foley

Introduction

This chapter presents one section of a larger study and focuses upon the identification of the creative learning preference and explores undergraduate business students' psychographics as antecedents within an Australian setting. The Australian higher education sector, shaped to meet the needs of Generation X students, today comprises of a multicultural student cohort where Generation Y is fast becoming the most dominant generation.

The importance of nurturing creativity in business education and Generation Y's increasing role in helping organisations to fulfill their mission is increasingly being recognised. Generation Y in the extant literature is generally seen as encompassing the birth years of 1977 to 1994/1995 with Generation X comprising of the birth years of 1965 to 1976 (Wolburg & Pokrywczynski, 2001; Bartlett, 2004). Generation Y's level of willingness to engage in creative activities and the antecedents to this willingness and how it compares to Generation X students is an important question. Much of the foundation literature (Ballard & Clanchy, 1997; Biggs, 1994; Cheung & Chan, 2009) on how we unlock creative potential in business students is based on insights gained with Generation X.

Within the business discipline, the notion of creativity competence is a growing expectation from both industry and graduates. Creativity is seen as a key element of business practice and in business education it is no more clearly seen than in the entrepreneurial activity of creating value through innovation. This creativity can be expressed at a functional, business and corporate level and is equally applicable to the private, public and not for profit sectors. These innovations can range from incremental to radical. For business students who will emerge from their education with the growing expectation that they can contribute to these different types of innovation there is growing need to understand the creative learning preference that students bring into a university context and the antecedents that shaped this preference and how this preference can be nurtured and grown.

This chapter begins by exploring the creative learning preference and places it in a context of existing learning models. It defines the creative learning preference as a problem solving style that enjoys seeking hidden possibilities, learning by experimentation, engaging with novel ideas and tackling something new and different rather than seeking facts and continuity, needing to know what the experts think, valuing sequential thinking and enjoying traditional teacher-directed learning. We argue that a strong creative learning preference is associated with a higher willingness to engage in creative problem solving learning activities and a lower need to always engage in analytical problem solving learning activities. The chapter will look at what might be the factors that could explain this greater willingness and how these factors interact with generational membership. Specifically it will look at cultural factors such as English language enculturation and uncertainty avoidance and personality characteristics associated with seeking structure and task completion.

Creative and Analytical Problem Solving

Education within a business course consists of experiences that call for both analytical and creative problem solving skills. Many learning activities are based on teaching students how to be successful in rational problem solving models that involve a sequence of defined steps.

Students entering higher education are not only conditioned by their previous educational experiences (Kolb & Kolb, 2005) but by the educational experience within their course. Students' creative learning preference has also been shaped by their personalities, abilities, previous educational experiences and cultural backgrounds (Ballard & Clanchy, 1997). Different cultural traditions result in different attitudes to knowledge and knowledge acquisition. Stes, Gijbels & Van Petegem (2008) suggest that learning for reproduction is associated with a teacher-focused approach to teaching, whereas a student-focused approach to teaching is associated with an active approach to learning.

Students' previous educational experiences, culturally-anchored values and English language enculturation may shape learning and problem solving style preferences. Cheung & Chan (2009) found that the cultural value of uncertainty avoidance significantly influenced perceptions of university education however it is unclear how this factor might influence the analytical or creative problem solving preference. They also identified that a low uncertainty avoidance rating corresponds to greater tolerance towards educational innovation.

The role of the teacher has been conceptualised by Knowles *et al.* (1998) as providing students with opportunities to learn and that the task of learning needs to be driven by the student. However, analytical problem solving often begins with the definition of a problem. This definition is often provided by the teacher. Creative problem solving which emphasises both problem definition improvement and elaboration is more in keeping with adult learning. It is consistent with the accommodator and converger learning styles identified by Kolb (1976) and Honey & Mumford's (1992, 1995) activist and pragmatist learning styles. Biggs (1994) contends that a deep learning and problem solving style preference is the opposite of a surface learning and problem solving style preference and seems to have similarities to the learning and problem solving style preferences that Kolb (1976) has called divergers and assimilators and what Honey & Mumford (1992, 1995) had called the reflector and theorist learning and problem solving style preferences.

We argue that a creative learning preference exists when a student has a stronger preference for a learning style that Kolb would see as an accommodator and Honey & Mumford as an activist and a lower preference for the learning style that Kolb would call assimilators and Honey & Mumford would call theorists (see Figure 1).

Good learning in the West is described as a typical sense of deep approaches according to Biggs (1994), and is consistent with the normative position of Hassall & Joyce (2001). Hassall & Joyce (2001) suggest that students should:

1. use abstract frameworks for conceptualising the task

2. be meta-cognitive in planning and monitoring their own progress

35

3. see that the outcomes are well structured and integrated

4. see learning as enjoyable process.

Good learning is said to have taken place when learners move through all stages of learning (Honey & Mumford, 1992). However, certain styles are likely to provide advantages in certain learning contexts. According to Honey & Mumford's (1992) framework, the activist learning and problem solving style preference is described as situational learning, examples include business games and competitive teamwork tasks. Theorists present a preference for highly structured activities that are offered as part of a concept, model or theory.

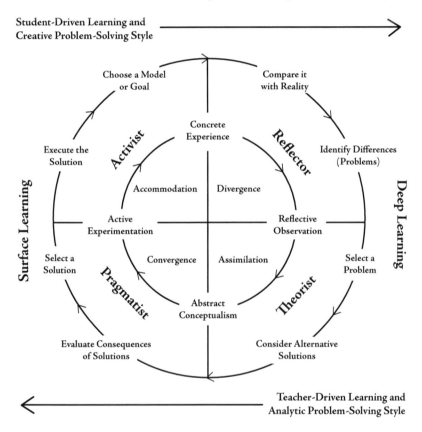

Figure 1: Learning and Problem Solving Styles

Hancock *et al.* (2002) see the student-driven learning and creative problem solving preference as flourishing in a less structured classroom, where students influence time allocation and methods of learning and openly communicate ideas. The teacher's role for a student-driven preference involves encouraging students to experience new activities or topics, and be a channel to assist in establishing and enforcing rules, as well as encouraging review and conclusions on lesson objectives (Hancock *et al.*, 2002).

The teacher-driven learning and analytic problem solving preference can be described as being highly structured, where the teacher's role is to organise learning tasks, time allocations and material presentations in-line with teaching objectives, and being specific in methods of instruction (Hancock *et al.*, 2002; Brown, 2003). Students with this preference exhibit low levels of active experimentation and attempt to understand the material taught within a theoretical framework of ideas and concepts (Hassall & Joyce, 2001).

Hancock *et al.*'s (2002) study into student performance found that a teacher-driven learning and problem solving style does not necessarily outperform a student-driven learning and problem solving style. Nevertheless, other research found that the teacher-driven preference results in greater sophistication in learning outcomes (Case & Gunstone, 2003). Kraiger (2008) presents a two tiered model of learning: first generation instruction and second generation learning. Here first generation instruction involves the instructor being the primary emphasis and second generation learning emphasises personalisation of content by learners. Due to its customisation, this second generation learning is likely to place a greater emphasis on creative problem solving activities. What has not been explored is the willingness of students to engage in these types of learning activities and what may influence this level of willingness.

Generation Y and the Creative Learning Preference

Generation Y has been identified as more *"...team-oriented, optimistic, trusting of authority, technologically savvy, practical, community oriented, able to multi-task, achievement focused, goal oriented, etc."* than Generation X (Griffin *et al.*, 2008:62). This description of Generation Y is consistent with earlier research conducted by Heaney (2007) and Bakewell & Mitchell (2003). Generation Y, compared to Generation X, is more likely to lead quieter lives within their social networks, and to have the tendency to research intended purchases and be on the look-out for bargains (Heaney 2007). Busch, Venkitachalam and Richards (2008) see Generation Y as enthusiastic and highly valuing their own opinions. While some aspects of Generation Y would suggest that they would have a greater creative learning preference, other aspects would suggest this may not be the case. It is unclear if Generation Y have a stronger creative learning preference than Generation X.

Culture and the Creative Learning Preference

In what Hofstede (1980, 1991) has identified as Anglo-Saxon societies, namely Australia, the UK, the US, New Zealand and Canada, good learning has been aligned with the deep and teacher-driven preference (Biggs, 1994). Good learning is said to occur within this paradigm when abstract frameworks are used by learners to conceptualise tasks, plan and monitor their own progress, interpret outcomes and perceive learning as enjoyable and results-based (Biggs, 1994; Hassall & Joyce, 2001). These preferences are compatible with different approaches to instruction design by educators (Kraiger, 2008). The familiarity to and preference for these instructional designs may vary by the cultural heritage of a student. Cultural heritage within a multicultural country may not be accurately identified by measures such as citizenship. Citizenship may also not accurately measure whether the person received their education in English. English language enculturation, that is whether an individual has studied in the English language throughout their pre-tertiary education, may also affect students' creative learning preference inclination.

The extant literature documents that different cultural customs influence both attitudes and behaviours (Hofstede, 1980; Hall & Hall, 1990; Hampden-Turner, 1994; Trompenaars 1994; Hofstede, 2001; Hofstede & Hofstede, 2005). One of the most commonly cited cultural values frameworks is Hofstede's (1980, 1991, 2001). The GLOBE study of 62 societies has also adopted sections of Hofstede's cultural framework (House & Javidan, 2004) and used his concept of uncertainty avoidance. Uncertainty avoidance measures the level of comfort a society has in regards to ambiguous or unknown situations (Hofstede, 1991, 2001). Therefore it is plausible that a culturally-anchored value like uncertainty avoidance may affect students' creative learning preference. Therefore it is also unclear if English language enculturation encultured students have a greater preference for a creative learning style and how culturally-anchored values such as uncertainty avoidance may also shape the preference for creative learning.

Psychological Characteristics and the Creative Learning Preference

Certain personality characteristics might be more associated with a creative learning preference. A personality with a high focus on defined structure and efficient task completion and precision in decision making may prefer only to engage in analytic problem solving and be unwilling to engage in self-initiated creative problem solving. These students are more likely to perceive information concretely rather than intuitively, prefer courses that emphasise rational problem solving with clear feedback from a teacher on correct procedure and the learning experience when judgements are made after all the facts are available. It is a personality type that dislikes ambiguity and seeks environments that minimize this (Benfari, 1999; Lubit, 2004; Nahavandi, 2006; Yukl, 2006). It seems plausible that this area is under-researched, that individuals who have a preference for defined structure, efficient time completion and precision in decision making may approach problem solving using an analytical problem solving approach rather than a creative learning problem solving approach. This preference for analytical problem solving could be reflected in a lower creative learning preference.

The second part of the chapter reports on a study we undertook to address the issues raised in the first part of the chapter and to answer the question: are there student characteristics that predispose them to a creative learning preference and are these characteristics influenced by their generational membership?

Exploring the Interaction of Possible Psychographic Antecedents to a Creative Learning Preference

The context of this exploration was in an Australian Business Education environment and involved 364 students. The study was designed to explore if students' Generation Y or X membership and gender explain any variation in their creative learning preference. It explored if English language enculturation and culturally engendered values such as uncertainty avoidance also explain variation in the creative learning preference. Finally the study examined the relationship of students' individual psychological personality characteristics like their problem clarity seeking orientation, task completion seeking orientation and precision assurance seeking orientation on the creative learning preference.

The remaining part of the chapter will identify the implications of this study for the teaching of creativity and the development of a curriculum for creativity.

The study involved 364 students studying a business undergraduate degree in an on-campus mode at a large metropolitan university based in Melbourne Australia. All participants were volunteers, of whom 87.4% were Generation Y (coded 1) and the remainder were Generation X (coded 0). This sample's ratio of Generation Y to Generation X membership is representative of enrolments within the Australian higher education sector. The majority (85%) were Australian citizens who did not come from a diverse cultural heritage and 46% were male (Male Gender was coded 1).

The majority of participants (88%) within this sample were English language enculturated (coded 1) by studying in the English language in their pre-tertiary education. The remaining 12% of participants had not been instructed in the English language, but variously in: Mandarin, Sinhalese, Cantonese, French, Vietnamese, Arabic, Malay, Filipino, Turkish, Dutch, Hindi, Lao, Indonesian, German, Thai, Yugoslavian and Myanmar. These non-English languages of instruction can also be identified with one or more of the following culture societal clusters identified by Hofstede (1980, 1991, 2001): Eastern Europe/Arab Speaking/Spanish Speaking, China, Asia/Africa, Former British or American Colonies, Nordic Europe, France/Belgium and Europe/Africa.

Students were asked to respond to Robertson & Hoffman's (2000) uncertainty avoidance, culturally-anchored value dimension which was designed to measure an individual's beliefs along Hofstede's (1980, 1991, 2001) uncertainty avoidance cultural value. The culturally-anchored value responses were coded 1 = strongly disagree through to 5 = strongly agree.

Honey & Mumford's (1992) learning style questionnaire was used to collect the creative learning style preference data from the respondents, by rating to what extent they agreed with their Activist and Theorist learning style dimension items on a six point Likert scale, where 0 = strongly disagree through to 5 = strongly agree. The creative learning style preference was calculated by dividing the Activist dimension score by the Theorist dimension score. The English language enculturation variable was coded 1 if students studied their pre-tertiary education in the English language.

All three individual psychological personality characteristics are new scales and the Cronbach's alpha coefficients for each of the characteristics are acceptable with the problem clarity seeking preference equal to 0.70, the task completion seeking preference equal to 0.72 and the precision assurance seeking preference equal to 0.79.

The problem clarity seeking personality characteristic scale is a four item scale, of which two items are from Ramsden's (1992) generic teaching scale: "The course develops my problem solving skills" and "The course sharpens my analytic skills"; one item from his clear goals scale "I usually have a clear idea of where I am going and what is expected of me in the course"; and one item from Ramsden's (1992) good teaching scale: "The staff put a lot of time into commenting on my work". Students therefore responded to Ramsden's (1992) course experience questionnaire, by rating how important these items were on a five point likert scale where 1 = extremely unimportant to 5 = extremely important.

The task completion seeking personality characteristic scale is a 12 item scale of which all 12 items originate from Honey & Mumford's (1992) pragmatist learning style preference, whereby students were asked to rate statements on a six point scale (0 = strongly disagree through to 5 = strongly agree). Indicative questions include: "In discussions I like to get straight to the point"; "In discussions I get impatient with irrelevancies and digressions"; "I do whatever is expedient to get the job done".

The precision assurance seeking characteristic scale is a nine item scale from Honey & Mumford's (1992) reflector learning style preference. Indicative questions include: "I take care over the interpretation of data available to me and avoid jumping to conclusions"; "I like to reach a decision carefully after weighing up many alternatives"; "I pay meticulous attention to detail before coming to a conclusion".

Two types of analyses were conducted in order to explore the relationships between the student's psychographic characteristics and the creative learning preference.

1. whether students' Generation Y or X membership and gender explain any variation in their creative learning preference

2. whether English language enculturation and culturally engendered values such as uncertainty avoidance also explain variation in the creative learning preference

3. and whether the relationship of students' individual psychological personality characteristics like their problem clarity seeking orientation, task completion seeking orientation and precision assurance seeking orientation influence the creative learning preference.

The first type of analysis conducted was a Pearson correlation analysis between the psychographic characteristics and the creative learning preference in order to identify whether there are any significant associations. The second type of analysis conducted was a three-step hierarchical regression analysis in order to establish whether the demographic characteristics, the culturally-anchored variables, or the individual psychological personality characteristics explain a greater creative tendency.

The Pearson correlation analysis revealed that one culturally-anchored variable, uncertainty avoidance, and two individual psychological personality characteristics – of problem clarity seeking and precision assurance seeking – each appeared to have significant associations with the creative learning preference (see Table 1). In other words, low uncertainty avoidance, a low problem clarity seeking preference and a low precision assurance seeking preference are highly associated with the creative learning preference.

Variable	1.	2.	3.	4.	5.	6.	7.
1. Generation Y	--						
2. Gender	-0.005**	--					
3. English Language Enculturation	-0.044**	-0.155**	--				
4. Uncertainty Avoidance	-0.000**	-0.040**	-0.003**	0.834			
5. Problem Clarity Seeking	-0.021**	-0.045**	-0.039**	-0.132**	0.697		
6. Task Completion Seeking	-0.037**	-0.296**	-0.078**	-0.123**	-0.062**	0.716	
7. Precision Assurance Seeking	-0.035**	-0.090**	-0.113**	-0.235**	-0.294**	-0.103**	0.794
8. Creative Learning Preference	-0.102**	-0.066**	-0.016**	-0.192**	-0.212**	-0.066**	-0.424**

*Correlation is significant at the 0.05 level (2-tailed);**Correlation is significant at the 0.01 level (2-tailed). Cronbach's alphas are in italics on the diagonal.*

Table 1: Correlations Matrix

The three-step hierarchical regression analysis was conducted to establish which of the eight variables (as listed in Table 1) explain a greater tendency towards the creative learning preference, by controlling for each type of psychographic characteristic.

The demographic characteristics of Generation Y and gender were entered into the first step of the regression and the results revealed no statistically significant association with the creative learning preference (multiple $R(0.121)$; $R^2 = 0.015$; $F(2,361) = 2.699$, p>0.05).

The culturally-anchored variables of English language enculturation and uncertainty avoidance were entered into the second step of the model and revealed that the culturally-anchored variables make a significant explanatory contribution of 3.6% of the creative learning preference, after students' demographic characteristics were controlled for ($\Delta R^2 = 0.036$; multiple $R(0.225)$; $R^2 = 0.051$; $F(4,359) = 4.78$, p = 0.001).

Uncertainty avoidance explained 3.6% and Generation Y explained 1% of the unique variance in the creative learning preference.

The third step involved entering the individual psychological personality characteristics of problem clarity seeking, task completion seeking and precision assurance seeking into the model. The individual psychological personality characteristics made a significant explanatory contribution of 17.4% in the creative learning preference after students' demographic characteristics and culturally-anchored variables were controlled for ($\Delta R^2 = 0.179$; multiple $R(0.474)$, $R^2 = 0.225$, $F(7,356) = 14.726$, p = 0.000). Generation Y remained a significant explanatory variable contributing 0.86% as did uncertainty avoidance contributing 1% and all three individual psychological personality characteristics of problem clarity seeking, task completion seeking and precision assurance seeking contributed 0.85%, 1.99% and 12.1% respectively of the unique variance in the creative learning preference.

The Creative Learning Preference

These results suggest that students who have a tendency towards the creative learning preference are those who are Generation Y, who have a high uncertainty avoidance culturally-anchored value and who are precision assurance seeking. This applied even when the demographic and culturally-anchored variables of generational membership and gender and the culturally-anchored variables of English language enculturation and uncertainty avoidance were controlled for.

Generation Y students within this study had a greater enthusiasm and inclination for a creative learning preference. This supports Busch *et al.*'s (2008) contention that members of Generation Y are enthusiastic and highly value their own opinions. A low uncertainty avoidance culturally-anchored value orientation also aligns with greater openness and willingness for innovations in educational practices. Although as educators we are unable to alter a student's generational membership or cultural values orientation, an awareness and understanding of classroom dynamics is valuable for both the teaching of creativity and the development of curriculum for creativity.

This study also identified that a low precision assurance seeking personality characteristic, a low problem clarity seeking personality characteristic and a high task completion seeking personality characteristic are positively associated with the creative learning preference. From the perspective of an academic teaching creativity and developing curriculum for creativity, it is important for educators to be aware of the types of learning activities students which these personality characteristics thrive upon. The types of learning activities associated with low precision assurance seeking, low problem clarity seeking and high task completion-seeking include a need:

+ for usability, utility, and results

+ to know how things work

+ to learn by testing theories in ways that seem most sensible

+ to use factual data to build designed concepts

+ for hands on experiences

+ to know how things they are asked to do will help in real life.

Thus, in teaching creativity, and in developing curriculum for creativity, the aforementioned learning characteristics should also be taken into account by educators.

This study aimed to add to our understanding of the antecedents to the creative learning preference that students bring into a university so that these preferences can be nurtured and grown. This study suggests that there are differences that shape creative learning preference and that individuals who have a preference for defined structure, efficient time completion, and precision in decision making may approach problem solving using an analytical problem solving approach rather than a creative learning problem solving approach. This preference for analytical problem solving could be reflected in a lower creative learning preference.

Generation Y membership and the cultural value of uncertainty avoidance also shaped creative learning preference though the most important variable was precision assurance seeking.

Further research is needed on how people who have high precision assurance needs to can become more comfortably using creative problem solving as well as analytical problem solving approaches.

About the Authors

Ann Mitsis is a Lecturer in Marketing and the Faculty of Business and Enterprise's Honours Coordinator at Swinburne University of Technology, Melbourne, Australia. She can be contacted at this e-mail: amitsis@swin.edu.au

Patrick Foley is a Senior Lecturer in Management at Victoria University of Technology, Melbourne, Australia. He can be contacted at this e-mail: patrick.foley@vu.edu.au

Creating the Conditions for Creativity: Looking at Assessment in Fine Art Studio Practice

Dina Belluigi

Introduction

Education literature suggests that creativity in students is promoted by learner-centred environments that are supportive; encourage playfulness, risk-taking and experimentation; and formative assessment practices that involve positive feedback (Dineen *et al.*, 2005). In this chapter, I explore the importance of assessment for creating the conditions necessary to foster creativity. The discussion utilises the specificity of fine art studio practice, as it is often assumed that creativity is most enabled in the creative arts fields, but in reality this is where contemporary notions of creativity can be exceptionally challenging to develop. Whereas fine art acts as a pivot on which the discussion rotates, the content of this chapter is concerned with fostering experiences of learning at the heart of this anthology's discussion of creativity.

The chapter will firstly take a wider stance, looking at contemporary notions of creativity in higher education. An important aspect of this discussion is how creativity relates to student experiences of learning. I draw from textual as well as empirical research (Belluigi, 2008a), exploring notions of creativity in fine art, and noting particularly how in its contemporary conception "creativity" is paired with "critical thinking". In the bulk of the chapter, I explore the potential for and the challenges of creating the conditions for creativity through assessment in fine art, with a concern for the affective aspects of learning. I discuss cultural, structural and agentic factors, as they are intertwined in teaching and learning. I firstly highlight the importance of the teacher's role as both assessor and "critical friend", going on to discuss how the assessment focus should be on the process of learning. I argue that the negotiation of assessment criteria should allow for student agency, with a recognition of student intentionality. The discussion then draws these elements together, showing that relevant and constructive feedback supports the process of learning towards realising the students' intention. Whilst these suggestions have arisen from the specificity of fine art education, I believe that productive connections can be made with similar occurrences in the reader's context.

Considering Creativity in Higher Education

Knight (2001:7) points out that higher education curricula "...are giving increasing prominence to complex learning outcomes and to 'soft skills' – they are claiming to foster inter-personal skill, emotional intelligence, creativity, critical thinking, reflectiveness, incremental self-theories, autonomy and such like". Although a slippery term to describe definitively, Biggs' (1999a) understanding of creativity incorporates abstract learning outcomes, such as hypothesizing, synthesizing, reflecting and generating ideas, and working with problems that have a range of possible divergent solutions. Creativity involves aspects of both convergent and divergent thinking (Jackson, 2004), resulting in dynamic and complex intersections and slippages between thinking critically and creativity (The Five Colleges of Ohio, 2007). As alluded to by a number of authors in this anthology, recently creativity has been recognised as a *process* rather than simply an end product, with more importance given to the imaginative processes of conceptualisation and schematization than to the "*craft*" executed in the final product (Cowdroy & de Graaf, 2005).

A useful differentiation is the continuum between what Freeman (2006) calls "*weak*" and "*strong*" acts of creativity. When the student only solves the problem to which s/he was directed it is seen as "weak", wheras a "strong" act is when the student further problematises the subject at hand, opening it up to multiple possibilities, utilising convergent and divergent thinking. This playful process of "problematising" is informed by critical theory and postmodernism, where the learning process involves "...*the continuous deconstruction of knowledge, of playing with contradictions, and of creatively and productively opening the discourse of a field to an eclectic mosaic of many truths*" (Kilgore, 2001:60).

Much like child's play, environments need to be created where risk is not thwarted by the threat of failure – a challenge where assessment casts a negative shadow on the curriculum. Crucial to the development of creativity, experimentation and play draw on the student's whole personality, processes through which they gain a sense of "self" (Winnicott, 1971). What this requires in practical terms, are assessment tasks and methods that involve students in actively questioning or creating problems from the set assignment topic or "brief" (Freeman, 2006; Reid & Solomonides, 2007) rather than slavishly finding solutions. "Weak" acts could be linked to what is known as a "*surface*" approach to learning, and "strong" acts to a "*deep*" approach (Marton & Säljö, 1984).

Whilst there have been many studies dedicated to the impossible task of defining the term "creativity" (Amabile, 1996; Knight, 2002a; Dallow 2003; Lindström 2006), less has been said about how conditions foster or hinder its growth. The responsibility for creating these conditions rests with the teacher, the curriculum, the student, and wider teaching and learning processes. A study by The Five Colleges of Ohio (2007) distinguished improvement in creative thinking by risk, novelty and curiosity – elements of the "play" discussed above. These elements would need to be embedded in an effective curriculum, one that establishes "...*good links between assessment, learning and personal development by inter alia allowing students some element of choice, encouraging self-assessment and reflection*" (Luckett & Sutherland 2000:107) for creativity to be more than a superficially adopted discourse (Belluigi, 2008a). This is because autonomous learning or "metalearning" (Nickerson *et al.*, 1985) is one of the central determinants of student creativity.

Validation through assessment is a feature of education. My emphasis on affective learning in this chapter arises from studies which link it with creativity, and which indicate that feedback is experienced affectively (Taylor & McCormack, 2005). Of concern is a body of research which has shown that creativity can be adversely affected by assessment. Assessment can decrease creativity if the timing is insensitive or assessment too harsh, promoting adaptation or reproduction rather than questioning or production (Dineen *et al.*, 2005). Because the student's sense of self is important, special attention must be given to ensuring that engaged rather than alienated experiences of learning occur (Mann, 2001; Reid & Solomonides, 2007). If the student does not feel safe in the teaching environment to explore and play, it could have a detrimental effect on his/her learning. Research shows that students will adopt surface approaches when their learning experience is alienating and will protect themselves by choosing the most predictable options, avoiding risk-taking and progression (Mann, 2001). However, as I argue in this chapter, with formative assessment that focuses on process and involves constructive feedback, students' intrinsic motivation can be accessed and thereby creativity can be encouraged (Amabile, 1996).

Contemporary Notions of Creativity in Fine Art Studio Practice

As I outline in Tables 1 and 2, notions of creativity within fine art have undergone a radical shift. Whilst art was previously seen as unknowable and the artist's process mystical and opaque, the postmodern artist is seen as subject to social and historical forces with ethical responsibilities in his/her image-making. Important for this chapter, conceptions of creativity have also shifted and been problematised. With Freudian psychology, the "inspiration" of the artist is now understood as the realisation or trigger of ideas lying dormant in the subconscious. Creative activity is no longer seen as antithetical to analytical engagement (Freeman, 2006). Rather the artist is a *"practical intellectual"* (Dallow, 2003:49) engaging actively in critical reflection. However although Romantic myths of the autonomous, authentic, artist-genius may have been subverted with postmodernism, many of today's artists uncritically believe that they are morally superior and more emotionally sensitive than non-artists (Massey, 2006). This is where self-reflexivity plays an important part, particularly in education, to prevent self-absorption or tacit acceptance of myths of creativity which can promote elitism and become reductive. For these reason, contemporary conceptions of creativity have often been productively linked strongly to critical thinking and reflexivity rather than polarised (Belluigi, 2009; Almeida, this volume; Adriansen, this volume). Interpretation, analysis, evaluation, inference, explanation and self-regulation are aspects which comprise critical thinking, according to the Delphi Report (Facione, 1990).

Informed by this linkage of creativity with criticality, critical discourse in fine art curricula is centred on the artworks of students and artists, with

Notions of the creativity	Traditions of teacher-student relationships	Curriculum
Characterized by words such as: 'talent', 'gifted', 'inspiration', 'muse'	Vertical and hierarchical	**Content:** - medium-specific emphasis - skills and technique most important
Person/ attributes: Artist as 'genius', morally superior, emotionally more sensitive	**Gifted tradition** - relationship of mutual respect between teacher as master and 'gifted' student	- learning occurs in the studio
Process: Mystical, opaque and beyond analysis	**Innate tradition** - student is born with creativity which can be developed through followship	**Assessment:** - summative - product only - assessment by proxy through exhibition of artefact
Product: Valued for mastery of technique - acontextual and apolitical	**Studio apprenticeship** - creativity is 'taught' through prolonged association with teacher as living master who passes down his (most typically) skills and implicitly his values	- traditionally by panel of expert assessors - later included a defence of student work by studio supervisor - implicit norm-referenced assessment
Polarization of critical and creative; analytical and expressive	**Reproduction tradition** - reproduce work of previous masters with tutors - emphasises on craft/skill and product	

Table 1: The Links Between Myths of Creativity and the Curriculum in the Humanist/ Romantic Tradition

Notions of the creativity	Traditions of teacher-student relationships	Curriculum
C Characterized by words such as 'creative thinking', 'reflexivity', 'self-criticality'	Horizontal levelling of power towards a partnership	**Content:** - discourse-specific emphasis - critical thinking and
Person: - artist as 'practical intellectual' - subject to political, social, economic and historic forces	- teacher as facilitator of student aims or 'critical friend' - recognition of student agency, autonomy and responsibility	questioning of assumptions and ideologies of power - recognition that learning occurs in and out of the studio, and within assessments
Process/Product: -' inspiration' now seen as a trigger or realization buried in the subconscious - process given emphasis and open to analysis, deconstruction and play		**Assessment practices:** - process privileged over product - formative and summative assessment exhibition of artefact, in addition to portfolios etc
- concepts and ideas given as much if not more emphasis than form or medium	- recognition of affective impact of feedback - feedback relevant and informed by focus on process and the criteria negotiated with student - importance of personal relevance and development of critical consciousness	- feedback from panel of expert assessors and student's peers in dialogue with student - explicit criteria, preferably negotiated - inclusion of student intentionality
Blurring of boundaries between criticality and creativity		

Table 2: The Links that I Argue Should Exist Between Conceptions of Creativity and the Curriculum in Postmodern Curricula.

dimensions of inquiry into social issues (such as race, gender, ethnicity) serving to interrogate, challenge and shape the artist-student's personal and cultural connections (Sullivan, 1993). This "...look[ing] beyond the structures of their discipline or the interests of the individual to society" is in an attempt to build critical consciousness (Toohey, 1999:65-66). Content is organised around investigations, themes or projects, with complex concepts such as "the other" or "the gaze", chosen from current socio-political issues. Students then work on their related projects in the studio, interacting with their studio practice teacher and peers informally, with assessments occurring intermittently. This chapter is most concerned with how assessment impacts on the conditions for creativity, and the backwash effect on the curriculum.

Central to the pedagogy of "western" fine art, design and architectural education is the studio context and the Critique method of assessment (otherwise called "crit", and also known as "jury", "review", or "dialogue"). It is this method of assessment on which I am focusing in this chapter. The traditional system is assessment by proxy where a panel of experts or jury make a collective judgement about the quality of a student's work, based on a visual exhibition and verbal presentation of the artwork or product made by the studio teacher. In other systems, the students themselves present and defend their own work ("in viva voce"), which I will term the "defence model". More recently, methods such as portfolios, which record the learning process, have been added as complimentary assessment tasks. This is not the practice in the case study from which I draw extensively for this chapter. Here, the defence model is adopted for formative assessments and the traditional jury system is used for summative assessment. Having access to this more "traditional" case, allowed me to gauge the impact of the Critique method which is held up by many as a paradigm of student-centred learning (Webster, 2005).

Feedback, given in studio dialogue and during Critiques, is mostly informal and discursive in nature. Assessments are social, public events with teachers giving and guiding oral feedback, including various degrees of peer involvement. Because of this social element, the dynamics between the agents in the teaching and learning relationship are very important. It has long been recognised that learning and "play" can only be made possible within a context of trust and acceptance (Winnicott, 1971), as both creative and critical thinking involve cognitive and affective skills (The Five Colleges of Ohio, 2007). In studio based interactions, much learning occurs through failure, challenge and difficulty (Corner, 2005). For this reason, art education is ideally intended to be experienced as "...luxurious but not elitist" (Talbot, 1998), with enough time for students to explore their aims and extend their limits, and space for play, uncertainty, maturation and critical reflection. The reality, especially because of the affective nature of assessment, is that such ideals are often not experienced by students as intended. For this reason, in this chapter I look particularly at how creativity is affected by the role that the assessor adopts and the feedback s/he provides. Structural factors are equally important and so the impact of the assessment focus (process and/ product) and assessment criteria on creating such safe spaces are also considered.

What the conditions for creativity necessitate is a pedagogic approach that "… *is facilitating, enabling, responsive, open to possibilities, and collaborative, and which values process as much as product*" (Jackson, 2004:9). How this translates into formative and summative assessment practices, which are commonly accepted to heavily influence students' approaches to and experiences of learning, is the central concern of my discussion.

The Teacher-Assessor as Critical Friend

In fine art, the four dominant traditions of teacher-student interactions can be linked to how creativity is conceptualised (Cowdroy & de Graaf, 2005). The "gifted" tradition holds that creative ability is a gift that may be nurtured by a master within a teaching and learning partnership of mutual respect with the gifted student. The "innate" tradition assumes that creativity is innate but can be developed through "followship". The "studio apprenticeship" tradition is underpinned by the idea that creativity can only be taught through prolonged association with living masters, who pass on their abilities (and values). The "reproduction" tradition holds that creativity can only be learnt through reproducing the work of past masters with the assistance of tutors, emphasising craft over intellect or originality.

However, we know from social theories of learning that creativity is more conducive in non-hierarchical contexts which have an allowance of difference, student ownership and personal development (Siegel & Kaemmerer, 1978), and a valuing of uncertainty, ambiguity and fantasy (Creativity in Education, 2003). In addition, constructivist conceptions have challenged the idea of the teacher as an expert in authority. Since autonomous learning or "metalearning" (Nickerson *et al.*, 1985) is now understood as one of the central determinants of student creativity (Jackson, 2004; Freeman, 2006), a shift is necessitated in teachers' roles from "masters" to a more balanced power relationship, with the teacher as facilitator, guide or critical friend. Where the teacher and student begin to share goals, there is more possibility that a *"community of practice"* can be created (Wenger, 1998). Such a shift in role would need to be explored consciously by educators for a climate conducive to creativity to be established. The challenge is that we often slip into practicing certain traditions, such as those identified above, without carefully considering their relation to the conceptions of creativity we hold.

I attempted to excavate such disjunctions between the espoused and practiced in recent research I conducted using critical discourse analysis of data collected from a school of fine art in South Africa (Belluigi, 2008a). Despite the constructive potential of the Critique method of assessment, my findings revealed what many have long suspected: students often find them traumatic and in some cases detrimental to their learning. Mann (2001:17) argues that we should rethink *"...the potential[ly] heavy hand of our assessment practices in the delicate world of the student's self; and... the complexity, uncertainty and threat of the learning process itself"*. Being in a situation where one's self is not validated in relationships and contexts leads to a loss of "self", agency and desire (Mann, 2001). When such estrangement from the student's creative and autonomous self occurs, it is replaced by a compliant self, leading to a more reproductive than productive approach to his/her learning. The result is that the student becomes bereft of the capacity for creativity. When this occurs repetitively, the student will choose self-preservation, realising it is safer to disengage by repressing his/her desire and adopting a superficial or strategic approach (Mann, 2001).

Mann's perspectives of alienation proved a powerful framework for my analysis of the student data recorded in journals during the period of a week before, during and after the assessment event, and the stories (some written in the third person) written a week later. I found that for many students their sense of self was indeed dependent on such validation, most notably by the studio-practice teacher. As is evident from the sense of trepidation expressed by this student in her third person story:

> *"The next day excited with her idea, after sitting outside the studio for half an hour, she plucked up the courage to walk in... As she had suspected, all X [studio practice teacher] said was that it didn't comment on anything. 'It comments on me DAMMIT!' thought Chloe".*

The students' journals and stories revealed that they were often put in positions where their selves were not validated, perceiving that teachers were not responding to their individual needs. For many students the lack of validation created an experience of alienation, as this student described:

"The criticism ends up confusing him and leaving him feeling demoralised, like nothing he has done has been worthy of time. 'Why am I making art?' he wonders. He goes back home feeling desolate, not knowing why he ever decided to [make] art. He feels completely unmotivated to create at all".

When "hearing" the excerpt from this story, it is important to keep in mind that metalearning is central to student creativity, and those students able to take responsibility and control over their learning are more inclined towards creative practice (Freeman, 2006). The importance of student agency and autonomy cannot be overestimated. Creative disciplines link creativity and engagement so that the two are interdependent (Reid & Solomonides, 2007). Students learning in an environment they perceive to be supportive and non-threatening, have higher motivation and are more likely to *"...make sense of the tasks in hand"* (Marton & Säljö, 1984) with more learning likely to take place (Blair, 2006). Intrinsic motivators assist creativity whereas extrinsic motivators, such as examination pressure or incentive of a "good" grade, are generally held to undermine it (Amabile, 1996). From interactions at assessments, students learn what pleases the assessors. Such compliance would most probably result in "weak" acts of creativity. All the more reason for teachers looking carefully at affective aspects of their approach, to ensure where possible that experiences of alienation are minimised and rich engagement enabled. To create such a climate of independence requires backwash from assessment practices, from the focus of the assessment through to the rest of the curriculum, as I will now discuss.

The Assessment Focus on Process

From cognitive theories of learning we know that for creative development problem-based learning is most effective because it requires both divergent and convergent thinking (Dineen *et al.*, 2005). Considered integral to creativity are play, experimentation and process, which have been linked to autonomy and developing evaluation skills (Winnicott, 1971; Freeman, 2006). Creative and critical thinking are now recognised to be as important as mastery of skill or technique (Sloan & Nathan, 2005). Moreover, studies have found that student creativity is fostered by an emphasis on *"process"* rather than *"product"* (Knight, 2002a; Jackson, 2004).

In fine art, this focus on process is reiterated by the community of practice but not necessarily within academia. Much of the discussion around contemporary art questions the value of the art object itself, extending the notion of *"art-as-object"* to include *"process-as-practice"* and *"theory-as-practice"* (Sullivan,

1993). A postmodernist contention is that representation is not only an act of (re)presentation but also invention, with unpredictable options that emerge when in progress. For these reasons, *"production logs"*, *"portfolios"*, or *"creative journals"* are recent additions as assessment methods (Dallow, 2003; Gordon, 2004). However many curricula have maintained the sole focus of summative assessments on product through *"assessment by exhibition"* (Cowdroy & de Graaf, 2005), as in the case I studied.

In this study, teachers' responses to a questionnaire and in our discussions made it clear that they equated experimentation or play with immaturity. Whilst permitted in the first two years of study, experimentation was not given value at the end of the degree where the student was expected to exhibit his/her mastery. In the summative method of assessment-by-exhibition, students were graded solely on the artefact displayed, creating much emphasis on the product. When examining the data, it became clear that the few supervisors who in studio interactions may have encouraged their students to experiment or be "in process", failed to recognise or confront the backwash of summative assessment practices. In contrast, the students were well aware of the disjunction between the espoused encouragement of risk taking and the constraints of assessment practices which made no allowance for process or failure. This disjunction added stress to this student's experience, reflected in her third-person journal entry:

> *"The teacher in his arty way had said 'Just do it! It doesn't matter if you bugger it up! That's how you learn!'. Just that sentence sent the perfectionist Chloe into a panic frenzy, 'Just do it?' How could she just do it, it was half a year's worth of work, what if it was a mess? How would she fix it? How would the assessment go? Would she pass?"*

What my research found was that an emphasis on product can create an environment contrary to the conditions required for creativity and critical thinking, because students need to feel safe to play and to take risks with the foreknowledge that they may fail. In the art school I studied, an assessor acknowledged that Critiques *"…can get dreadful in that respect… to be able to be creative you have to have self-confidence"*. The timing of these formative assessments, determined according to logistical convenience rather than being placed sensitively within students' cycles of reflective learning, also had a negative effect on students' learning. An assessor recounted in an interview that *"…there have been instances in the past, when a student was midway through a process, [with] the teachers prematurely saying 'god no, it's not going to work, it's a disaster. Cut it up'"*. In my observations, I found that most feedback indicated an instrumental rationality with fact separated from value and the focus on "how to" and conditions such as the amount of output, sizes of works, display or framing, and time constraints.

Data collected from participating students confirmed studies which indicate that summative assessments often undermine the creative process (Dineen *et al.*, 2005). When the emphasis is on the product, it can too easily become part of a system of exchange undertaken for strategic reasons. Drawing on Marx's four perspectives on alienation, Mann (2001) notes that such a strategic approach can occur when, firstly, there is alienation from the product of one's labour; secondly, alienation from the process of production; thirdly, alienation from oneself as a species-being; and lastly, alienation from other human beings.

The art school I studied strongly valued the final product (Belluigi, 2008a). In their journals and stories most students indicated that at some point in the build up and aftermath of the Critique event they experienced alienation from their artworks, from their art-making, from their "selves" or from other people. This is of concern because of the importance that commitment, desire and engagement have in fostering creativity.

The Issue of Assessment Criteria

One of the difficulties in HE is how to assess creativity, risk-taking, meaning-making and "wow" factors (Gordon, 2004) while also creating the conditions conducive for their development. In subjective areas of human experience and expression, "connoisseurship" has been considered an appropriate form of judgment (Knight, 2005). However a strict definition of connoisseurship is incompatible with current ideas about relativism because it suggests the holding of absolute values (Hardy, 2003). Preferably, the traditional notion of the connoisseur as "expert" could be extended to "the critic" who has to *work* at being a reflexive assessor (Smith, 2001). Reliability and fairness is of concern when assessing creative works, but not at the expense of validity. Most important is how such processes of thinking and judgement affect student learning and creativity.

In the case I studied, I found that students were left to deduce the implicit criteria in Critique interactions employed in the traditional norm-referenced system (Belluigi, 2009). This system is problematic for critical thinking and creativity, because where students lack understanding of the rules of the game they tend to stay within familiar and conservative parameters (Knight, 2002a). However, experimentation and process, as discussed previously, both require risk-taking and play. Indicators or criteria for assessment are potentially constructive for discussions between staff and students. However in the creative arts fields, establishing successful systems of criterion-referenced assessment have proved easier said than done. In fact, there is a recognised absence of criteria for assessing the subtleties of creative acts or high level creative ability (Cowdroy & de Graaf, 2005). Because much of art making involves unpredictability, some argue that neither norm-reference nor criterion-reference assessment is appropriate because they both involve comparison (Eisner, 1993). Most often the assessment focus is forced on to the end-product, rather than the creative process behind the product. Typically, this results in the product being assessed with arbitrarily assigned criteria (Cowdroy & de Graaf, 2005; Belluigi, 2008a).

In addition, none of the dominant art traditions (whether master-apprentice, reproduction, or the innate or gifted traditions discussed before) focus on *"intention"* (Cowdroy & de Graaf, 2005). Arguably the highest order of creative ability is imaginative conceptualisation (Cowdroy & de Graaf, 2005), referred to in post-structuralism as the author's intentionality for meaning-making in the text. Deep approaches to learning are characterised by desire, where learning is related to personal experience. A search for meaning and authorship is unfortunately recognised too late as important in this student's third person reflections in the days after the Critique:

> *"This is where the first problems appeared – at the very beginning. Penny should have… asked herself the most crucial question any artist could have asked: 'what do I want from this work?'".*

A paradigm shift is required from teacher-derived criteria for examination of a work to student-derived criteria around the student's understanding of the concept in terms of philosophical and theoretical frameworks. Studies that have used such *"Authenticative Assessment"* indicate that this is more successful for creativity in a range of contexts (Cowdroy & de Graaf, 2005). Negotiated criteria signal to the student the value of their intentions and reflexivity (Freeman, 2006). In the process, students are able to identify areas of importance in their own learning which would benefit from development or improvement. This not only rewards what students see as important learning achievements but also highlight these areas as foci to teachers, who can help problematise and be more supportive of students' learning processes.

The potential educational benefits of valuing student intentionality and agency are many (Hughes, 1999):

i.   reduced dependency on teachers throughout all stages, from producing the problem, selecting methods, materials and modes of execution, to assessing work

ii. student ownership and responsibility in terms of their own work and establishing their own criteria:

iii. increased motivation and a more engaged experience

iv. allowance for a diversity in the range of discourses, materials, *et cetera* which should result in a greater variety of artwork.

Making the structural choice of negotiated criteria is not without agentic considerations because the individual teacher has some of the greatest influence on the curriculum. Negotiated criteria would be better for those teachers who believe that creativity is innate, where the potential of each individual can be developed. The pedagogic goal is individual growth towards the ultimate aim of student-independence rather than skills acquisition or mastery of technique. For creativity, self-actualization will need to be prioritized over subject-knowledge (Dineen *et al.*, 2005).

The difficulties of embracing such a goal, as an individual without cultural or structural support and alignment, was revealed in my research (Belluigi, 2008a). One teacher discussed how s/he tried to separate grade allocation from the value placed on students' accomplishments: *"...the student should complete his/her degree with a keen sense of accomplishment and ownership of his/her work – regardless of the mark awarded"*. This encouraged, unwittingly or not, the students to disregard the implicit criteria valued by the art school without consideration of the impact on the person's career or sense of self. One of this teacher's students wrote about the conflict created by such separation of feedback from his/her own sense of accomplishment:

> *"I would like to pretend that I don't care about the crit, but I do. I care because I want to be an artist, a practicing artist (and that's all) for the rest of my life. – so obviously [I] take advice and criticism to heart. I'm not just getting a fine art degree to then carry on after varsity in a completely different field. This is my life".*

This journal extract provides a glimpse of how strongly a student's self-concept can be intertwined with their studies in creative arts fields. Boundaries are formed by disciplines and discourses which feed into how individual identities are included, excluded and developed (Becher, 1989). Thus agentic, cultural and structural, as well as teaching, learning and curricular aspects, need to be aligned for the conditions to foster creativity to be successfully created.

The Impact of Feedback on Learning

Earlier I discussed the importance of the relationship between teacher and student, because the conditions for creativity require *"…sensitive, trusting and responsive teacher-student relationships necessary to facilitate, continually respond to and adapt to what emerges from the process"* (Jackson, 2004:8). Such a relationship of trust is created and often tested during periods of assessment and through feedback. While it is generally accepted that feedback is critical to learning through assessment (Taylor & McCormack, 2005), recognition should also be given to the role of feedback on students' motivational beliefs and self-esteem (Juwah *et al.*, 2004). Ideally, formative assessment should increase students' confidence and intrinsic motivation.

Even those adopting what might be seen as a mechanistic approach to creative-thinking in creative arts disciplines, have stressed the importance of emotion and the subconscious on creativity. However, only recently has there been recognition that the Critique method is experienced by students as exceptionally emotional. Misunderstandings of formative feedback, negative experiences or stress interfere with students' cognitive resources and the resultant level of learning (Blair, 2006). My study confirmed Blair's (2006) findings that student learning is not just reliant on the nature or quality of the feedback given, but on broader factors such as power relations and stress which impact on "the self". In a number of observed exchanges at Critiques, I found that student agency was denied by the assessors, with unexplained suggestions and instructions often given against students' desires or intentionality. Thwarting experimentation, in one instance a student was warned that by trying a desired approach s/he would *"f*** it up"*. What this suggested was an imbalanced power dynamic, more akin to the master-apprentice tradition than a relationship of guidance and facilitation. Opportunities for sharing positive feedback were rarely taken. Ignoring student intentionality resulted in formative feedback often unrelated and irrelevant to students' learning processes. As with Blair's (2006) study on feedback, such Critiques were experienced by students as ineffectual, demotivating and confusing. One student expressed in his story that:

> *"…the crit seems to have been a bit silly, like they completely missed the point of what he was doing and therefore couldn't give him any helpful advice".*

The importance of open discussion and negotiated criteria, discussed before, is not only about transparency or disclosure, but about enabling students to interpret feedback. According to Corner (2005:340), *"…fine art learning*

experiences... need to be set in a cognitive framework that allows the student to refer-
ence, explain, interpret, evaluate, experiment and assess their creations and artistic
development". Prescriptions from assessors create experiences of alienation, compliance and reduce judgment, thereby removing much of the educational benefit of assessments. For this reason, feedback should be designed to act as proposals of possible readings and not instructions (Knight, 2001). To actively evaluate such feedback, students should be immersed in assessment activities, participating fully in their own Critiques and those of their peers.

Constant constructive dialogue between teacher and student as the process progresses has been found to impact positively, in contrast to those students who receive less feedback (Lindström, 2006). This returns us to my initial point about the importance of the teacher-assessor's role as a critical friend. In order for teaching and learning interaction to truly foster creativity, teachers would have to forego their own desires imposed on the student for willingness to facilitate the student's achievement of his/her intention. Recent feminist psychology conceptualizes caring relationships as those that are *"mutually engaging and rewarding"* (Tom, 1997:6), rather than one-way exercises. This relationship involves just enough support (neither excessive nor lacking), for the student to learn from the process (Mann, 2001). A safe space needs to be established for the relevant assessment criteria to be negotiated and a supportive culture created through valid constructive feedback.

Conclusion

Whilst I am cautious of claiming too easy transference from this context to another, I believe that many lessons and suggestions arise from research into assessment in fine art. In this chapter I have identified four important areas of teaching and learning interactions, which impact on the conditions for creativity: (i) the teacher-assessor acting as a critical friend; (ii) assessment focused on process to allow for a different conception of failure, and to encourage productive rather than reproductive thinking; (iii) negotiated criteria which recognise the importance of student intentionality, increasing students' intrinsic motivation and autonomy; (iv) formative feedback informed by the assessment focus and made relevant by the negotiated criteria.

It is essential for these cultural, structural and agentive elements to recognise and be sensitive to the affective nature of the relationship between learning and creativity.

About the Author

Dina Zoe Belluigi is a lecturer at the Centre for Higher Education Research, Teaching and Learning at Rhodes University, South Africa. She can be contacted at this e-mail: d.belluigi@ru.ac.za

Chapter Five

How Criticality Affects Students' Creativity

Hanne Kirstine Adriansen

Introduction

In the knowledge society, creativity and innovation are in high demand. There is increasing focus on the role of education as a place not only for unlocking the creative potential of gifted students but also for teaching all students how to be creative and innovative (Craft, 2006). While few universities offer courses on creativity *per se*, an increasing number of courses in innovation and entrepreneurship have seen daylight over the past decade. This chapter sees creativity as a step towards innovation. When wanting to distinguish between creativity and innovation, Amabile *et al.* (1996:1155) explain that all innovation begins with creative ideas. They further explain that innovation is *"...the successful implementation of creative ideas within an organization. In this view, creativity by individuals and teams is a starting point for innovation; the first is a necessary but not sufficient condition for the second"*. Hence, creativity is intimately related to any innovation process.

The theme of this chapter is how we can teach creativity and innovation in academia. It addresses an apparent paradox: there is an increasing interest from universities to run courses on creativity, but universities may not be the right place to host such courses. As Oliver *et al.* (2006) have pointed out, many students experience a conflict between being *"creative"* and being *"academic"*. Moreover, in academia, criticality is seen as a virtue (Phillips & Bond, 2004; Pithers & Soden, 2000). There is emphasis on critical thinking, on fault finding, and on deconstructing and searching for weak points in an idea or argument. The culture is often quite individual at least in terms of assessment which is based on individual performance. In contrast to this, the optimal conditions for creativity (in its "conventional" form) have to do with finding the strong points in an idea. In order to reach a brilliant idea, you have to accept that it may come after 29 miserable ideas. In a creative team, one should build on each others' ideas, be cooperative and constructive (Darsø, 2001). Hence, one must ask how we can foster creativity in higher education where criticality is seen as a vital teaching and learning goal.

The chapter discusses questions such as what is creative thinking and how does it relate to critical thinking? Do teaching the subject matters creativity and innovation mean that we have to be creative and innovative in our way of teaching? If yes, how do we practice what we preach? Hence, what is creative teaching and learning and how can this be assessed? The relevance of the chapter is twofold; as stimuli for the theoretical discussions of learning and creativity and as contributions to practitioners teaching innovation and creativity in academia.

Aim and Method of the Chapter

The chapter is practice oriented. While it discusses the concepts of creativity and criticality, the main emphasis is on teaching methods and assessment. The approach is inductive, taking departure in a concrete example of how creativity and innovation is taught at the degree programme in "Leadership and Innovation in Complex Systems", LAICS. This is a two-year, part-time, executive masters programme offered by the Danish School of Education, Aarhus University in cooperation with Copenhagen Business School, Denmark. The empirical material consists of interviews and observations.

By basing the chapter on empirical material from LAICS, I aim to shed light upon how creativity and innovation are taught in practice. Although we often know *how* it would be good to teach and assess, this may not be what we do in practice due to various constraints. By analysing what constitutes creativity and learning in a concrete case, I hope to be able to increase our understandings of these concepts at a more theoretical level. Upon this level we can further develop our understanding of how to teach creativity and which teaching methods have a positive effect on students' creativity and learning. The chapter is an attempt to contribute to the "second generation" creativity discussion (McWilliam & Dawson, 2008) on how to foster creative teaching and learning in academia.

The empirical material for this chapter consists primarily of qualitative interviews conducted in the form of action research. I firstly interviewed five former students, then I taught my present students interview techniques and told them to interview each other using a time line, which I gathered afterwards. In addition, when I was teaching them to do a timeline interview, I got them to participate as a focus group to consider their learning journey. I also interviewed the current study leader.

From the outset of writing this chapter, the apparent paradox between criticality and creativity intrigued me, but when I conducted the interviews, I concentrated on the learning journeys and only addressed this paradox towards the end of the interview. When analysing the interviews, however, a tension was detected between creativity and "alternative methods" on the one hand and "traditional, academic methods" on the other hand. Hence, the analysis has been an iterative process, which has homed in on the interviewees' learning journey tales and on the issues of creativity and criticality.

Creativity and Criticality – an Introduction

Given the lack of an established, commonly agreed framework for understanding and conceptualising creativity, I adopt an exploratory approach. I am inspired by Bohm (1998) who refuses to capture what is ultimately indefinable. Yet for the purpose of discussing creativity versus criticality it is useful to have an idea about what the two concepts entail.

In psychology literature, there are numerous definitions of creativity depending on the perspective of the author, but divergent thinking, diversity, originality, and novelty are the prevalent keywords (e.g. Runco, 2004; Simonton, 2000; Sternberg, 2006). Some also include an element of appropriateness of new ideas (e.g. Lubart, 1994; Sternberg, 2006). However, I find that the discussion of value or appropriateness of novel ideas belong to the realm of innovation and not to creativity. For the purpose of this chapter, I find it useful to look at the discourse employed by the editors of "*Developing creativity in higher education*" (Jackson et al., 2006) – Jackson who also writes the foreword in this volume. This states that creativity has to do with our ability to imagine and invent new worlds for ourselves. In their book, the term creativity is coined slightly differently in the various chapters, but there seems to be an agreement that higher education should foster creativity both at individual and at institutional level. Hence, creativity is a "talent" that we all have, which can be nurtured, rather than a gift from nature for a selected few. In the literature on criticality, this is rarely seen as a "gift of nature", but as a skill all students possess (although to a varying degree) and one of the important duties of higher education is to foster critical thinking abilities in students. Although the conceptualisations vary, criticality is always related to rational thinking. Often it also entails deconstructing ideas or problems by being analytical, selective, and evaluative (see e.g. Bailin *et al.*, 1999; Phillips & Bond, 2004; Pithers & Soden, 2000).

As noted by Bailin (1987:23), creativity and criticality are often portrayed as two different ways of thinking, requiring different pedagogies: "*Critical thinking is seen as analytic. It is the means for arriving at judgements within a given framework or context. Creative thinking, on the other hand, is seen as imaginative, constructive, generative. It is what allows for the breaking out of or transcending of the framework itself*".

While it is commonplace to contrast creativity and criticality (e.g. de Bono 1977; Jackson *et al.* 2006) – and this was also my initial thought when I began writing this chapter – there are also a number of similarities. Some researchers even see the two ways of thinking as intertwined (e.g. Belluigi, 2009; Edwards *et al.* 2006; Reiker, in this volume), while others have definitions that blur the differences. A case in point is this definition of creativity by one of the creativity's "grand old men" E. P. Torrance (1988:47): "*Creativity is the process of sensing difficulties, problems, gaps in information, missing elements, something askew; making guesses and formulating hypothesis; possibly revising and retesting them; and finally communicating the results*".

This is close to some of the conceptualisations of criticality mentioned above. In particular, problem solving seems to call for both creative thinking and critical thinking. Hence, even though there are differences between the two ways of thinking, the literature is not entirely clear on what the difference entails. Table 1 is an illustration of some of the differences between creativity and criticality as these concepts are described in the literature.

Creativity	Criticality
Imaginative	Rational
Non-judgemental	Evaluative
Generative	Selective
Holistic	Analytic
Constructing	Deconstructing
Transcending the framework	Within the framework
Open to serendipity	Work systematically
Iterative process with detours	Linear process

Table 1. Idealised differences between criticality and creativity

The conceptualisation of creative and critical thinking also depends on the writers' epistemological point of departure – whether one sees knowledge as given or as constructed. When knowledge is seen as a given, it is the product, not the process, which is important; and vice versa. I find that concentration on product or process does not correspond to critical or creative thinking respectively, instead it relates to the epistemological view of knowledge.

In the following, I apply an understanding of criticality and creativity which means that critical thinking can be creative in questioning that which is often taken for granted. However, it can also be futile for creativity due to the focus on deconstructing rather than constructing. Hence, I suggest that critical and creative thinking are not two entirely separate and distinct ways of thinking. After analysing my empirical material, I will address the question of creativity and criticality again and hopefully develop a better understanding of how we can teach creativity in higher education where the emphasis is on criticality.

The LAICS Case and the Empirical Material

The LAICS masters degree focuses on innovation and leadership from a "real-world", practice-based and social skills perspective using arts-based methods. It is cross-disciplinary and targeted at organisation leaders, senior project leaders, and key specialists working with leadership, innovation, and business development. The curriculum is designed with emphasis on the learning process rather than the content. Hence, it belongs to degree programmes with a learning-based paradigm rather than a syllabus-driven didactic paradigm (Nygaard & Holtham, 2008). The pedagogies used at LAICS are inspired by John Dewey's (1933, 1938) and Donald Schön's (1983, 1987) educational philosophies in which building on experience, practice-centred experimentation, and reflection are fundamental (LAICS, 2010). The process focus is important, and it relates to the view on creativity. Many creativity researchers have noted the difference between seeing creativity as related to person, process, or product (e.g. Lubart, 1994; Runco, 2004). The approach applied at LAICS is related to seeing creativity as process when it comes to creative teaching and learning.

In the summer of 2006, the first students were admitted at LAICS and two years later, the first cohort finished their masters degree. Every year, some twenty students are admitted. Not all finish within two years. As each semester (called a module) is paid for separately, modules can be taken as single modules and it is possible to take a break between modules. Each module consists of three seminars. The duration of each seminar is typically 3½ days and they are held as residential courses at nice conference venues in Denmark. One seminar in each module is held abroad. There is a module coordinator for each seminar and one member of the faculty, often the module coordinator, is present during the entire seminar, facilitating the processes and making sure that the different activities are connected. In between the seminars participants complete assignments, work in groups and participate in virtual dialogues with each other and the faculty.

Both abroad and in Denmark, each seminar begins with a "check in". This means that all participants, while sitting in a circle, take turn in telling "*Where am I?*" and sharing with each other how they feel upon arrival. Hence, it is a means of arriving, of leaving work and private life behind in order to be able to concentrate fully on the seminar ahead. The check-in also helps build an atmosphere of trust, because the participants can tell what is on their mind, their concerns or changes in life, without anybody interrupting or even commenting. There is no time limit, but usually each participant spends a minute or two. It is not compulsory to say anything. After the check in and a presentation of the seminar programme, two "gardeners" are found. The use of gardeners is based on Darsø's (2001) innovation research, which shows that relations are extremely important. Even though the goal of an innovation process and of a degree programme is different, the gardener role is useful for both, as the gardener helps the group to build trust and create the right space for creativity and learning. The responsibilities of the gardeners are the wellbeing of the participants, the group climate and energy level; they help creating positive relations, creating common ground, getting to know each other's strong points.

They do so by being in close contact with the faculty during the seminar and they have 30 minutes every day where they can address the needs and wants of the participants. This can be discussing the curriculum or a burning question, but most often it is some sort of physical activity or play.

The seminars consists of a combination of lectures, group work, and some type of physical engagement with materials, for instance by prototyping innovation spaces, drawing, or using clay to express leadership. Due to the understanding of creativity as a process, we use tools and techniques from fields such as facilitation and process consultation, which do not concern creativity but are by definition very process focused in their approach to teaching and learning. This means that the participants also gain a repertoire of methods such as Open Space and World Café, which are useful for leading the creative process. Time for reflection is important. Therefore, there is time set aside for writing in a "learning journal" (a log book for reflections, questions, and learning points) around lunch and before dinner. If possible, group discussions can take place as "walk and talk" making the most of beautiful surroundings. After dinner there is often group work for a couple of hours. After that the participants socialise. This is an important part of the seminar and of building relations and an atmosphere of trust. Each seminar ends with a standard written and an oral evaluation as well as a "check out". The format of the oral evaluation varies; often the gardeners are involved in deciding how to evaluate. The check out resembles the check in, but is concerns *"What do I take with me from the seminar?"*.

The seminars are planned with three intertwined elements in mind: process, practice, and experiments. The process orientation means that the faculty not act as teachers but rather as facilitators stimulating the participants' learning. While faculty plan each seminar carefully and make a detailed script, it is important to have a programme that leaves room for what emerges. Emphasis on practice entails that the participants' own cases are used as examples whenever possible. The learning approach of LAICS is experimental and experiential, this means that we try to experiment, play, and reflect as a supplement to listening to lectures. The presentation of the Theory U described later is an example hereof. Finally, the use of the physical space is also considered – what seating arrangement will be most useful for the purpose of the day? How can we use our bodies and not just sit down all day? How can we benefit from the natural surroundings? We want to negotiate the physical space to ensure a pleasant and energetic atmosphere.

In the following analysis, I combine information from interviews with observations made as member of the faculty.

Students' Learning Journey Tales

The pedagogies of LAICS concentrate on the learning process rather than the content. This focus is related to an understanding of creativity as a process and thereby time becomes an important element. The learning process can be understood as a learning journey, a word used quite often at LAICS. Therefore it was natural to ask the interviewees (former students) about their learning journey. So I have decided to structure the following analysis of the interviews as a learning journey tale.

It is common to open a tale with the beginning. And the first step in the LAICS learning journey for all students was to apply for admission. Why did they choose LAICS? The interviewees wanted an academic degree; hence a course in innovation outside academia was not an option. The alternative, for some of them, would have been an MBA. They stated that the interest in obtaining a university degree was for career purposes and that for a number of reasons they found LAICS the most attractive on the market. While they showed interest in the teachings on innovation and leadership as well as the alternative teaching/learning approach, none of them expressed a particular interest in the offerings of academia *per se*. The attraction of academia was to receive a diploma in the end.

Some of the interviewees were particularly interested in the structure of three residential seminars per semester rather than having more frequent lessons at university. This fitted better with a busy work life, which many of the students lead while completing the masters degree. The seminar format is also quite important for the teaching style and for the learning outcome, as follows.

The first seminar at module 1 was held in Denmark and here the students were exposed to the learning culture and some of the teaching methods they would meet throughout their education. A substantial part of the seminar is spent on relationship building. But as one of the participants explained, part of this was done as integral elements of other subjects, which meant that for him, the intense and profound relationship development also took place subconsciously. An actor worked with the group and used image theatre as a means to discuss obstacles to innovation. They made body sculptures of and with each other instead of having a traditional lecture. Some participants saw this as a playful and very open approach towards the journey they were now entering. Time was also spent on making a "codex" for how to work and learn. The important aspect of this is not the codex itself – it is discussed and may by revised at the second seminar – but it is the process entailed in making the codex (Darsø,

2008). This allowed the participants to share their experiences with learning environments, to empower them and take responsibility, and also get to know each other. Hence, it was an element in constructing an atmosphere of trust and curiosity. Body mapping was another technique used for getting people to know each other. This method entails that people move around in the room (or preferably outside) depending on their preferences or interests and talk to people with similar preferences and interests. For some, the first seminar was a shock, while others found it very stimulating and interesting:

> "I was pleasantly surprised at the first seminar because it was so creative. Many were frustrated, because it was so open and not structured. I could deal with it because it reminded me of the creative process. Afterwards we could all see why there was so little structure".

It comes as no surprise that those students who were already familiar with creativity (e.g. being part-time artists or having an educational background as architects) found the session stimulating. One of the interviewees explained how she had experienced the first seminar as unstructured and very confusing, even frustrating, leaving the seminar with more questions than answers:

> "I had a feeling of having wasted three days".

But already when preparing the first assignment, she became a little more positive:

> "I could feel that I had some new thoughts, was thinking in a new way".

And in hindsight, she could see how the first seminar had made sense, how it had prepared her for the journey.

The drawings of the learning journeys made by present students showed that for many, the seminars abroad had been more intense and for some had led to more learning than the seminars in Denmark. The reasons for this are manifold, as revealed during the in-depth interviews. In my observation, being abroad increases the concentration on the task at hand. There is no possibility for attending a meeting, going home at night, or leaving earlier. Also, there may be a time difference which makes it more difficult to be on-line with family, colleagues, or clients. Also, seminars abroad are held in beautiful natural surroundings such as in the Rocky Mountains. Here, the seminar is held at *The Banff Centre*, which has post-graduate training in leadership working with an arts- and nature-based approach to leadership and complexity. Many people find the natural surroundings stimulating for learning and reflecting. Third, the content of the seminars abroad is focused inwards, for instance looking at personal leadership, personal innovation spaces, and they are quite experimental. All together this meant that some of the students had a different, a more intense experience than "at home" and for some this also increased the learning outcome. Interviewee comments included:

> *"Being in a completely new context and spending time together have meant a lot. The joint curiosity, the joint wondering, the communities of interest. Having gone for walks, discussing and reflecting first with one person, then with another, have given different perspectives and inputs. It has been really, really good".*

> *"The seminars abroad have been more creative and I have liked that".*

The work with Otto Scharmer's *Theory U* (Scharmer, 2007) is an example of the various approaches and methods used. The participants are introduced to theory U during the second seminar at module one. The theory U concerns leadership and innovation from a very personal perspective. The seminar usually takes place in France and is thus one of the seminars abroad with a personal and inward perspective. The theory U is both explained in a "conventional" academic way, but is it also conveyed by the violinist, Miha Pogacnik. His music is used as a means of understanding different levels of creativity (Darsø, 2008). Important aspects of the theory U are presence and sensing. These aspects are returned to later in the programme in different ways. At the seminar in Banff, for example, there is a walking meditation, where the participants are trained in being present "being in the now" by paying attention to what there are sensing through a walk in the natural surroundings. This is a very practical and non-academic way to approach some of the key concepts of Theory U. At the last seminar on module three, there is a session on mindfulness. The session is a combined practical and academic introduction to the concept of mindfulness and how it can be practiced. While some of the participants disliked the walking meditation in Banff, others really enjoyed it. However, when we discussed the learning points from Banff at the proceeding seminar, some of the negative perceptions had changed. In hindsight they appreciated the experience and what they had learned. During the course, there is a growing awareness that learning may develop gradually and sometimes be "delayed".

In general, the facilitative and process-oriented teaching style and practice-based methods in combination with the residential seminar format has created a special atmosphere. As one student explained, there had been a space for wondering and room for reflection. Among the students themselves, there have been many academic discussions. Some said that it was primarily amongst them that the students had analysed and discussed the curriculum, as there had been little time for that during the seminars. Few teachers explain the curriculum; instead they deliberate a different but related topic or story. Sometimes there is group work discussing the curriculum during the seminar. Otherwise some of the participants made sure to discuss it anyway. The time set aside for reflections every day at every seminar had often been used for these discussions. Many emphasised the importance of time for reflection. While some had enjoyed using the learning journal given for each module, others admitted that they had never used it as writing was not a useful tool for reflecting:

"I have been reflecting but not through the tip of a pen".

During my informal conversations with the students, they have expressed a wish for discussing the curriculum more during the seminars. It is not entirely clear whether the students are calling for more traditional, academic teaching or for more criticality in the approach – there are a number of different voices. During interviews, however, nobody has stated this. There has been more focus on taking responsibility for their learning not leaving it up to the teacher or the way of teaching:

"It has been very ambitious, but at the same time there has been room for people engaging in different ways… It's up to you and the projects you make. What you give is what you get".

This difference in perceptions comes as no surprise. The kinds of grumble heard in informal conversations usually change when people participate in a more formal and thoughtful situation such as an interview. This does not mean that the grumble is invalid, just that we as human beings may have different and sometimes conflicting views.

An important part of the learning journeys was the assessment process. The students had to write a 15-page mini project for the first three modules. The mini-project was presented and defended through an oral exam. The mini project should concern the student's own practice and this should be analysed in relation to models and theories presented in the literature. In this context it is interesting to see how assessment affects learning. From the interviewees' learning-journey tales it seems that this varies quite a bit although they all agreed that the assessment method was very traditional and academic, while the teaching methods were seen as alternative and creative. One of the interviewees was quite satisfied with the very traditional assessment which made him feel safe, on familiar territory. Another one stated that the assessment was a means to use the curriculum as this was not discussed very much during the seminars. While a third student felt that the seminars did not prepare her for the type of assessment used and that the assessment did not "measure" the learning outcome of the seminar but only assessed some academic qualifications which had not been part of the teaching during the seminars.

The students have quite varied educational backgrounds ranging from bachelor degrees to PhDs and from nursing to engineering. As there is little emphasis on teaching academic writing and other academic skills, some students are better off when it comes to writing their mini projects and perform well at the oral defence. The last module consists of two seminars which aim at helping the students write their thesis. The first seminar concerns research methodology such as action research and qualitative interviews. The second seminar is a writing retreat where students receive supervision from the faculty and help each other through peer-learning. The thesis itself is a traditional piece of academic work: 40-60 pages with a critical analysis of a practice-based problem. The thesis is defended at an oral exam similar to the mini projects. Some enjoyed writing the master thesis, while others found it an academic exercise they had not been adequately prepared for.

The last step in the learning journey concerned what the interviewees had learned and how they had applied it. A common expression of what they had learned was that they saw things in a new way. They had gained a new way of perceiving and reflecting about problems or situations in their respective organisations. Also, they had learned about different creativity theories and innovation models and experimented with different creativity tools and techniques. Whether they could be applied directly or not, the learning outcome was still beneficial. As expressed by one of the interviewees:

> "There are some tools which I wouldn't use in my current job, but there are a number of tools and processes which are useful… And even those things where I thought 'that's too far out' were good because at least I have tried it and know what it is".

While another one said:

"I have applied most of what I have learned directly. When we have learned something new, I have used it for my next project with a client".

Some also noticed how the study and the new ways of thinking had changed them as persons:

"When reading so much and trying so many new things you automatically start reflecting about methods, processes, etc., about your taken for granted knowledge... I have changed my impression of how to do things, and also on how I perceive and see things and how I work. This is what I mean by having changed and developed as a person".

Hence, it was not only their professional life which had gained from their learning journey and education, their personal development had also benefitted.

How Can We Teach Creativity?

In this section, I will analyse the learning journey of the LAICS programme based on an interview with the present study leader and on my observations and experiences as a LAICS faculty member. Furthermore, I will include the participants' perceptions of creativity.

The study leader explained that when they were creating LAICS as a degree programme, they had to "walk the talk" and use creative methods for developing the programme. Also, they presented the preliminary programme to potential organisations and listened to their needs in terms of creative employees and innovative leaders. Regarding the teaching methods, it was a high priority that there should be a lot of process work and reflectivity, as well as an experimental and explorative approach. They wanted to establish a learning culture right from the beginning. There should be no PowerPoints, no lectures, but lecturettes of 20 minutes. The programme should be leading edge and on the edge. It was important to establish a practice sphere where students could explore and experience leadership and innovation in situations that involved complexity and ambiguity. After the very first seminar, they realised that some adjustment was necessary. Hence, PowerPoints were permitted, also lectures, but not all the time. The occasional changes were based on the students' needs, because they wanted more input and less process work as well as a more structured, less open and explorative teaching style. Adjustments are still being made, but it is important that it should not be a formal structure determining the teaching methods. Instead the type of teaching depends on the topic of each seminar and on the faculty. Members of the faculty are both university professors and consultants. Some teachers are good at process work, while others perform better with more traditional teaching methods. When it comes to the type of assessment, the aims of the LAICS development team were quite different from the present outcome. As the study leader explains, they had to conform with the rules and regulations of the university and so far there has not been time or energy for challenging the rules or experimenting with innovative assessment.

From the outset, the use of arts-based approaches was an important tenet of the programme. Arts-based approaches are a useful means for accessing an inner focus which involves including knowledge derived from experience and reflection (Darsø, 2008). These approaches and techniques allow tacit knowledge to surface without violating it with words. They include theatre rehearsal and using live music for listening and improvisation. Some of the arts-based tools and methods are used by the "normal" faculty, others are presented by various artists, actors and the like who are included as faculty members. The teaching methods were selected in order to make teaching creative; an important element is the use of questions. "Powerful questions" are those which can stimulate curiosity and reflection, they generate energy and are seen as key to creativity and innovation. Questions are a well-known tool for generating creativity (Almeida and colleagues, in this volume; Lange, 2010). Another important element in the learning culture, and in making space for creativity during seminars, is the use of gardeners mentioned previously. To sum up how teaching is made creative in the context of the LAICS programme, it is useful to look at the study leader's description of the LAICS learning design:

1. Creating a learning culture right from the beginning

2. Every theory, model or method should be related to own practice

3. Seminars should be designed to be engaging and to involve the participants

4. Learning design must include giving the participants first-hand experience, followed by reflection

5. Learning design should include exploration and improvisation

6. Learning design should involve both intellect and feelings – and the body, when possible

7. Seminars must be designed to include personal reflection, conversations in small and larger groups, as well as plenum conversations and dialogue

8. Seminars must include space for reflection and inner dialogue through work with individual learning journals (Darsø, 2008:6).

This learning design remains the same, even though the seminars are developed and refined regularly. Hence, the learning journey of LAICS is not finished. An important lesson for us as faculty is how we cope with ambiguity and complexity. We experienced this in the Spring of 2010 where we were due to travel to Slovenia on the second module just when an ash plume from the Icelandic volcano interfered with air traffic in Europe. With two days notice we had to find an alternative location not involving too much travel and change the programme accordingly – not knowing whether we would be allowed to fly to Slovenia or not. We ended up staying in Copenhagen and had an even better seminar than the one planned. This led us to rethink the purpose of travelling to Slovenia for that particular seminar and change location for future seminars. Hence, the ash plume became a creative constraint, one which led to learning for all of us.

What did the participants learn about creativity during their learning journeys and how did they perceive creativity after finishing their masters degree? The interviewees had different, but not contrasting conceptualisations of creativity. Some of the views were:

"Creativity is to see things in new ways, to think new both within the existing framework and outside the framework".

"Creativity has to do with being open, not knowing what emerges. This is how you work as an artist. You cannot imagine what will happen if you add a certain colour. If it doesn't work, well then you know... Creativity is both imagining and trying in practice. And sometimes you cannot even imagine but just have to start with practice, with trying".

Not only did the interviewees talk about creativity, they had also embraced some of the elements of creativity. One clear example was their approach to failure. This concept was not mentioned by any of the interviewees. Their approach was that there is no such thing as a mistake; instead it may be a detour on your learning journey. And in line with this, there is an understanding among the interviewees that the same teaching does not constitute the same learning for all of them. We develop an understanding that creativity is social and collaborative. This understanding is also related to complexity theory. Within complexity theory connected to education and management, human systems are seen as comparable to nature which is rarely linear or predictable (Tosey, 2006).

Based on my observations and my experiences as a teacher and not the least as a supervisor, I find explaining my own creative research process is very rewarding for the students. Usually, journal articles and academic books portray the process as a rational, linear sequence of events that led to the outcome presented in the book – very much in line with some critical thinking. It is rare to see a description of the detours, coincidences, and serendipities which most researchers acknowledge as part of the process. Hence, the creative thinking part is omitted from the reporting of research. Therefore, I tell my students about the detours and serendipities I experience and encourage them also to be reflective and "honest" about their learning journey in their written assignments and in their oral assessments. In this way, I encourage a more emergent approach to knowledge generation; an approach, which is in line with the spirit of the degree programme while adhering to the format of the assessment.

Because the LAICS teaching methods are alternative and have a strong impact on the students' learning, it is interesting to notice how learning is assessed at LAICS. Generally, assessment has a strong influence on learning (Biggs, 2003). Therefore, I find it important to regard assessment as a central part of teaching and learning itself and not only as an act of measurement after learning has occurred. Assessment can help students to focus on the most important concepts and practices that they are studying. As explained by Boud (2006:xix):

> "The more we can engage students in assessment activities meaningful to them and which contribute to their learning, the more satisfying will be their experience of higher education".

However, assessment can also have a harmful effect on creativity (Belluigi, in this volume). The question is whether the assessment methods are able to capture the nature and the range of learning outcomes sought from the LAICS seminars. All interviewees concur that the assessment method is very traditional. They found that there was little assessment of the creative competencies they had gained. It seems that it is difficult to reconcile creativity and criticality in the current assessment process. Here criticality is rewarded.

The call for creativity in higher education is often related to the idea that we live in an increasingly complex world with rapid changes. The LAICS programme attempts to answer this call by using a learning approach where the students learn to live with ambiguity and to navigate in complex systems. To sum up, the main tools for this are: to establish a practice sphere with emphasis on practice and experiments thereby creating room for exploration and experiencing; to apply arts-based approaches, which allow us to access tacit knowledge and give an inner focus; to build a learning culture that emphasises the importance of relations, trust, and curiosity; to use a variety of teaching methods to allow for diversity; and to prioritise time for reflection. These are all tools that promote creativity one way or another. The learning approach includes both intellect, feelings and where possible also the body.

Creativity and Criticality Reconsidered

Is there a paradox or not between creative thinking and critical thinking? After studying some of the extensive literature on creativity and criticality and after analysing my empirical material, my answer is no. There is no paradox between the two ways of thinking. Sometimes they are intertwined, sometimes they complement each other and on a few occasions they can be futile for one another (Bailin, 1987). There are phases in a creative process where critical thinking can be detrimental, for instance in the middle of a divergent phase where focus is on quantity of ideas and not quality. In a convergent phase focus is on narrowing down the number of ideas and therefore quality is of importance and criticality becomes a tool – even in a creative process (Darsø, 2001). Hence, we need both creativity and criticality in academia and I agree with Bailin (1987:27) that "... *the critical and the creative are inextricably linked and are joint aspects of effective learning*". Or as Tosey (2006:37) explains: "*...dreaming, serendipity and the like can be complemented, refined and honed, but not replaced, by critical rationality*".

If we as higher education teachers pay attention to our teaching methods, we can enhance the students' learning and enhance both their creativity and criticality.

This being said, my learning journey studying this question has also led me to the conclusion that there is an *apparent* paradox between criticality and creativity because in academia we do not pay sufficient attention to the creative processes which are part of the research process. As shown by Kleiman (2008), criticality is not part of the daily discourse. We do not talk about our creative processes, nor do we report them in our publications. Usually peer reviewed articles and the like describe very linear, rational knowledge processes. However, when asking researchers how their new knowledge and research came into being, the road has usually been far from linear. Serendipity is a well known friend. Yet, we often talk about academic work using a vocabulary that seems more aligned with critical thinking than creative thinking. Hence, the cultural norms in academia are not cultivating creativity. Moreover, the academic rules and structures are hampering creativity. As Bleakley (2004:472-73) explains: *"Accidental by-products are commonly reported in science, arts and humanities research, but this type of creativity may be neglected in higher education in an era of obsessively learning outcomes and curriculum descriptors. Serendipity has perhaps become the unconscious or tacit dimension to such limiting pedagogical frameworks".*

Consequently, we see an apparent paradox between criticality and creativity. With criticality being a clear aim of higher education, it becomes difficult to teach creativity and teach creatively. While creativity can be inhibited by criticality, rules and structures are the major impediment to creative teaching in academia. As Jackson (2006:4) explains: *"Creativity is inhibited by predictive outcome-based course designs, which set out what students will be expected to have learned with no room for unanticipated or student-determined outcomes".*

Jackson further remarks that assessment criteria, which limit the students' possible ways of answering, are a major inhibitor both for students' and for teachers' creativity. This corresponds with the findings from LAICS in which assessment mainly is concerned with criticality.

Having acknowledged that creativity is constrained by academic norms, rules, and standards, let us now turn to how we can teach creativity and teach creatively. While creative thinking can be taught without teaching creatively, there is a conviction among LAICS faculty that it is better to practice what you preach and that creative teaching will enhance creative learning outcomes even if the subject taught is not creativity *per se*. At LAICS, creative teaching methods are used for teaching both innovation and leadership – there is no difference in the choice of teaching methods for the two subjects. By using an exploratory, practice-based approach and being open towards the needs and wants of the group, the LAICS faculty members facilitate the students' learning rather than teaching them. This leads to the idea that instead of teaching creativity *per se* we should seek to create the best conditions for learning creativity by teaching creatively.

Teaching creatively also has a bearing on what we teach and on our pedagogies. As mentioned, the pedagogies at LAICS are inspired by Dewey's and Schön's practice-oriented approaches emphasising experiential and experimental learning. One of the interviewees explained how practice relates to creativity and criticality in the teaching at LAICS:

> "...creativity is not only about being imaginative but also about practice. Practice is the link between creativity and criticality, between the imaginative and the rational. When you have tried something in practice, you use your criticality to judge what you have tried in practice. If you only are critical, you judge the idea without even trying it. Creativity is both imagining and trying in practice".

Following this view of creativity, teaching creatively also means making space for practice or creating a "practice sphere" to use the words of the LAICS study leader. By including an element of practice, of unfolding new ideas, a link is established to critical thinking – in this case by judging if the new piece of work was good or bad. The idea can be a painting needing further effort or an idea for research. Hence, if we want to teach creatively, we can do so by introducing elements of practice where creativity can be performed. And in the practice element, there can be interplay between creativity and criticality similarly to what Smith-Bingham (2006:16) has labelled "the cultivation of creativity in the context of critical practice". Hence, by including practice we use criticality to analyse if we are satisfied with the new world we have invented. This is one of the reasons why the practice element is so important at the LAICS programme.

Concluding Remarks

In this chapter, I set out to analyse how creativity is and can be taught in academia which is preoccupied with teaching criticality. I found that creative thinking and critical thinking are not at odds with each other. Hence critical thinking and a focus on criticality is not necessarily hampering creative thinking. But there are some constraints to teaching creativity and especially to creative teaching. These are related to the academic norms and culture, to the rule and structures found in academia. Some of these are imposed from the Government and others are not. As mentioned, we are not used to discussing creativity in academia, while criticality has a more prominent space. However, this does not mean that creativity has no space, on the contrary: many researchers acknowledge that research is a creation of new knowledge and therefore creative by nature. But when it comes to teaching, creativity has only little space outside the arts. This is unfortunate, as society needs students with creative thinking skills. These can be learned either through specific courses teaching creativity or through creative teaching methods. Many proponents of critical thinking advocate an integration of critical thinking into the way the disciplines are taught; likewise I would advocate using creative teaching methods rather than designing separate courses in creativity. Hence, teaching creativity should be done through creative teaching.

About the Author

Hanne Kirstine Adriansen is Associate Professor at Danish School of Education, Aarhus University, Denmark.

She can be contacted at this e-mail: hkoa@dpu.dk

Chapter Six

Building a Culture of Creativity while Engaging Science Students in Questioning

Patricia Albergaria Almeida, José Joaquim Teixeira-Dias and Jorge Medina

Introduction

How can we identify, characterise and nurture creativity? Being creative is of vital importance in the world of Higher Education (HE) as, arguably, it is else-where. Is being creative a learned behaviour or are there general dispositions that lend some students a creative edge that others struggle to find? And, as asked by Claxton *et al.* (2006:57), *"…is it possible to organise life in schools and classrooms in such a way that young people not only have the opportunity to express their creativity, but systematically become more creative?"*

In Portugal, according to the Framework Law on the Education System (Law no. 46/86, dated 14 October 1986, further amended by Laws no. 115/97 and no. 49/2005), the general aims of HE underline the need for:

i.   developing scientific and reflexive thought

ii. enabling the concretisation and integration of acquired knowledge into a strong intellectual structure

iii. promoting a long-term search for cultural and professional development.

This is similar to many other countries (The Quality Assurance Agency, 2007) where external evaluations of HE have emphasised the need for a larger degree of deep, critical and creative learning as a way of avoiding basic procedural learning, and a need for conceptual (Beatty *et al.*, 1997) and integrated learning (Kolb *et al.*, 2002). This kind of learning involves being creative and, in the frame of our research, of asking higher-level questions. Force (2000:1) sees the process of question-generation and, in particular, the design and use of quality questions as exercises in the development of creative skills: "*To enhance creativity, we must develop and maintain an attitude of creative questioning*".

Carin & Sund (1985) also demonstrated that students reach significantly higher levels of thinking when they are encouraged to develop skills in generating critical and creative questions and when they are provided opportunities for dialogue with peers about the questions raised.

We perceive creative thinking to entail a clear tendency to ask questions. In fact, in our view, one of the most significant indicators of creativity, along with experimenting, thoughtfulness, attentiveness, environment-setting and resilience (Claxton *et al.*, 2006), is the capacity to question, leading in turn to conceptual and integrated learning. Therefore, in this chapter, we propose to explore the kind of questions university students ask, as indicators and consequences of creativity. More specifically we intend to:

i. describe teaching and learning strategies used to foster students' creative questioning

ii. identify and characterise the different types of questions students ask during their learning

iii. characterise and map students' approaches to creativity

iv. discuss the relationship between students' questions asked in different contexts and students' approaches to creativity.

This chapter starts by exploring the role of students' questioning in the development of higher-order thinking skills such as creativity (Ten Dam & Volman, 2004; Zoller & Pushkin, 2007), followed by a discussion on how to enhance students' questioning in HE. The study presented in this chapter was developed with first-year Chemistry students in Science and Engineering courses, and Geological Engineering master students, at the University of Aveiro, in Portugal. The work is aimed at contributing to the development of pedagogical models that promote student-oriented approaches, stimulating university students to be active participants in their learning process, and teachers to act as promoters of innovative teaching strategies. As mentioned by Reid & Petocz (in this volume), nowadays most teachers design strategies that emphasise creativity, even if they seem to hold a variety of views about creativity.

Approaches to Creativity

Contemporary society is characterised by fast and complex change processes (Barnett, 2000) covering all spheres of life. According to the report on creativity in higher education (EUA, 2007), creativity has been identified both as a key factor to adequately address the challenges caused by these changes as well as being a major driving force towards knowledge creation.

When approaching creativity our first difficulty is to define it: *what is creativity?* The literature on creativity indicates that the meaning of the term may vary considerably and seems to depend to a high degree on the contexts in which the topic is discussed. Even if there may be no single, "one-size-fits-all" definition of creativity, there seems to be a degree of consensus amongst creativity researchers that creativity involves a mental process as well as an outcome of that process. It is important to emphasise that creative ideas do not always lead to creative results, so this aspect should be considered in particular. In the same line of thought, creative results are not always based on creative processes.

Osche (1990:2) stated that creativity involves "...*bringing something into being that is original (new, unusual, novel, unexpected) and also valuable (useful, good, adaptive, appropriate)*". Kleiman (2008:209) agrees, adding that "...*creativity involves notions of novelty and originality combined with notions of utility and value*". Knight (2002:1) also characterises creativity as the construction of something new, at a cognitive level or at a social level: "*Creativity constructs new tools and new outcomes – new embodiments of knowledge. It constructs new relationships, rules, communities of practice and new connections – new social practices*".

According to Biggs & Tang (2007), creativity involves hypothesising, synthesising, reflecting, generating ideas, applying the known to "far domains" and working with problems that do not have unique solutions. As stated by Sternberg *et al.*, (2009:35): "*Creativity is not only what enables us to come up with new ideas (whatever the field); it is also the skill that enables us to deal with new situations or problems that we have never confronted before".*

Creativity also implies the skill to create and connect ideas and produce frameworks to judge the significance of facts and ideas and possible solutions. These can be seen as higher-order skills that students should develop along their HE route.

Claxton *et al.* (2006) emphasise that creativity relies not just on the ability to think, focus or reflect in certain ways, but also on the inclination to do so, and to take the pleasure in doing so. Mitsis & Foley (this volume) emphasise the relationship between learning style and creativity. These authors state that students with a pragmatic or active learning style will be more likely to develop creative ideas than students adopting a theorist or reflector learning style. Students must be willing to detect intriguing inconsistencies as well as simply able to do so. Thus, creativity can be characterised by both habits and dispositions of mind.

Several authors (e.g., Claxton *et al.*, 2006; Amabile, 1996) agree that the role of motivation is crucial in the development of creativity. Interests, beliefs and values are crucial factors when promoting creativity. Some have argued that the dispositions that seem most supportive of creativity are: curiosity, resilience, experimenting, attentiveness, thoughtfulness and environment-setting (Claxton *et al.*, 2006).

Although distinct disciplines appreciate and value different kinds of creativity, research studies recognise a range of intellectual features, attitudes and behaviours related to creativity. Dewulf & Baillie (1999) identified three main characteristics of creativity:

+ *ability to visualise ideas* globally, spatially, and metaphorically, and to be capable to alter ideas through imaginative manipulation and adaptability

+ *effective use of memory* as a first step to establish relationships and associations

+ *divergent and convergent thinking* instead of valuing only divergent thinking. Creativity involves both types of thinking: convergent (analytical, focused, judgemental and detailed) and divergent (perceptual, imaginative, diffuse, free-flowing and associated). Divergent and convergent thinking can be characterised by the kinds of questions students ask.

The section that follows presents a brief literature review about students' questioning.

Student-generated Questions

In recent years there has been an increasing emphasis on the important role that students' questions play in learning, as questions are an essential component of discursive activity, dialectical thinking (Chin & Osborne, 2008), and dialogic teaching (Lange, in this volume; Wolfe & Alexander, 2008). Student-generated questions are an important element in the teaching and learning process and play a significant role in motivating meaningful learning. In fact some studies, for instance the research conducted by Pedrosa de Jesus *et al.* (2007), show that the promotion of a true spirit of inquiry can improve the quality of teaching and, consequently, the quality of learning.

The act of questioning encourages learners to engage in deep, scientific and creative reasoning. Given that asking questions is fundamental to science and scientific inquiry, Zoller *et al.* (1997) argue that the development of students' abilities to ask questions, reason, problem solve, and think critically and creatively should become a central focus of science education reform.

Students' questions result from a gap or discrepancy in their understanding or a desire to extend their knowledge in some direction. Graesser & Olde find that students' questions may be triggered by unknown words or inconsistencies between the students' knowledge and the new information, which then engender *"cognitive disequilibrium"* (2003:525). They observe that questions are asked *"... when individuals are confronted with obstacles to goals, anomalous events, contradictions, discrepancies, salient contrasts, obvious gaps in knowledge, expectation violations, and decisions that require discrimination among equally attractive alternatives".*

In spite of the educational significance of learners' questions it is noted that students generally are seen to ask few questions, and even fewer in the search for real knowledge. Pizzini & Shepardson (1991) argue that student questioning is influenced by instructional models and lesson structures and by the social structure of the classroom. Dillon (1988) also refers to the influence of the students' role as participants, and to the controlling function of the teacher's own questions. Pedrosa de Jesus *et al.* (2003) consider that students will only engage in questioning if they are interested in the science topics studied. Clearly, if the classroom environment inhibits questioning, few questions will be asked.

Questioning in a Creative Context

We believe that it is possible to develop creativity if the right conditions are created and if the learning environment nurtures the spirit of creativity and values different types of thinking. We concur with Dewulf & Baillie's (1999) view that to promote creative thinking it is not enough to encourage a specific type of thinking, but instead to support the employment of different types of thinking, according to the circumstances.

Sternberg & Grigorenko (2008) point to the practice of questioning as one of the modes to enhance creativity. These authors emphasise the role that teachers perform in the development of students' questioning competence. Teachers should make questioning an important part of the daily classroom exchange. Dillon (1988) asserts that it is more important for students to know how to ask a question than to know how to answer the teacher's questions. However, students are taught throughout all school levels that their main role is to answer and not to ask. So, it is not an easy challenge but teachers should teach their students how to ask questions and, more than that, they should teach them how to ask quality questions (open, creative, critical, deep, thought-provoking). According to Teixeira-Dias *et al.* (2005), quality questions are those that seem to signal some reorganisation or re-structuring of the students' understanding. So, of course the immediate question is: *how can this be done?*

In addressing this we lessen the emphasis on surface learning and creating a questioning friendly environment, where demanding situations are presented to students, and students are asked to propose solutions. We are not stating that students should find answers to these situations; instead, we believe that students should ask questions to facilitate the understanding of these problem-based cases.

In this chapter, we investigate the nature of "creative questioning". Our presumption is that if we intend university students to be creative thinkers then one means for achieving this is to assist them to raise creative questions. Among others, Force (2000:28) has argued that asking creative questions is one of the processes associated with creative thinking: *"To enhance creativity, we must develop and maintain an attitude of creative questioning".*

A review of the literature about this theme suggests that there exists a category of questions that are exclusively creative, that fully involve and serve to reveal creativity. Dalton (1995) and Gross *et al.* (2001) suggest the following examples of creative questions:

+ What other perspectives are there to consider?

+ What other ways could this problem be solved?

+ How could you extend this idea to…?

+ If you took an opposite approach what might the outcomes be?

+ What would happen if we added...?

+ How could we change the end result?

+ What if you...?

+ What would happen if one element was changed?

+ What would your hypothesis be?

In this study, we have dispensed with this separate category of "creative questions", such as the one proposed by Force (2000) and Lehman (1972), in favour of a designation of the actions and processes of creative thinking. We are more interested in developing students who are "creative questioners" than in a simple category of question types that characterise creative questions. We see "being creative" as an holistic approach to life and a specific approach to thinking and to study.

We believe that students' capacity to be creative can be brought into being, developed, and improved. Force (2000) maintains that because being creative is a learner competency then improvement is always possible.

Methodology

Procedure

The two projects, Questions and Answers in Chemistry and Questions and Answers in Geology, are being developed in full collaboration between an educational researcher and two lecturers in the Chemistry department and in the Geosciences department of the University of Aveiro. These projects intend to contribute to the development of pedagogical models that promote student-oriented approaches, stimulating students to be active participants in their learning process, and teachers to act as promoters of innovative teaching strategies. Such work has been part of a research programme designed to face the challenges associated with the implementation of the Bologna Process in Portugal and the enhancement of the scholarship of teaching and learning.

From the first day of the course, students were told about the research projects. The teachers explained to them the aims of the project and that a researcher was going to be present in all their classes asking for their understanding and collaboration. Additional explanations were provided at other strategic moments (for example, when some students were invited to be interviewed).

Participants

The main sample comprised 130 students. 120 were 1st year chemistry students (74 female, 46 male; mean age 18 years) who were tackling foundation chemistry, although following different science and engineering degree programmes (environmental engineering, chemical engineering, biology, biology and geology, physics and chemistry, meteorological and oceanographic geophysics, physics, chemistry, physical engineering). A further ten were students enrolled in a master's geology course (5 female, 5 male; mean age 24 years).

For this particular study, 5 students from each course were selected for deeper analysis. The selection criteria were their approaches to creativity (as identified through interviews), the types and number of oral and written questions they raised, and their level of individual involvement observed during classes.

Creating the Conditions for Student Creative Questioning

Several teaching and learning strategies were designed and implemented to encourage students' high-level and creative questioning. Since the most frequent reasons to justify the shortage of students' questions are fear of exposure to peers and lack of confidence, we tried to create a friendly questioning environment where students felt confident and comfortable to take risks, an essential feature of creativity. Thus, besides having the opportunity to raise oral questions, the research team also provided students with the chance to ask written questions. The teaching and learning strategies implemented had different foci, in order to create a broad range of stimuli to foster students' questions and to embrace students' different approaches to creativity. These strategies were also conceived having in mind that today's students are no longer satisfied to sit passively through a lecture or laboratory activity, but rather to be thoroughly engaged in it. Actually, according to Sawyer (2004:13): *"In true discussion, the topic and the flow of the class emerge from teacher and students together; the outcome is unpredictable, just as in theatre improvisations".*

The strategies implemented included:

Small pauses during chemistry lectures to encourage students' oral questions. At the middle of the lesson, the teacher stopped lecturing for about two to three minutes, and invited the students to think about and/or to discuss the class topics with their colleagues. At the end of the pause, students had the opportunity to raise oral questions. If the students felt more comfortable, they could write their questions instead, and the teacher would answer orally in the beginning of the next lesson.

Chemistry teacher's written questions during lectures to facilitate the organisation of teaching and learning and to serve as a role model to students. For instance, throughout the "Water" topic, the teacher presented 17 written questions. These had diverse degrees of difficulty and served different functions. Some instances of teacher's written questions drawn from our project are: "How can you describe the polarity of a water molecule?", "In the absence of gravity, why are water drops exactly spherical?", "Why are there substances that are gaseous, others that are liquids and others that are solids?"

Chemistry practical laboratory sessions where the students have opportunities to: a) identify the main objectives of the work; b) identify and overcome any conceptual and practical difficulties encountered; c) plan and execute the work; d) record and discuss the results and observations in their lab book (a log book, not a book of reports); e) suggest practical alterations and improvements; f) answer the questions raised in their laboratory manual (e.g. "Comment on the title of this laboratory task", "Is it possible to determine the percentage of copper recovery? How?"), and f) raise oral and/or written questions.

One of the practical activities proposed to students was concerned with comparing the viscosity of several liquids and water at different temperatures. "Consider an air bubble moving in the ascending sense in two liquids with different viscosities. In which liquid do the air bubbles move faster?". "Using this principle, plan and execute experiments for comparing the viscosity of a) water and ethyl ether; b) water at several temperatures; c) water and oil".

"Questions and answers in chemistry" online forum to encourage and facilitate students' questioning. Students could use this tool to raise written questions related to the topics taught during lectures and practical laboratory sessions. The teacher answers all questions in one to two days, also in the online forum. All questions and answers are visible to all chemistry students.

Written questions during geology classes. The students are encouraged to write their questions in the course of lectures and practical sessions. Even if students feel confident and comfortable to raise oral questions, they are stimulated to also ask written questions, since, as stated by Almeida *et al.* (2008), usually this kind of question requires more reflection and, therefore, produces higher-level questions.

Geology field trip where the students are given the opportunity to find answers in the field to questions they that have raised previously. These questions emerged from the analysis of maps and photographs of the areas that they were going to visit in the field trip. The places visited in the field trip were determined by the questions raised by each student.

"Questions and answers in geology" online forum where the students should post their questions before the field trip. Likewise, after the trip, the students should publish the responses to their questions on the online platform. The questions and answers of each student are visible to the whole class.

Data Gathering and Analysis

Data from multiple sources (transcripts of classroom discourse from audio-recordings, audio-recorded interviews with the students, field notes, students' oral and written questions) were analysed in relation to each other. The different sources of data were very helpful in assuring the rigor of the data because, as Maxwell (1996:76) stated, "...*triangulation can provide a more complete and accurate account than either could alone*".

In analysing students' conceptions of and approaches to creativity, a large part involved the study of students' thinking, behaviour and their internal states manifested in their observed performance. However, since it is not possible to gain direct access to the mind or internal state of the learner, the analysis must be inferred to some extent. Thus, in developing grounded interpretative analyses of the students' approaches to creativity, the purpose was not to characterise what was really going on in students minds since this was not open to direct inspection. Rather, it was to articulate the subtleties of the general conceptions of and approaches to creativity identified, by looking closely at naturalistic student interactions and using interpretative analyses to assist in this.

Observation

Observation is a valid and direct way of obtaining data from people. Gillham (2000:46) argues that "...*it is not what they say they do. It is what they actually do*".

From September to December 2010 (the first semester of the academic year 2009-2010) all the chemistry and the geology classes (approximately 30 classes) were audio-recorded. Observation grids for every class were completed by the educational researcher, who was present at all classes. This way, oral questions were also collected.

Interviews

Five students from each course (chemistry and geology) were selected for interview, a total of ten students. They were chosen because of their particular attitudes in class and the number and kinds of questions they asked. From the responses given, it was possible to identify and characterize their approaches to creativity, as well as to describe their questioning style.

The students were interviewed individually in a quiet, private room within the Education department. All the interviews were semi-structured, audio-recorded and transcribed verbatim. The data we elicited are taken from the interviewees' comments and the questions that they posed.

Research Findings and Discussion

Students' Approaches to Creativity

The analysis of students' interviews allowed us to identify and qualitatively characterise distinct approaches to creativity. When conducting the analysis we have found similarities between students' conceptions of creativity and the teachers' conceptions of learning identified by Kleiman (2008). Thus, we have decided to maintain the labels used by Kleiman in his study. According to our findings, students approach creativity in three different ways:

+ as a constraint approach

+ as a process approach

+ as a transformation approach.

Students adopting a constraint approach were not able to use creativity in their approach to learning. These students showed a very restricted view of creativity, relating it only to the field of arts and not understanding how creativity could have a role in the process of learning science, or even in the field of science. As stated by Ana during the interview:

> *"Well... it is chemistry... things are what they are... I cannot change the formula of the water molecule... I think that creativity can be exploited in an arts class, in a painting class... or a dance class, but in chemistry, in physics... it is not possible..."*

Other students felt that it was possible to be creative in a science class, but they did not feel comfortable to express their different opinions in front of their colleagues. So, even if they can conceive of learning and teaching science associated to creativity, they do not feel comfortable to share their thoughts.

Students with a process approach to creativity seem to conceive of creativity as the establishment of new relationships between facts and/or ideas. Rui, a geology master student, shares this view of creativity:

> *"I think that I can be creative when I am learning... in reality I cannot create something new, because I am learning something that is already well-know by experts, but it is new to me! So... I think I can discover how to... for instance, I can discover how to identify schist in a photo... I can relate the characteristics of the rock to the features of the photo and discover what rock is in a certain place. This is being creative... discovering something new!... at least for me!".*

Students with this approach to creativity do not perceive creativity in learning as a product since they feel that they are not able to create something really new. However, when these students are making new connections, they are trying to create something new. Thus, when considering this approach to creativity we also take into account the generation of something new, but we only consider the process, and not the product.

The third approach to creativity includes hypothesising and changing, not only in what concerns knowledge, but also changing as a person. In this category, encountering and exploiting chance and risk-taking appear as crucial factors. Students adopting this approach are self-confident, comfortable with their peers and teachers and like to take risks, as stated by Nuno, a 1ˢᵗ year chemistry student:

> *"I don't have problems in saying what I think... even if it may be a dumb thought! ... If I have an idea, something that I am not able to know by myself if makes sense or not I ask, I explain my idea and sometimes it makes sense, other times it's a stupid thought... ok, maybe it is not stupid, but it is not right... but this is how we grow up, isn't it? We try and we see how it works... sometimes works... sometimes it doesn't!".*

So, we consider students' approaches to creativity as a continuum of creativity sophistication with the constraint approach at the lower level of progression and the transformation approach at the higher level of development. Since we consider these approaches to creativity to be disposed along a continuum we will refer to these as approaches or stages separately.

Students' Questioning and Approaches to Creativity

From the ten students that were selected from the main sample, which included 130 students, three students were found to be in the constraint phase, five in the process phase and only two students in the transformation phase.

Students' oral and written questions were categorised against the taxonomy proposed by Almeida, *et al.* (2008) that includes three categories of questions: acquisition, specialisation and integration.

We have concluded that students adopting a constraint approach to creativity asked mainly acquisition questions. These questions deal mainly with relatively straightforward gaps in knowledge, simple ideas, objects, processes, or concepts that do not require evaluation, judgment, or drawing conclusions. When asking acquisition questions, students were attempting to clear up matters of fact, confirm explanations or clarify conceptual issues. Students may feel they have grasped an idea, or the structure of an argument, and are testing for reassurance that this is in fact the case. These are "stick to the facts" or closed questions whose answers will mainly rely upon memory processes. Some examples of acquisition questions are:

+ What is an amphiphilic molecule?

+ What is the state of the granite (weathering processes)?

+ Are these covalent bonds?

Students adopting a process approach ask mainly specialisation questions, but also raise some acquisition questions (Figure 1). Drawn from our project, some instances of specialisation questions are:

+ The viscosity of the liquids can be compared to the rugosity of the solids? Why?

+ How can we explain the relationship between the water lines and the granite's fault?

+ Is there a difference in the vegetation that exists in the areas with schist and in the areas with granite?

As shown in these examples, specialization questions asked tend to go beyond an initial search for information. The student establishes relations and tries to understand and interpret the surrounding world. These questions transcend the specific or detailed level of comprehension, in order to generalize or relate these specifics into meaningful patterns. Students seek to both expand knowledge and test constructs that they have formed. In this stage, the students feel secure about their understandings. Consequently, they try to expand their knowledge into the neighbouring terrain and test constructs that they have shaped.

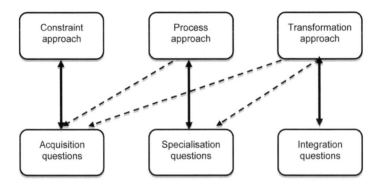

Figure 1: Students' Approaches to Creativity Related to Their Questions

Students with a transformation approach to creativity seem to have the ability to ask different kinds of questions (Figure 1), according to the learning context, the learning demands and their own needs. Students in this stage can ask acquisition and specialisation questions but also have the capacity to ask higher-level questions: integration questions. These questions can include prediction involving:

+ speculation or hypothesising

+ anomaly detection where the students expresses scepticism or detect discrepant information or cognitive conflict

+ different application of principles learned

+ attempting to reconcile understanding, tracking in and around complex ideas and their consequences.

The student seems to want to get further "inside" the ideas, to be hypothetic-deductive, to seek extensions to what is known, to cross knowledge domains. These questions focused on explanations and causes, or on predictions, or on resolving discrepancies in knowledge, and were more open, critical, imaginative, and reflective. The learner seems to challenge accepted reasoning. Integration questions may have distinct origins. These may emerge from the classroom topic being taught, but can also be shaped by tangential issues or stimulated by something from outside the class entirely.

Some instances of these questions would be:

+ Was the Big Bang a spontaneous reaction? Nowadays there are some theories saying that the matter will join again (in the opposite way of the Big Bang). How can we understand and explain this according to the 2nd law of thermodynamics? Is this also a spontaneous reaction? How can we interpret it?

+ Since the green leaves reflect the wavelength of the infrared radiation, is it possible to use this information to examine the health of the plants?

Discussion of Findings, Conclusions, and Implications

We propose a hierarchy of students' approaches to creativity, starting from a constraint approach and finishing at a transformation approach. The intermediate stage between the constraint and the transformation approach is called the process approach. Likewise, we also suggest that students' questions can be categorised against a taxonomy including three categories: acquisition, specialisation and integration questions. When analysing these categories we observe an obvious congruence between acquisition questions and the constraint approach, specialisation questions and the process approach and integration questions and the transformation approach. Thus, we conclude that students adopting one of these approaches to creativity tend to ask questions that are coherent with that approach.

Students with a constraint approach ask mainly acquisition questions that are related to basic and factual information. Students with an intermediate approach to creativity tend principally to ask questions that try to establish connections between ideas – specialisation questions. Finally, students adopting a transformation approach to learning can ask all kinds of questions, including questions that raise hypotheses: integration questions. We see a lower level of creativity associated with the students that ask mainly acquisition questions, and a higher degree of creativity related to those who are able to ask all kinds of questions. As we stated before, creativity involves the ability to ask different kinds of questions, according to the circumstances and to the student needs.

However, we suggest that all students can ask each kind of question. Our findings show that students adopting a transformation approach to creativity can raise acquisition, specialisation and integration questions and that students adopting a process approach can ask acquisition and specialisation questions. We believe that these students are also able to ask integration questions, and we consider that students with a constraint approach also have the ability to raise specialization and integration questions. We propose that some students are internally motivated to raise all kinds of questions, while others need more stimuli to do this. However, we strongly believe that all students possess a "seed of creativity" that only needs to germinate, with more or less external assistance.

We contend that it is possible to create a learning environment that triggers students' creative questioning. The different characteristics of students can be considered and valued when designing diverse teaching and learning strategies.

The major contribution of our study is that it shows how students' questions represent a useful tool that allows us to establish a relationship between students' questioning and students' approaches to creativity. Thus, students' questions can be used as an indicator to identify and characterise students' positioning along the "creativity continuum", allowing the teacher to conceive, design and implement strategies according to his/her students' characteristics and needs.

Conducting this study with students from different backgrounds and in different moments of their higher education route had a clear intention: to broaden students' horizons by showing them that they can (and they should) ask and share all their questions without being afraid. In reality their questions are well-accepted and, more than that, their questions are valued.

During the next school year the 1st year students in our sample will attend classes in several departments at the University of Aveiro, besides the chemistry department. Our research study was also an attempt to plant the spirit of inquiry in each student, in order to spread this "mood to creativity", and, ultimately, to generate a culture of creativity not only within the chemistry and the geosciences departments but within other departments of the university.

About the Authors

Patrícia Albergaria Almeida is a researcher at the Research Centre for Didactics and Technology in Teacher Education, Department of Education, University of Aveiro, Portugal. She can be contacted at this e-mail: patriciaalmeida@ua.pt

José Joaquim Teixeira-Dias is a Full Professor of Chemistry at the Department of Chemistry, University of Aveiro, Portugal. He can be contacted at this e-mail: teixeiradias@ua.pt

Jorge Medina is an assistant professor at the Department of Geosciences, University of Aveiro, Portugal. He can be contacted at this e-mail: jmedina@ua.pt

Chapter Seven

Diverse Views of Creativity for Learning

Anna Reid and Peter Petocz

Introduction

Creativity is an idea that is understood in many different ways. Most people have experienced various forms of creativity throughout their lives and hold popular views of its nature and importance. Our research with university students and lecturers shows that different discipline areas generate views of creativity that are related to the practice of a particular domain and the role played by a person in the pedagogical process. It seems that creativity comprises indispensable aspects of teaching practice in some disciplines and is all but ignored in others. Further, students and lecturers may also have quite different approaches to creativity. For some students, creativity is an essential aspect of their studies, while for others it is rarely considered. By contrast, most lecturers will tend to give creativity a more central role in their teaching, though their understandings of the concept can be quite varied. Other chapters in this volume are in agreement with these ideas: for instance, Raiker gives evidence that supervisors and students seem to have differing understandings of creativity, and Almeida illustrates different notions of creativity shown by students in science.

An important problem is uncovering the range of variation in the ways that people understand creativity in order to enhance learning environments and disciplinary content. In this chapter, we critique ideas about creativity against empirical evidence from our research studies with the aim of investigating the conditions that support students' creative learning. In the process, we describe the range of ways that learners and teachers view the notion of creativity. The students in our study showed three different views of creativity: the "definition" view positions creativity as essentially irrelevant; the "attribute" view holds that creativity is tied to either a person or a process or a product; the "comprehensive" view combines person, process and product in a mutually reinforcing way. The teacher group added a fourth view that we have labelled "holistic", in which they saw their entire teaching and professional practice leading to creative outcomes for their students.

Creativity is often held to be the essential characteristic that makes high-quality student learning outcomes apparent (Biggs, 1999a). Students who demonstrate creativity in assessment tasks will usually be awarded better grades than their peers to reward this act or expression of thinking. Recently, many universities have begun to include creativity as a "generic skill" that students should acquire whilst at university and that teachers should endeavour to teach (e.g., University of Queensland, 2010; London Metropolitan University, 2010). But how are university lecturers to teach this elusive concept, and how can students learn to be creative? This important question is the focus of our chapter. Students and lecturers – as members of the general community – share popular notions of creativity and at the same time express specific ideas of creativity from the context of their discipline. Students' learning outcomes are generated from a complex interaction between their conception of learning, of their discipline, of their future professional work, and their core dispositions. Our earlier empirical results (see, for example, Reid & Petocz, 2008) indicate that students who are aware of the most expansive and inclusive conceptions of learning are more able to express creative learning outcomes and to use the notion of creativity in their work, whereas students who hold the most limiting conceptions of learning will focus on atomistic and fractured discipline requirements which hinder their opportunities to demonstrate creativity. Thus, teaching that encourages students towards the higher and more inclusive conceptions of learning will also set up a fertile learning environment that supports and enhances students' creativity.

Popular Views of Creativity

Creativity is often considered to be a personal trait related to some form of eccentricity or artistry. It is not uncommon to hear people say *"Igor is so creative, he can sing and paint and wears amazing clothing"*. Psychologists have spent considerable effort examining and defining the personal cognitive traits that provide evidence for a *"creative person"* (Sternberg, 1988). Such theories look for the *determinants* of creative thinking, and the search for these results in a mechanistic, computer-like model for creative processes. From an educator's point of view, then, it would be sensible to set up some sort of university entrance test that would demonstrate which students were naturally creative. This would then ensure the best academic outcomes and present to the world of work people who were certifiably creative. Silva *et al.* (2009) suggest that it is possible to assess divergent thinking using a simple scoring system. This system could be used by educators to assess individual differences in creative potential and abilities. A criticism of this approach, however, is that it is acontextual in that the system requires participants to provide novel uses for objects (such as knives or boxes). This approach is outside any particular domain and could be considered of limited use to teachers in specific disciplines, for instance, teachers of statistics or music.

Alternatively, creativity may be considered to reside in a particular product such as a painting, a piece of music or a graph. Taking the product approach, researchers investigating creative works strive to demonstrate how the characteristics of the product exemplify creativity (Gardner, 1988). From an educator's perspective, the creative product is usually a piece of assessed student work. Csikszentmihalyi (1990:193) suggests that in many fields the mark of creativity is the ability not to solve the problem, but to be able to *discover* a problem. For lecturers, this suggests that creative assessment methods should not prescribe particular solutions, but should give students an opportunity to first find a problem and then solve it. Criterion-based assessment tasks suggest that high-quality work exhibits creativity and therefore is worth higher grades (Feldhusen & Goh, 1995; Kaufman *et al.*, 2007).

In yet another approach, creativity may be considered to be a process. Taking the process approach, creativity theorists would suggest that negotiations with others, intersections between ideas, trial and error, reflective development and discard, all combine to produce a creative artefact. For example, Swede (1993:2) maintains that creativity is more than just a response to a situation: *"Creativity is a process that results in some sort of outcome that possesses at least two qualities:*

it must be unique and it must have value". Furthermore, to be creative it must be *"universally"* recognised. For lecturers, this means that students' demonstrations of creative processes and outcomes need to be understood and appreciated. However, lecturers' understanding of creativity (in all its guises) can be quite variable – as we will show later. It is very possible that a student could present a product or practice that is exceptionally creative (as judged perhaps by a professional in the field), but that their lecturer's experience may be insufficient for them to recognize the creative merit of the work.

Creative learning is perhaps another process that is at play in higher education. This may happen when students are able to integrate several seemingly different aspects into a new and unique form. For lecturers, this could be generated through the development of inter-disciplinary studies, where unusual intersections have a better chance of becoming apparent. Koestler (1981) calls this form of creativity *"bisociation"*. This has been described by Biggs (1999a:47-48) as the highest level of the SOLO taxonomy (Structure of Observed Learning Outcomes) – the *"extended abstract"* level where students relate existing principles to unseen problems and are able to question existing ideas and move beyond them. Sawyer & DeZutter (2009) suggest that the intersections that form creative practices emerge primarily from collaborations. They suggest that when groups work together on problems, each group member brings to the discussion distinctly different ways of considering the problem. However, at the group level, each individual suggestion contributes to a change in the entire group's cognition and enables a broader extension – much the same as Biggs' extended abstract outcome level.

While there is research evidence that reports on the distinctions between creative persons, processes, products and thoughts, there is a surprising lack of domain-specific evidence. Csikszentmihalyi (1990) presents a systems view of creativity which recognises that person, product and process may be found in relationship to the domain in which they reside. Matare (2009) explored cross-cultural differences in the concept of a specific domain: music. European and African musicians, both novice and expert, were asked to improvise on two short phrases of their choice. Subsequent interviews with participants showed that African musicians' creative processes included a focus on spiritualty, emotions and social therapy. In contrast, the creative practice of European musicians focused on self-expression, musical interpretation and audience communication. In both instances there was a strong relationship between the musical knowledge and the created artefact. Matare's work then extends Csikszentmihalyi's into a systems view of creativity that is centred in cultural spaces.

We have previously reported on the characteristics of *"learning domains"* as sites for creativity (Reid & Petocz, 2004). In the sections that follow, we will describe the results of two separate research projects that present material based on the experiences of participants from different learning contexts. First, in the domain of business education, we investigate how undergraduate business students understand the notion of creativity. Secondly, in the domain of post-graduate studies in various disciplines, we look at lecturers' understanding of creativity in the general context of their teaching. Finally, we discuss the outcomes of these projects as they relate to popular understandings of creativity, and speculate further on the implications of domain-specific creativity for pedagogical situations such as curriculum design or teaching practices.

Domain-specific Views of Creativity

Business Students' Understanding of Creativity

The student data included in this chapter were collected at a university in Sydney, Australia as part of a study investigating domestic and international students' views of professional attributes that they develop through their studies in preparation for their future workplaces. Forty-four domestic and international students undertaking business degrees were interviewed singly or in groups, resulting in interview transcripts of 88,000 words. The students responded to the questions: *How do you understand the idea of creativity?* and *What role do you think creativity will play in your future professional work?* These questions were followed, if necessary, with further probing questions such as: *Can you give me an example of that?* or *Could you elaborate on what you mean by "thinking outside the square"?* (see Petocz et al., 2009).

The analysis revealed three qualitatively different conceptions of creativity that were shown by participants. These conceptions were labelled as (1) Definition, (2) Attribute and (3) Comprehensive, from the narrowest and most limited to the broadest and most inclusive. For each conception we provide one or two quotes that are representative of the comments made by participants and use them to illuminate the conception.

(1) *Definition.* Here students talk about creativity using fairly simplistic definitions. Naturally, all students had been exposed to the term creativity as part of their studies, but to some of them it was an unexamined idea. Several students used buzz phrases to talk about the concept.

Rose: *"I think the idea of creativity is to think outside the square (cliché I know but no other way to express it)".*

Richard: *"Creativity is the ability to think outside the box and rise above mediocrity with something new and unheard of. /.../ Seeing that I'm an accounting student intending to work in forensic accounting, creativity isn't really a big part of that kind of work".*

There were several different turns of phrase that could express this definitional conception but the commonality between them was a lack of further discussion about the idea. Phrases such as "thinking outside the box/square" have become general parlance since de Bono's work in the 1960s on lateral thinking. It is important to recognise that the phrase has become common but not the complexities within the concept that de Bono initially suggested (de Bono, 1967). While most of the comments about creativity within this conception were general, a few were specifically based in professional contexts, such as the quote from Richard.

(2) *Attribute.* This conception is broader than the "definition" conception in that students viewed creativity as an attribute of either a person, or a process or a product: the most common attribution was to a person. Of course, the three attributions are related in that a person would be carrying out a process resulting in a product. However, the view was limited because it was one dimensional in that the focus was on only one of these, and fixed in that the person (or process, or product) was either creative or not. Samantha shows the most common view that creativity is an attribute of a person, and immediately expands on the personal workplace benefits.

Samantha: *"Having the ability and mentality to be different I guess. It will help set me apart from my work colleagues, by being the same as everyone will not get me noticed hence being creative and thinking differently gets noticed and differentiated from the crowd".*

In another example of this uni-dimensional view, Erica puts the emphasis on the process, in this instance, finding a way to make a presentation interesting, or designing an advertising campaign.

Erica: *"Well, a simple example I suppose is if you're asked to present information to somebody, rather than standing up there and presenting it, you could work out some sort of drama item or some sort of artistic way of presenting the information. That's my idea of being creative. Also when you see, when people come up with totally new concepts for ads or different clothing designs and that sort of thing, that to me is creative – anything that's sort of different to what people normally would do".*

In this example, Erica connects creativity to drama – an "obviously" creative field – and in this case used as a means of enlivening the presentation of an assessment task. She does not suggest that the object of the assessment task was creative, nor that it was possible to be creative with the construction of the assessed work, but only in the means of delivering it. She provides another example of such domains of creativity – clothing design – but emphasises that it is not present in everyday learning activities. In this sense, the learning domain –management – does not seem to provide for Erica a location where management is considered a creative endeavour. Rather, the only opportunity for creative activity could be in a cross-disciplinary area, drama, which she could use. Linguistically, she has placed herself in the group of "normal" people who do not display creative tendencies.

(3) *Comprehensive.* In this conception, views of creativity are combined or integrated resulting in a multi-dimensional approach. Students talking about creativity in this way also come up with novel views of creativity itself, for instance, as a product of a combination of ideas from different people.

Sid exemplifies this comprehensive conception of creativity, in turn as process (different ways of doing something, such as brainstorming), then as product (the creative thing that collective minds can make) and then as person (the creative person who may be in your group). He also introduces the notion that working in a group may heighten creativity.

Sid: *"Creativity, new, something never done before. Different way of doing things, you know, different from your competitors if you work in the same industry. You know, something that your customers, your customers don't know, know they've never seen the thing before. /.../ Like for example the exercise we do here, brainstorming, you know, you look at a problem for example the lecturer give us a case study for our collective minds and that's, that's where... the chance to come up with something creative I think will depend on someone sitting next to you, some, the people around you. You know, the collective minds will make something creative. Of course you have someone, a person that is very creative, even if you have the person in your group, it's going to be very good".*

The final section of this quotation emphasises the usefulness of a creative person, but shows how this person is also found in relation to the group exercise. Sid's quote demonstrates domain specificity at two levels, a possible work level where creative activity is seen as a form of business advantage, and also a learning level where creative process is seen as something that is enacted between students. This particular quote demonstrates a more complex level of thinking about creativity, qualitatively different from the earlier conceptions. For the participant group in this study, the comprehensive definitional conception represents a way of experiencing creativity that includes the aspects of the other conceptions, but places them in a relation with each other and towards a directed purpose.

Lecturers' Understanding of Creativity for Teaching

In an empirical study of 14 post-graduate lecturers' experience of teaching, we asked questions regarding their view of creativity and the relationship this concept may have for their teaching. The lecturers came from different subject areas and shared a context where the university was emphasising the concept of creativity as a generic skill. Here, using direct quotations from the participants, we present the various ways in which lecturers understood the notion of creativity as a practice for teaching, as a skill for students to demonstrate, and as an outcome that could be assessed.

Before we present our analysis, it is pertinent to discuss an aspect of research methodology. The aim of research is to present new findings on a particular issue combined with an implicit intention that others may be able to use those outcomes themselves to either confirm the original research, or to extend it into another, possibly related, domain. In the case of this research, we had already analysed the student data (as given above) and then used that schema to conduct our first explorations of the teacher data. As the research method in both cases was similar – the conduct of semi-structured interviews focusing on the topic of creativity – it is not surprising that the results obtained in the student analysis have been confirmed (and extended) by our analysis of the teachers' transcripts. However, lecturers tended to express their ideas in more eloquent language, and at often much greater length, and applied their ideas to the context of learning and teaching in a more explicit way.

The previous definition, attribute, comprehensive conceptions can be seen in the results from the lecturers. Harry illustrates the definition conception.

> Harry: "OK, creativity I guess is finding a new way to solve a problem, that hasn't been thought of before, tried a new approach, something that is not the

standard solution that might work better. I mean, I know there is creativity from an artistic point of view, but for most of our students that is not really an issue. Creativity is more like thinking outside the square to find new solutions to new problems".

Like many business students, Harry completes his discussion of creativity by using a familiar "buzz" phrase – "thinking outside the square". An aspect of his definition is an emphasis on the concept of "new": new solutions to problems. For creativity to be recognized in this conception, novelty needs to be present. In addition, the newness of the problem or solution appears in a form of a vacuum. Harry says that it shouldn't have been "thought of before". This perspective on creativity is a step behind Koestler's (1981) definition of "bisociation", where the catalyst for creative action or thinking is the integration of two distinct ideas. Although teaching actuarial studies, Harry seems to imply that creativity is not a part of his teaching or professional practices; rather, it lies outside his professional domain. This is typical of responses which could be categorized as representing the *definition* conception.

To illustrate and illuminate the *attribute* conception we use a quotation from William, in the field of psychometrics, that emphasises the person attribute.

> William: *"I think of a creative person as a person who is a good problem solver. Irrespective of the area, it might be academic, it might be practical, it might be whatever. Now that differs from the point of view that sees creativity mainly in terms of music and art – in being able to make something original. So I see that as an aspect of creativity on the artistic, but I guess that comes back to my general notion, that creativity is someone who is an original thinker and can apply that to solving problems of any type, to creating works of art".*

William appears to be constructing his view of creativity as he responds to the question. Where Harry suggests that the hallmark of creativity is newness, William emphasises the notion of problem solving, from a situated perspective (as opposed to Harry's vacuum). He proposes the familiar notion that creativity resides in some traditional areas such as music and art, where the outcome of musical and artistic work is originality. However, he moves beyond this concept and suggests that creativity resides in a person. This too is familiar from the student transcripts. There is a difference however as William shows that creative practice starts in the ability to think originally and then apply that thinking to problem solving – and in any domain – and he then includes art work as one aspect of possible creative outcomes (among a range of many). William's quote shows a rather more expanded view than that of the students, yet it is still recognisably a view of creativity as an attribute.

To illustrate the comprehensive conception we use a quote from Patricia, in early childhood education, who provides a general view of the creative domain, including aspects of person, process and product.

> Patricia: *"I think that creativity is very difficult to define. Maybe one aspect of creativity is people being able to approach problems or issues or concepts in ways that aren't narrowly defined. To be able to look at things from different sorts of perspectives and come up with something new. But I'm aware that is a very sort of intellectualised version of creativity and it's also about what people – often you think about it in terms of art – it's about what people produce and I don't know that I can define it, I mean I can see it, but I don't know that I can define it".*

Patricia's statement includes reference to creative people, the process of creativity, specifically in the context of her classes, and creative products. It is a comprehensive conception in that all three aspects are evident and combined in her statement.

However, it is possible to see in some of the lecturers' discussions a broader conception of creativity that we can label (4) *Holistic*. More than viewing creativity from the combined multiple attributes of person-process-product, the holistic conception goes beyond this to expound an integrated view in which the individual attributes are subsumed in a general theory of creativity, characteristically set in the lecturer's pedagogical context. We will give two examples of holistic conceptions of creativity, in each case based on fairly extensive quotes.

Valentin, a philosopher, initially seems to show a comprehensive view of creativity, moving from process to product to person, and clearly situated within his own discipline. Yet he quickly moves beyond this.

> Valentin: *"Well in a very, very broad sense I am concerned with creativity in the field of ideas. So my understanding of that would be creativity as a breakthrough in conceptual development, primarily in various theoretical developments, in philosophical developments, political theory. I think my training enables me to support creative efforts or creative results in those two fields. I have no ability to identify very much creativity in artistic [fields]; I can enjoy some of the creativity but I can't say what the creativity would consist of in those areas, either music or writing or painting or visual arts. All these areas I would say, including of course scientific research, would have creative aspects to it. It is just that in some areas I can see or understand the processes, which are creative processes, much*

better than in other areas. I can see only the results and have some enjoyment of the results. So when it comes to definitions, it's really something to do with on one hand, breakthrough and on the other hand, with originality. That's how I would understand these two terms".

[Can you give me any examples?] *"Relatively original philosophical ideas, which are not very frequent nowadays, I can't identify them so much nowadays, but I would have in my mind a few great philosophers whom I would consider to be very creative. One of my favourites is called Ludwig Wittgenstein. He was an Austrian philosopher and when one reads his works I feel that they open completely new perspectives: in other words, I can't see anything in his works that are plagiarising in any sense which relates to any of his immediate predecessors. One can place him in a variety of movements so that the originality and also from my own personal perspective the new insight that I get, the new perspective that I get, which I didn't expect, something quite unexpected is to me a sign of creativity".*

Valentin's professional domain of philosophy is present in his conception of creativity, yet his theory clearly takes in a broader range of domains. He points to individual attributes, such as the process aspect as a means of making a breakthrough in conceptual thinking: the breakthrough is also the product of the creative activity. His quotation also includes an affective dimension wherein the creator has some "enjoyment" of the process and result of the creative work.

Leslie, in the field of human geography, provides another example of the holistic conception of creativity. She begins by suggesting that creativity is a process aligned with the domain of arts, but then broadens this to describe what she calls *"social creativity"*.

Leslie: *"Well creativity for me is about change. It's about exploring different ways of doing things that have become commonplace, making problems out of the taken for granted. And I think that applies to the world of arts, creativity, you know, always pushing the envelope. But trying to problematise what has become commonplace and which exercise new ways of doing the same things emerge plus totally different ways of doing totally different things. Both of those things are very creative endeavours. I would never be one who regards the creative as producing entirely new things all the time. I think that it is very creative to produce better more socially just ways of doing quite well known things. So I think both of those things involve a good deal of social creativity. But in the artistic world, you know, creativity is only associated with people getting out there and doing something that has never been done before, or that we couldn't even imagine. It is working backwards from the imaginary and bringing that into the commonplace and the everyday. /.../*

"I've never felt myself to be a very creative person in the kind of conventional, cultural sense. I am a musician but what I have always done musically is to interpret and re-interpret. But social creativity is about thinking about new ways of doing social interactions and economic interactions. Creating new societies, creating new designs for sustainability for example. All of those things involve a huge amount of creativity and I have always been more comfortable I suppose in working in that kind of social creativity area than what you might call artistically creative".

While Lesley's description utilises the attributes of person, process and product, combined in a multi-dimensional view, it seems to go beyond this to expound a holistic conception of creativity.

Differences Between Students' and Lecturers' Views

Although all participants in both these studies were asked about the same phenomenon – creativity – there are obvious differences of context between the group of business students and the group of postgraduate lecturers. The former group was asked about creativity in the context of a range of dispositions that were felt to be an important part of the development of business graduates. These dispositions included ethics, sustainability and cross-cultural sensitivity as well as creativity, and also the intersections between them. The interviews started by asking them to talk about the aspects of university study that they thought would be most important to them when they joined the workforce, and they were specifically asked about creativity in their future professional work.

The lecturers, in contrast, were interviewed about their views of two of these dispositions – sustainability and creativity – in their teaching. Their context was the view of a teacher, not specifically focusing on the use of the dispositions in the workplace (though of course some of them discussed that point). While both groups were interviewed in a pedagogical context, they represented different participants in the process, and to some extent their views of creativity reflect this.

All of the lecturers had thought about the questions in advance, and all seemed able to recognise and discuss creativity rather than define it. They generally saw the creative process as a part of their professional teaching practice and also as a part of their professional discipline areas. In this sense, the domain at the centre of their discussion was complex as it involved the intersections between professionalism and teaching within that profession. This was different from the majority of students who saw creativity in a rather acontextual way (with the exception of a few who suggested that the demonstration of creative practice, or being a creative person, may give them a business advantage in the future).

In particular, while all subjects were participants in a pedagogical community, we could distinguish the two groups as novices and experts (Reid *et al.*, 2008) and identify differences in their viewpoints or conceptions as a result of this. So, many of the business students put forward relatively simplistic definition conceptions of creativity, and those who showed a broader attribute conception for the most part linked creativity with a person. Many of them were quite willing to deny their own creativity with phrases such as *"I'm not a very creative person"*, or the role of creativity in their discipline or workplace. Consider, for instance, the statement of Shelly, a student of tourism.

> Shelly: *"I think of art. Art. /.../ Innovative ways of like doing things new. I think of painting and craft, so relating that to the hotel industry, I don't see it".*

Similarly, the second part of Richard's quote (given earlier) also implies that he doesn't think that creativity has a role in his discipline (accounting).

By contrast, all of the lecturers accepted that creativity was a proper topic for their consideration, even Harry to some extent (also from the accounting discipline), the most dubious of them.

> Harry: *"Well, I hope that we encourage our students to be creative. Though sometimes creative in financial terms can be a pejorative word".*

As opposed to the business students, most lecturers focused on the *process* of creativity when they talked at the attribute level (there is the one brief reference to a "creative person" in William's quote given earlier). This was possibly related to their viewpoint as teachers, and particularly as teachers of classes of students. In another contrast to the business students, none of the lecturers discussed creativity in terms of personal gain or advantage, not even those lecturers who were in the commercial areas. Further, the teachers as a group were happy to discuss various discipline-specific meanings of creativity, particularly contrasting the arts and sciences, as in the following quote.

Ron: "*Well you could argue that every piece of art is creative. It's much different for science. But some people who do art think they are very creative but a lot of them don't have very much creativity*".

Valentin's earlier quote talks about music or writing or painting or visual arts including scientific research as sites of creativity, and Leslie, also quoted earlier, expounds her theory of "social creativity".

Looking at the student data as a whole, we see generally naïve views of creativity. Naïve in that they are usually uni-dimensional and only occasionally related to the students' own life-world. In one sense the student group saw creativity largely in the domain of others with only a few making a personal connection to the concept. In contrast, the lecturers provided a multi-dimensional view where the concept of creativity was tied to the professional world, their teaching world, their personal world, and a social world.

The biggest difference between the two groups, however, is in the lecturers' fourth and broadest "holistic" conception of creativity. Although there were a few students, such as Sid, who were able to look at a comprehensive conception of creativity, from multiple attributes or perspectives, only in the lecturers' quotes do we see an integrated view that leads to a general theory of creativity. Such general theory of creativity could also incorporate other dispositions such as ethics, as another lecturer, Robin, explained:

"*So inevitably I think creativity requires some sort of ethical clarity, some sort of value clarity, and an ability to discern values, so I don't think it… I'm certainly not talking about a requirement to conform to any particular set of values but the need to be able to discern what values people and societies and institutions in fact refer to as their reference point, as their benchmarks for performance*".

True, Sid and some of his fellow students were able to discuss aspects of creativity that extended the person-process-product ideas, such as the notion of the group dimension of creativity: and this idea of group creativity was more common in the lecturers' discussions. But the holistic discussion of creativity as exemplified by Valentin and Leslie is qualitatively different to the multi-dimensional but additive ideas of some students.

We have discussed in other contexts how the broadest conceptions of various professional dispositions, including creativity, incorporate an ontological aspect of being or becoming (see Petocz & Reid, 2010). This can be seen in some of the lecturers' quotes illustrating the holistic conception, for example, when Valentin says that:

"*From my own personal perspective the new insight that I get, the new perspective that I get which I didn't expect, something quite unexpected, is to me a sign of creativity*".

Occasionally, the ontological aspect also appears at the comprehensive level, as when Paul (one of the students) says:

"*I think creativity is in every aspect of life... you know, university study to, to relationships, to you know, to I mean, it's, every aspect of life creativity touches in a lot of ways*".

The ontological dimension is also a component of the broadest conception of creativity identified by science students in the chapter by Almeida and colleagues (this volume).

Helping Students Utilise Creativity in Their Learning

This leads to discussion of the pedagogical aspects of these findings. It seems that creativity – and creativity within a specific learning domain – is rarely discussed as a concept with students, and rarely appears as part of the formal material of a course of tertiary study. Rather, it is sometimes held up as a characteristic to aim for, and students are informed (sometimes explicitly, but often only implicitly) that the highest marks will be reserved for work that displays creativity. Yet students have firm views on the importance and relevance (or not) of creativity in their particular context. A discussion of the nature of creativity, the ways that different students and lecturers view creativity and how it might be shown in an assessment task could be a useful addition to an early discussion of the course requirements. We have previously found that class discussion of conceptions of learning or of a specific discipline (such as statistics, see Reid & Petocz, 2003) can be a very powerful first step in encouraging students to broaden their views. It is always surprising how many students believe that all of their fellow students share their ideas about a specific topic.

In terms of specific techniques, the lecturers we interviewed suggested a wide range of teaching approaches that they used to encourage the process of creativity in their students. At the simplest level, this included a willingness to try new methods, based on regular professional discussion and reading. More specific techniques included regular use of group work, flexible approaches to teaching and assessment, using creative and hypothetical questions, involving students in carrying out their own research projects, and, at the higher levels, matching students carefully with projects in their own area of interest. Some of the lecturers give more details, starting with Kenneth's thoughts about group work.

> Kenneth: *"I think groups allow ideas to be transferred between people and therefore somebody might come up with something that triggers a thought that you might not have come up with otherwise and then that will lead to a more personal level of creativity. But then you can also feed that back into the group and so it can work around all the different people".*

Theresa explains her flexible approach to teaching and assessment.

> Theresa: *"In terms of creativity, I try to build in options a lot, so I have alternative kinds of assignments so wherever I can, because I feel that gives students more freedom to develop and take things in the direction they want. I also do always say they can change their assignment to an equivalent assignment if they want to. /.../ Even in the essay field I try to leave room in the essays that I suggest for them to choose between options, develop arguments in any direction that they want to".*

Patricia highlights the importance of a creative approach to questions that provoke creative responses.

> Patricia: *"I guess that sometimes it's through the types of questions I ask back in response to what they say, sometimes it's getting them to think about their own childhoods. And what the sorts of things they liked and didn't like about their own childhoods and that often makes me think about things differently, sort of analysing why they like that experience or why they didn't and then they begin to maybe take the child's perspective more in terms of what they're experiencing in their setting".*

In the field of human geography, Robin expresses her pedagogic theory of creativity and gives a key example for a higher-year course.

> Robin: *"I don't think you can teach creativity but you can teach creativity out of people. I think? So I'm not sure that in the sort of work that I do I can teach people to be creative so what I aim to do is that I aim to facilitate their creativity. I aim to open their eyes to their own creativity. /.../ In the last assignment in my third year course, I ask people what do they think they've learned and how*

are they going to apply that learning in their personal/professional lives. I mean the question's phrased a little differently each year but that's basically the task".

Also in human geography, Leslie highlights the importance of allowing students to participate in the research process.

Leslie: *"But we actually engage our students from the earliest possible time in doing their own research and thinking through why they want to do the research this way and how they do it, what their ethical obligations are to the subjects of their research and what subjectivity is. /.../ So one of the best ways of encouraging students to get into those kinds of debates and that kind of thought is to actually go out and do some research".*

And at the doctoral level, Mark highlights the creative aspects of matching students with potential research projects in music that will best appeal to their interests and talents.

Mark: *"So there is a constant effort for the best kind of outcome for the interests they've had that will deliver them a PhD at the end that will be successful with its elements. So you often have to be creative in knowing what the student thinks they want, knowing what outcomes will work and knowing how to bridge the areas in the middle, so that's one kind of creativity, not in the kind of artistic sense but more in a professional sense".*

Taken as a whole, our lecturer respondents suggested a wide range of techniques for helping students to utilise creativity in their learning. A particularly powerful aspect is to utilise the assessment processes of a subject, both from the view of the teacher's approach to assessment (as described, for instance, by Theresa and Robin) but also in terms of rewarding (explicitly) the creativity displayed by students in their work. A framework such as the SOLO (Structure of Observed Learning Outcomes) taxonomy (Biggs & Collis, 1982; Biggs, 1999a), referred to earlier in this chapter, could be used as the basis for an assessment rubric in many situations. Indeed, the pre-structural, unistructural, multistructural and relational/extended abstract outcomes could be seen as paralleling the four conceptions of creativity that we have identified.

Students could be made aware of the contextual aspects of creativity and the manner in which creativity is recognised inside the particular learning domain. Robust discussions between lecturers and students of creative practices, processes and products could generate learning situations where group activities begin to demonstrate creative attributes. From our business example, it is clear that the domain plays an important role in "being" creative and recognising creativity. Different domains may bring to light different ways of articulating and working with creativity. For instance, anyone who plays a musical instrument is popularly considered creative, but from within the domain of music education, creativity takes on a far more sophisticated description with features such as nuance, culture and phrasing playing integral roles. It only needs to be determined how creativity in those and other domains is manifested, and what specific aspects of the discipline are generally recognised as creative. In such ways, students can develop their appreciation of the nature of creativity and its role in preparing them for successful working lives.

About the Authors

Anna Reid is a Professor and Associate Dean at the Sydney Conservatorium of Music, Australia. She can be contacted on anna.reid@sydney.edu.au

Peter Petocz is an Associate Professor in the Department of Statistics at Macquarie University, Sydney. He has broad research interests in applied statistics and pedagogy. You can contact him on Peter.Petocz@mq.edu.au

Chapter Eight

Creativity and Reflection: some Theoretical Perspectives Arising from Practice

Andrea Raiker

Introduction

My purposes in this chapter are twofold; firstly to consider whether reflection, critical analysis, critical evaluation and synthesis are constituents of creativity; and secondly to explore an assumption in my university's Education Strategy (Atlay, 2008) that creativity is implicitly embedded in practice to be learnt automatically by students. Therefore this chapter is about words, the meanings attributed to them by tutors and students, and how these meanings might impact on achievement. My background in socio-cultural linguistics has led me to regard words as icebergs; what you see on the surface in a word's use does not reflect the bulk of individual constructs arising from complex and interwoven experiences held in the mind to which that word applies. So use of a word can develop degrees of understanding or misunderstanding or even misconception, depending on the overlap of constructs held by participants in discourse. So my research was directed at discovering tutors' and students' constructs of creativity.

In my university, the University of Bedfordshire, the terms "creativity" and "creative" are written into the recent Education Strategy from 2008. However, there is no explanation of what creativity or being creative entails. The document does not suggest that creativity should be taught or learnt. It appears to assume that creativity and creative processes are embedded in practice and therefore will be either implicitly or explicitly taught as a matter of course.

My interest in creativity was stimulated by a perception of an increasing trend of poor performance in dissertations undertaken by education undergraduates at the English university where I teach. The dissertation is undertaken in the final year. It entails reflection upon, and critical analysis and evaluation of, both literature and empirical data collected from classrooms. The synthesis of the findings from the literature and classroom data results in conclusions and recommendations for future practice. It is expected that conclusions attracting high grades will demonstrate insights, that is, the construction of knowledge and understanding new to the students. A significant number of dissertations did not demonstrate insights.

According to Jackson (2005), insights can be regarded as the outcomes of creativity and creative practices. Courses and modules are taught according to learning outcomes and related assessment criteria. Neither "creativity" nor "insights" appear in the assessment criteria for the dissertation on the university template, the validated information document for the module. In this document the important concepts mentioned are "reflection", "critical analysis", "critical evaluation" and "synthesis". These resonate with Jackson's notion of *"academic intellectual territory"*. What is more the template does not specify that these concepts should be taught.

I had recently completed a research project into supervisors' and students' perceptions of the tutorial system supporting the dissertations. Included was a focus on creativity. Interviews with supervisors and students on aspects of creativity suggested that they related it in varying degrees to the four concepts of reflection, critical analysis, critical evaluation and synthesis. This prompted me to consider whether these four concepts are in fact constituents of creativity, and if the assumption that creativity is therefore implicitly embedded in practice to be learnt automatically by students is correct.

The establishment of theory-practice relationships is fundamental to academic writing in my discipline of education. My own particular interest is the development of theoretical models that aid understanding of theory-practice relationships. Therefore this chapter will begin with consideration of Mezirow's (1991) work that provides the initial theoretical framework linking creativity with reflection.

This is followed by a brief discussion of my research as context and a presentation of the principal findings. The theoretical framework is then developed in two ways. Firstly, Meyer & Land's (2006) threshold concept theory (TCT) is applied to a key finding of my research to investigate how creativity can be constrained. In my previous work (Raiker, 2009a, 2009b) I have shown that TCT, particularly Meyer & Land's concept of liminal space, is useful in understanding why some students have difficulties in some areas of learning whilst other students do not. Both TCT and liminal space will be defined in the following discussion. Secondly, a model is presented to illustrate the relationship between creativity, knowledge and understanding, and elements contingent upon reflection. Furthermore, the model is used to generate a profile for tutor and student use to identify areas inhibiting the latter's creativity. The chapter concludes with a discussion on implications of the developed theoretical framework for future practice.

Theoretical Framework

Despite being difficult to define (Fryer, 2006a), creativity in higher education in the UK is regarded as being valuable. As Edwards *et al.* (2006:59) conclude, attitudes to creativity are based on: *"...the assumption that most students are capable of some creative work at some level; that creativity can contribute to the lives of individuals and societies; and that its encouragement among academics and students is a central part of universities' missions"*. This suggests that higher education is becoming more aligned with approaches to creativity adopted by the pre-university phases. In English primary schools, a succession of governmental policies and strategies beginning with Children and their Primary Schools, known as The Plowden Report (CACE, 1967), has raised the profile of creativity in students' learning in teachers' minds and practice. In this phase, creativity is no longer regarded as peripheral or specifically arts-orientated but central to education. "Creative thinking" is now a component of curricula from the Foundation Stage (the stage leading up to formal entry into school at five) to that offered by the National College of School Leadership for prospective head teachers at both primary and secondary levels (Craft, 2005). In higher education, some progress has been made towards embedding creativity in subject benchmarking statements (descriptions characterising learning at undergraduate and postgraduate levels). Also organisations such as The South East England Consortium for Credit Accumulation & Transfer (SEEC) have developed credit level descriptors of creativity for use in higher education nationally and in the developing field of European credit. However as Jackson (2006:2) observes, thus supporting Edwards *et al.* (2006): *"...the problem is not that creativity is absent but that it is omnipresent and subsumed within the analytical and critical ways of thinking that dominate the academic intellectual territory".* This chapter is focused on making that presence explicit and considering possible impact on achievement. But first understanding of the terms "creativity" and "reflection" must be determined. This will involve the establishment of a theoretical framework out of which the desired understandings will arise.

Moon (2004:82) defines reflection as *"...a form of mental processing – like thinking – that we may use to fulfil a purpose or to achieve some anticipated outcome or we may simply 'be reflective' and then an outcome can be unexpected".* Various authors (Tosey, 1993; Jackson, 2005; Craft, 2005; Fryer, 2006a) have pointed out that creativity is purposeful, implicitly suggesting expectations and outcomes. Outcomes indicate products, the results of process, and processes can be learnt. Jackson in particular highlights the seeming contradiction of creativity, a concept linked with freedom from conventions and expectations, being enhanced by a problem-solving, outcome-based approach to learning. It is suggested that the contradiction occurs because creativity can be considered to be both process and product. Creative products are the outcome of the unique restructuring of an individual's mental connections to gain new insights. These can be expressed as paintings, plays or assignments. Each will display varying degrees of individual technical excellence and socio-cultural originality. Creative products become part of an individual's bank of *knowledge and understanding.* In contrast, creative processes are ongoing. Institutions such as art colleges, drama schools and universities offer problem-solving, outcome-based approaches to learning that develop the *skills* of creative process. This suggests that every individual can be engaged in creative processes and produce creative products, though not all creative products will be acknowledged with the socio-cultural accolade of significant achievement. It is argued here that the creative skills in higher education are reflection, critical analysis, critical evaluation and synthesis. It is proposed that developing these skills will enhance students' individual creative products, that is, achievements in assignments and, particularly for the research discussed in this chapter, in undergraduate dissertations.

I found it useful to consider at this juncture Mezirow's (1991) perceptions on reflection. I wanted to see if he made connections between reflection and insights. As has been argued earlier, insights are indicative of creativity and creative processes at work. Mezirow maintains that reflection is prompted by the perplexities and ambiguities resulting from challenges to beliefs, perceptions and assumptions. According to Mezirow, a learner's first response to a problem arising from such a challenge will be to examine its content. This suggests that the learner considers his/her knowledge base in which the problem sits. Mezirow terms this *"content reflection"*. This will be followed by *"process reflection"* where the learner will critically consider the problem-solving strategies available and choose the most appropriate. Successful choice and application of suitable strategies will lead to the final stage of *"premise reflection"* where an intended outcome is achieved. Furthermore the learner's perspective will change as a result of engaging with the reflective process. This is indicative of creativity as the changing perspective experienced can be recognised as the perception of insights new to the learner, that is, an individual's creative product.

I found Mezirow's categorisation persuasive but in need of development for use in a discussion of reflection as an essential component of creativity in undergraduate dissertations. Critical analysis resonates with "process reflection", as does "premise reflection" with synthesis. However, critical evaluation is not explicitly addressed. More importantly, reflection is not defined in its own right, only as a constituent of something else. Consideration of a finding from my research suggests that it is necessary to consider reflection independently to understand "content reflection" fully. The dissertations attracting lower grades, analysed for my research, demonstrated higher proportions of description than those awarded higher grades. Description was of content, but colleagues interviewed as part of the research believed that description did not indicate reflection. However, it can be argued that description does involve reflection, as Moon's (2004:82) *"...form of mental processing – like thinking"* is applied to *"... fulfil a purpose"* of selecting content to form the description. It is apparent that definition is important when discussing reflection and hence creativity. Therefore some definitions are presented for use in this chapter.

It is suggested that content reflection is reflection on knowledge and that these two components should be defined separately:

+ Knowledge – cognitive structures of fact and belief leading to understanding

+ Reflection – to think about knowledge with or without purpose.

Description can then be defined as purposeful reflection resulting in an uncritical account or explanation of knowledge. It is proposed that some description is necessary in the undergraduate dissertation to give valuable context but is unlikely to result in the unique restructuring of an individual's mental connections to gain new insights indicative of creative product. Neither will description indicate creative process, that is, the skills involved in problem-solving to meet learning outcomes. These skills involve critical analysis, critical evaluation and synthesis, and are defined as follows:

+ Critical analysis – the application of rational, logical and purposeful reflection to deconstructed knowledge

+ Critical evaluation – the making of judgments on the outcomes of rational, logical and purposeful reflection on deconstructed knowledge (i.e. on critical analysis)

+ Synthesis – the fusion of outcomes of critical evaluation into new knowledge, broadening and/or deepening the knowledge base.

It is suggested that insights can occur in any or all of these three aspects of the creative process. The result is broadened and/or deepened knowledge that can be regarded as extended cognitive structures of fact and belief. Although this extended knowledge can be presented as a dissertation, that is a creative product, it is in fact merely a point in a creative process, though for the undergraduate an important one as a major contribution to graduation classification. Arguably, the importance of process increases if breakdowns occur, resulting in insights, creativity and achievement being constrained. There are taxonomies, for example those developed by SEEC, that describe progressive depths of critical analysis, critical evaluation and synthesis related to creativity at undergraduate level that could be used diagnostically. However, the complexity of the creative process as discussed above suggests that linear taxonomies might be simplistic. To address this, a profile is presented as Table 1 demonstrating creative development during the three years of an undergraduate course through descriptions of reflection, analysis, evaluation and synthesis at three levels. The descriptors for reflection arise out of the argument above, namely, that reflection should be regarded as a discrete concept through which reflective skills are applied to knowledge and understanding. Critical analysis and evaluation have been combined as it proved impossible to meaningfully separate them. The profile is designed to be used by tutors and students. It could support the identification of areas for development to strengthen the creative process. It is important that the theoretical framework should be developed to consider points or processes of breakdowns. However, I established in my introduction that theory-practice relationships were fundamental to academic writing in my discipline of education. Before developing the theoretical framework further, to maintain balance I will discuss the practice to which it is related, the undergraduate dissertation in education and the prior development of necessary creative skills. This will involve a discussion of the principal findings from my research on this practice in relation to creativity and reflection.

Cognitive skills	Undergraduate Year 1	Undergraduate Year 2	Undergraduate Year 3
Reflection	Begins to think about subject knowledge purposefully and with understanding in the light of personal experience or feelings. Shows extension of knowledge base through selection of reading related to lived experience and to task.	Presents depth of subject knowledge appropriate to task through identification and rationalisation of personal and vicarious experiences. Shows critical ability to think about knowledge purposefully and with some understanding of complexity. Shows extension of knowledge base through critical thought on simple primary research and secondary research.	Presents depth and breadth of subject knowledge appropriate to task through rationalising experience, theory and philosophy. Shows increased critical ability to think about knowledge resulting in changes in perspective. Shows extension of knowledge base through critical thought leading to insights on primary and secondary research.
Analysis and evaluation	Describes with limited analysis a range of information using given principles, frameworks or criteria. Shows some ability to structure descriptions but gives minimal or no reasons for any resulting evaluation or judgment.	Evidence of self analysis and evaluation. Can take apart an idea, argument or concept and make links with lived experience. Gives reasons and judges the reliability of data and information using pre-defined techniques and/or criteria.	Analyses a range of information comparing alternative methods and techniques. Selects appropriate techniques/criteria for evaluation and discriminates between the relative relevance and significance of data/evidence collected.

Cognitive skills	Undergraduate Year 1	Undergraduate Year 2	Undergraduate Year 3
Synthesis	Collects and structures descriptions with limited analysis and evaluation to inform a choice of commonplace solutions to standard problems in familiar contexts. Ideas and concepts showing minimal or no change from the reflective process.	Selects own methods of information and data collection. Uses these to collect and analyse information/data from a variety of authoritative and evaluated sources. Recognises relationships between ideas. Uses findings to inform a choice of solutions to standard problems in un/familiar contexts.	Evidence of meta-cognition through the integration of theory-practice relationships. Transformation and reconceptualisation evident in the form of in significant insights new to the learner. Collects and synthesis information to inform a choice of solutions to self defined problems in un/familiar contexts.

Table 1: Descriptors of Reflection and Creative Skills

The Practice

The dissertation is a "capstone" assignment, the last leading to a degree in initial teacher education. The nature of the dissertation has changed over recent years. The consensus from supervisors' interviews is that the change has been for the better as this extract from one supervisor (Supervisor 5 Interview: S5I) indicates:

> "It's now a much greater emphasis on the research and the analysis of the research rather than not copying things out of books, but reviewing the literature. There is much greater emphasis on engagement with the theory and the practice and synthesis. The analysis section has become much more of a focal point to the thesis… to the dissertation rather than the analysis, rather the reporting of the literature as it was in the past".

The students are introduced to the overall structure to the dissertation, what the expectations are, and where to find examples of previous year's dissertations to inform their understanding of what is required. They are asked to choose a focus that interests them and that can be researched in whatever school they find themselves for their final practical experience. It is emphasised that they are expected to read around their particular area of interest during the summer preceding the final year. Before the students return to university in October of their final year, they will be expected to have identified the general field in which they want to carry out their research, and also a very broad title. This is used by the module leader to identify tutors with the appropriate specialist knowledge so that tutor and student can be matched.

The primary means of student support throughout the course of the dissertation is the tutorial. The tutorial is a time and place that enables: *"...a structured and supported process undertaken by an individual to reflect upon their own learning, performance and or achievement and to plan for their personal, educational and career development"* (HEA, 2009:1). Students are asked to contact their supervisors as soon as possible on their return in October to arrange first tutorials. The unit handbook stipulates that the supervisor writes a record of this meeting, using a prescribed format. The format records work done for the tutorial, supervisor's comments, and a brief plan of work to be done for the next tutorial. The supervisor and student both sign and retain copies of the completed and dated document. The document includes spaces for date and time of the next meeting. All subsequent meetings are recorded in a similar manner. The focus of the first tutorial is the ethics proposal form. This is a summary of the student's research context and design, giving triangulated methods and including draft schedules (of observation and/or interview and/or questionnaire). References to key literature are provided, specifying how any ethical issue arising from that research will be addressed.

My research took the approach of a case study involving mixed methods. Collected by proportional sampling were records of 56 students submitted with their dissertations during 2009. These 174 documents, providing data on the number of tutorials per student, when they occurred and what was discussed, were submitted to content analysis (Brenner *et al.*, 1985). Further rich data was collected through recording 3 two hour dissertation support sessions, structured interviews with six dissertation students in a focus group and six supervisors during the summer term 2009. All qualitative data was subjected to discourse analysis according to Parker (1992) and Sfard (2001). This method uses no particular procedure of detailed analysis, but looks for patterns of language use that can be related to broader themes of social structure and ideological critical evaluation. The findings from content and discourse analysis were triangulated with quantitative data gathered from student grades, tutorial attendance and tutorial records.

Principal Findings on Creativity and Reflection

A key finding from my research suggested that all six supervisors believed creativity was innate and identified the brighter students. S3I's view was representative:

> "I don't think they are creative in terms of synthesising reading and empirical evidence, except for the really switched ones".

All three of Mezirow's categories are present here, and they are linked with creativity. Additionally, all believed that creativity could be enhanced but there were constraints. For example S1I thought that it was contingent on the ability to take risks:

> "Do you want to play it safe and get a good mark or push the envelope and get a great mark? Or potentially push the envelope and watch the whole balloon burst and not get such a good one".

S4I thought that the focus chosen was a component:

> "If it's a buzzy subject, they can develop, they can show creativity".

For S6I constraints were word count and submission deadlines:

> "They don't think 'Actually this could be this, or this could be that. What does this mean and how could that fit in?' and I think some of that is being constrained by word count. I think, for most of them. For others, I just need to get this done".

So, although all the supervisors interviewed used the words "creativity" and/or "creative", and implicitly or indirectly used Mezirow's categories, there was no mention of reflection, criticality, evaluation or insights when discussing creativity. It follows that supervisors would not be able to develop reflection and the creative skills dependent upon it. Students' abilities to produce insights would therefore be limited, and hence the potential to achieve higher grades. Furthermore, supervisors would not be able as a module team to address constraints on the development of creativity as they did not have shared understanding of what these were (see Reid & Petocz, in this volume).

The students also thought that creativity was innate but did not feel that creativity could be enhanced. The members of the focus group agreed with Student 3Focus Group (S3FG) that:

"...you either have it or you don't".

"It" was defined in terms of the creative arts. S4FG gave the unsolicited comment that one of the reasons she wanted to become a teacher was:

"...so that I can follow my hobbies. I love doing creative things like drawing and drama".

With this comment, the previously stuttering discussion became animated, but about creativity as music and art, not as an outcome of their classroom research. This is not conducive to students developing awareness and skills to increase creativity and insights.

Both supervisors and students showed greater confidence and understanding when discussing "reflection". Supervisors but not students indicated that they understood that there were different levels of reflection and associated them with ability. The terms "synthesis", "critical analysis", "critical thinking" and "reflection" appeared in supervisors' transcripts but the depth of understanding of these terms was unclear. For example S3I said:

"So they can synthesise these things through the dissertation but whether it's meaningful really does depend on their ability to reflect on that. Does that make sense?".

S4I understood that critical analysis and insights were connected, but her understanding did not appear to be systematic:

"...they can review things and tie things up in their concluding chapter or their critical analysis, it can give them new insights".

None of the supervisors' interviews contained explicit links between insights and creativity or between reflection and creativity. This being the case, it is difficult to see how supervisors could support students in being reflective to enhance creativity. Additionally, supervisors would not be able to increase students' awareness of their creativity through linking them directly with the insights revealed through literature review and analysis of empirical data.

There were indications that supervisors believed that an invitation to students to reflect would result in reflection. However there was no suggestion from the data that supervisors believed that reflection, or critical analysis or critical evaluation or synthesis, should be taught. Reflection would result from adequate reading. Reflection on extensive reading would provide the necessary subject knowledge for critical analysis and the emergence of insights and creativity. This equates closely with Mezirow's three categories. Conversely, if sufficient reading was not undertaken the result would be an unsatisfactory knowledge base for the critical analysis phase making it unlikely that insights or "premises" would emerge from reflection.

The incidence of lack of reading in the records of the first tutorial was high. So some students had little on which to reflect and apply creative skills. This resulted in students attending their first tutorials with little idea of focus. "X has very broad ideas about what she wants to do" (Tutorial Record 5: TR5) and "Brainstormed ideas" (TR15) are representative of this. Data from the supervisor interviews confirmed issues with students' knowledge base, the essential pre-requisite for reflection and creativity:

> "...they don't appreciate how much reading they have to do, particularly through the background".

(TR1) is representative of all supervisors' perceptions on an overall lack of preparatory reading. Interestingly, there is little difference in the incidence of students not reading, or not reading sufficiently at the time of the first tutorial, across all grade bands. All supervisors stated the view that the higher achieving students were able to catch up with the necessary reading during the course of their research but not the under-performing group. A finding of this research, reflecting and extending Harrison & Whalley's (2006) identification of time management as an issue affecting the quality of students' dissertations, is that some form of focused teaching on *project* management could have been beneficial to support students in planning their reading during the summer period preceding the start of their final year. It is also evident that engagement with the differences between the various forms of reflection and their relationship with and impact on creativity would be beneficial for both students and supervisors.

Constraints on Creativity

Amongst my findings, a number of constraints on creativity in the dissertation have been identified. Constraints on the acquisition of appropriate and sufficient subject knowledge are clearly important. Ineffective project management, an aspect that would not seem at first glance to constrain creativity, has been identified as doing just that. Lack of understanding by both supervisors and students of the creative process and the reflective skills on which it depends are also constraints. The discussion will now consider how these constraints can be understood theoretically with the aim of identifying ways of addressing them. It will focus on a constraint of crucial importance to the dissertation but not yet discussed, the transfer of research skills to the dissertation.

In the dissertation, critical analysis and evaluation is expected in two areas. These are the literature review of texts and the analysis of empirical data from the classroom. Students approaching their dissertations are comfortable with literature reviews. The traditional essay is a literature review and students have written many essays over the preceding three years. However my research revealed that students were anxious about the research skills needed to conduct their empirical research. Research skills are defined in terms of ability to identify valid research methods (usually triangulation between interview, observation, questionnaire and school documentation), carry out reliable data collection and apply appropriate methods of analysis. Despite all students successfully convincing their supervisors through their ethics proposal forms that they were confident with the research methods, data collection arrangements and methods of analysis presented, tutorial record and focus group content analysis revealed that most students felt that they *had not* been taught appropriate research skills earlier in the course. Conversely, supervisors maintained that skills *had* been taught. The issue appeared to be that students were not able to transfer their learning of research skills into the dissertation, reflecting a finding of Stephani *et al.'s* (2007) work. S1I provides insights into the reasons why:

> "...*getting them to focus on an appropriate methodology. Because I think that is the weakest area. They have no idea. Probably not enough experience over the four years that they are here with the research methodology because we give them the research methodology in observation tasks, this, that and the other, we tell them what it is, that they have been given to do. So they can't draw on that experience when it comes to picking up their own. Not because they're not capable of transferable, transferring knowledge. They just don't know what they did whenever it was that they did it, of actually applying the research methodology*".

So the contributing issues, confirmed in other supervisor and focus group transcripts, appear to be lack of research skills input earlier in the course and of autonomy of choice.

The fundamental aspect of newness to the student in creativity has been discussed above. It is therefore proposed that transfer and integration of one area of knowledge into a new area is necessary for creativity to occur. Furthermore, the inference from the findings is that students are unable to develop from *being given* research methods appropriate for earlier tasks by their tutors to reflecting in order to identify *for themselves* which methods were suitable for their dissertation research. This clearly affects some students' ability to critically analyse primary data, synthesise within this area and with the outcomes of their literature reviews and thus maximise the potential of creativity. To develop understanding of this relationship, it is useful to consider Meyer & Land's threshold concept theory.

Meyer & Land see a distinction between "core concepts" and threshold concepts. A core concept is *"...a conceptual 'building block' that progresses understanding of a subject; it has to be understood but it does not necessarily lead to a qualitatively different view of the subject"* (2006:6). This *'qualitatively different view of the subject'* is indicative of a threshold concept and resonates with Mezirow's changing perspective discussed above and therefore with creativity. However threshold concepts provide more than changing perspectives. Meyer & Land argue that there are some aspects of learning that form portals, the passage through which provides access to landscapes of understanding critical for students' progress. The effect of these aspects is so profound that they can transform students' perceptions of their courses, their disciplines or even their world views. Threshold concepts clearly indicate a greater degree of learning and of creativity than that indicated by Mezirow's premise reflection.

However, my reflections on the language used by supervisors and students indicated that concepts were more complex than suggested by Meyer & Land. I found it difficult to discern separate "building blocks" when analyzing my data. What I perceived were cognitive structures of culturally accepted knowledge, incorporating understanding and meaning commonly communicated through language though not exclusively so. This knowledge consisted of understanding in various stages of assimilation and accommodation (Piaget, 1956), that is, being learnt and learnt. The "dissertation" was such a structure. So was "research skills". These were terms used frequently by supervisors and students. Component terms, like "introduction" for the dissertation and "questionnaire" for research skills were rarely used. For illustrative purposes I have simplified these two conceptual structures used by supervisor and students to circles (Figure 1).

The problem experienced by many students lay in their inability to transfer and integrate their knowledge and understanding of research skills, gained during the former three years of their course, to their dissertations. In other words *synthesis* between what they understood by dissertation and research skills had not taken place and their ability to perceive insights, or be *creative*, was impaired.

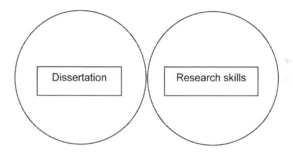

Figure 1: Two Cognitive Structures

Applying Meyer & Land's terminology, some students would pass through the threshold separating the two conceptual areas of dissertation and research skills to access a new vista of learning, in other words, to be creative. Others would find the new vista "troublesome" and counter-intuitive and could not apply the knowledge of one area to another because the relationship was meaningless to them (Lather, 1998; Perkins, 1999a). Students finding knowledge troublesome would be "stuck" in liminal space, their creativity impaired or even prevented. A metaphor describing liminal space would be a mental tunnel connecting two conceptual areas. One of these areas contains the current state of knowledge and understanding; the other contains the new vista of expanded learning. Learners finding the new learning troublesome will oscillate between the two. They will attempt to master the tacit knowledge they have of the new conceptual space together with attempted understandings and even misunderstandings of the subject specific language, the subject matter, subject landscape and even world view afforded by this new perspective. They can never go back to the old, comfortable understanding; they cannot progress to the new. In interview their supervisors used the term "mental blocks" to describe why not (Figure 2).

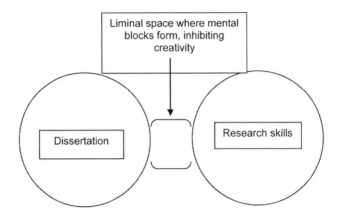

Figure 2: Liminal Space

It would appear that the dissertation students who had gained some knowledge and understanding of the dissertation, but who could not transfer their knowledge and understanding of research skills as the new vista, became stuck in liminal space. They seemed unable to see how their research skills related to the demands of the dissertation. This constrained their ability to carry out research which involves creative processes to produce dissertations which are creative products. However, through the support of their supervisors, students demonstrated they were capable of synthesising new understandings of "dissertation" and "research skills". It can be seen that supervisors were acting as scaffolds in the Brunerian sense (Bruner, 1986). Indeed, liminal space can be equated with Vygotsky's Zone of Proximal Development, defined by Vygotsky (1986:78) as being *"…the distance between the actual developmental level as determined by independent problem solving and the level of potential development as determined through problem solving under adult guidance, or in collaboration with more capable peers"*. Supervisor intervention was the trigger to synthesis and therefore creativity (Lange, in this volume). As one supervisor commented:

> *"I find that, overall, we chat about it on the phone, sometimes even an e-mail, and I give a suggestion, 'Have you thought about…'. It's usually something quite straightforward, it's not complicated, it helps them get over them, over the mental blocks".*

It appears that triggers to creativity are specific to individuals. What is more, they may or may not result in the socio-cultural accolade of significant achievement. For example, content analysis of the tutorial records of one student achieving a bare pass revealed excellent formative feedback on research skills resulting in insights new to that student.

Conclusions

I had two objectives in writing this chapter; firstly to ascertain whether reflection, critical analysis, critical evaluation and synthesis were constituents of creativity; and secondly to explore an assumption in my university's Education Strategy (Atlay, 2008) that creativity was implicitly embedded in practice to be learnt automatically by students. On both theoretical and empirical grounds, it appears that reflection, critical analysis, critical evaluation and synthesis are constituents of creativity. However, discussion has established that creativity can be both product and process. Reflection enables creative process. Critical analysis, critical evaluation and synthesis interact with knowledge and understanding. The resultant creative products become subsumed within and expand that knowledge and understanding.

The assumption underpinning my university's Education Strategy, namely that creativity and creative processes were embedded in practice and therefore implicitly or explicitly taught as a matter of course, was found to be erroneous. There was no evidence from my research that reflective skills enabling creative process and product were explicitly taught. It appears that creativity in the dissertation was regarded by supervisors as the reserve of the most able and that it was innate. My research indicated that supervisors believed that reflection was necessary for creativity to occur, that there were different levels of reflection but these were not made explicit. Supervisors' recognition of the necessity of an appropriate and sufficient knowledge base in the production of insights, seen as evidence of creativity, was demonstrated by the importance placed on reading. Many students did not appear to understand this importance. So my research suggests that supervisors' and students' constructs of creativity are different.

As a scaffold to understanding, a diagnostic profile giving descriptors of reflection and creative skills for a three year undergraduate course has been presented. Because theory-practice relationships are seen as being fundamental to my discipline, it is suggested that the profile would only be useful if related directly to supervisor-student interaction. In my introduction I proposed that this chapter was about words, the meanings attributed to them by tutors and students, and how these meanings might impact on achievement. It is strongly advised that the wording of the profile should be explicitly integrated into module learning outcomes and assessment criteria, and discussed with students. Through development of understandings of the concepts, the bulk of the icebergs being underwater, students would not only be able to construct their own *and* shared meanings and understandings. They would be given greater access to creative processes that could trigger creative insights and creative product with minimal misunderstandings and misconceptions. Meyer & Land's threshold concept theory is seen as being important in its perception of liminal space as a bar to creativity. It appears that "troublesome knowledge" causing "mental blocks" constrains creativity. The importance of the supervisory role of facilitator in promoting reflection in its various guises to remove these blocks, thus allowing creative process to proceed, has been demonstrated. However, this is contingent on reflection and creative skills being taught and practised from university entry.

In conclusion, it would appear that creative process can be taught through explicitly developing understanding of reflection, critical analysis, critical evaluation, synthesis. The dissertation lends itself to the teaching of creative processes as the supervisor's role is one of facilitation, usually working one-to-one in tutorials with students. Creative product can also be facilitated in the dissertation, as all dissertations are conceived as products original to the student. However it is arguable whether creative product, the outcome of individual complexity and originality, can be encouraged in the same way through more traditional module delivery formats.

About the Author

Dr Andrea Raiker is a Fellow of the Centre for Excellence in Teaching and Learning, University of Bedfordshire, Bedford, England. She can be contacted at this e-mail: andrea.raiker@beds.ac.uk

Chapter Nine

Connecting Creative Capital and Pedagogy in Postgraduate Programmes

Rajendra Chetty

Introduction

The objective of Higher Education should be to prepare multi-competent graduates with high levels of expertise and the ability to discover as well as exploit the discoveries of others through market related intelligence and the application of personal skills (Yorke, 2006). In essence, graduates need to use their skills effectively and creatively to add value to their lives. Cunningham (2006) adds that university graduates, unlike peers from previous decades, will be performing work that is less focused on routine problem-solving and more focused on new social relationships, novel challenges and the synthesising of "big picture" scenarios. It is unlikely that this objective can be met merely through the transmission of traditional disciplinary knowledge, what Freire (1971) refers to as "banking" education, or by adhering to traditional forms of evaluation and assessment. The hallmark of high quality graduates is of creative, independent thinkers who are able to generate ideas to solve complex problems within their area of expertise. Key questions that universities should ask are:

- What kind of environment enhances and influences creativity and how might this be constructed in postgraduate programmes?

- What are notions of creative capital that permeate the university?

- What sustainable and replicable pedagogical practices foster creativity among postgraduate students?

Unfortunately, the creativity agenda is compromised by institutional discourses that emphasise the quantity instead of the quality of students that graduate. This tendency links tenure to productivity by encouraging academics to play the research "game" by rewarding academics who procure high amounts of research funds. Institutional discourse rarely considers the impact of the research output. Further, the monetary incentive to South African universities in terms of intake of postgraduate students is highly problematic as it encourages universities to take large numbers of students without adequate provision for supervision and resources. Universities are also rewarded for students that graduate, hence pressure is applied on supervisors to increase the throughput rates of their students without due consideration to issues around quality.

It is therefore evident that within neo-liberal contexts, where issues around funding are dominant and high student intake is encouraged, creativity is not seen as important. A key reason for the exclusion of principles of creativity is that it jeopardises the monetary incentive, i.e. the chances of students going quickly through the system and graduating within the minimum period. Much of the research training and research grants are geared towards these imperatives of funding, access, retention and throughput with little room for creativity. Students who are not ready for the rigour of postgraduate research, struggle with mastering the epistemological and methodological frameworks that underpin their studies, leaving little scope for engagement with new approaches or innovative ways to conduct their studies. Thus, students are enrolled who are unlikely to complete and this places a huge responsibility on the supervisor to ensure that the student graduates, especially with the audit system that correlates the graduation rate with numbers that drop out. The audit results also identify academics that are "productive", i.e. those with high postgraduate throughput rates.

In South Africa, the theses of masters candidates should show evidence that there is a rigorous engagement with research methodology (process) and doctoral candidates are expected to contribute to knowledge (product). There is therefore room at both levels for new and innovative thinking around the process and the product. Central to this exercise is the influence of the higher education context on the creative product, the creative process and creative students. The neglect of creativity in theses production can be attributed to a number of reasons including the use of prescriptive guidelines for theses in terms of the nature, presentation and writing of the document (e.g. outline of chapters, trajectory towards recommendations and conclusions, and universities that lack supervision capacity generally move towards the standardisation of research design).

Creativity in theses production would involve researching and writing up the research report in a manner that is different to the linear, prescriptive and formulaic approach. The emphasis in the creative approach is to generate new ideas, to be innovative with process, style and product, to express individuality in writing up the thesis and to be imaginative in data presentation, interpretation and meaning construction. Integral for students to be able to grasp the opportunity for imaginative expression is a transparent, free and safe space to express their creativity.

The fact that there are multiple kinds of creativity reinforces the belief that every student has the potential to produce creative work and is able to excel in some form of creativity. The call here is for enlightened discourse by academics, use of critical thinking approaches and normative skills like caring, collaboration and ethics in an effort to encourage students to be imaginative, to explore new boundaries and to transcend mechanised ways of doing things.

Constructions of Creativity

The word "creative" (from the Latin *creativus*) and its main synonym "originative" are two values that form the backdrop to the definition of creativity: origination/innovation and production/work/usefulness (Sternberg & Lubart, 1999). Initial understandings of creativity limited it to complex ideas and behaviours exhibited by individuals. According to McWilliam & Dawson (2008), second generation understandings of creativity locate the creative enterprise in the processes and products of collaborative and purposeful activity. The key *product* of postgraduate programmes is generally a research project culminating in a thesis. However, Torrance (1993) foregrounds the research *process* in his description of creativity as opposed to the product and he includes problem identification, gaps in information, formulating, testing and revising hypotheses, and dissemination of results. Creativity is integral to research since the student brings something new into existence purposefully, usually a product resulting from a process initiated by the researcher (Barron, 1988).

There is still no consensus within the literature as to whether creativity is located in a person, a product or a process. There is agreement, however, that creative work is both novel and valuable (Mayer, 1999). Creativity is still viewed as a trait – an attribute with which one is born and something that only very gifted people possess: e.g. prowess in music, art, writing, choreography, etc. Positive traits, according to Feist (1999) are curiosity, high levels of personal energy, being attracted to complexity and novelty, tolerance for ambiguity, open-mindedness and persistence in the face of adversity. Interestingly, Sternberg (2002) broadens this view by postulating that there are multiple kinds of creativity, and that everyone can develop at least some of these. The "mystical" perspective of creativity is maintained by theorists like Donelly (2004) who views the phenomenon as a spiritual process that does not lend itself to scholarly scrutiny. It is therefore evident that creativity has emerged as a complex concept, and questions abound within this.

Kleiman (2008)	Creativity involves notions of novelty and originality combined with notions of utility and value.
Kaufman & Sternberg (2007)	It's a myth that creativity is only about individual genius. It is economically valuable, team-based, observable and learnable.
Knight (2002b)	Creativity constructs new tools and new outcomes – new embodiments of knowledge. It constructs new relationships, rules, communities of practice and new connections – new social practices.
Jackson (2002)	Creativity involves first imagining something (to cause to come into existence) and then doing something with this imagination (creating something that is new and useful to you). It's a very personal act and it gives you a sense of satisfaction and achievement when you've done it.
Boden (2000)	Three forms of creativity: combinational, exploratory and transformational.
Csikszentmihalyi (1999)	It is the community and not the individual who makes creativity manifest.

Sternberg & Lubart (1991)	Learner construction of knowledge is an important element for the development of creativity.
Gardner (1984)	Creativity is not an all-or-nothing phenomenon.
Koestler (1964)	The creative act does not create something out of nothing; it uncovers, selects, re-shuffles, combines, synthesizes already existing facts, ideas, faculties and skills.

Table 1: Various Understandings of Creativity

Key concepts that emanate from the differing understandings of creativity include originality, imagination, exploration for discovery, inventing new things, innovation (developing inventions into things people will want), adaptation (doing things differently) and transference (using things in different contexts). There is also a variance in the understanding of creativity from an individual act to the democratic notion that all people are creative. Central to tapping this intrinsic creative potential in both the process and the product of pedagogical work in higher education is the dynamics of the engagement between student and supervisor.

Dialogic Relations

The essence of the relationship between supervisor and student is the dialogue. The qualities of dialogic relations are an appropriate index of creative productivity in higher education. Notions of criticality, creativity, emotional learning and cognitive conflict need to be foregrounded. The quality of "thinking space" within programmes and environments for research is central to creative dialogue.

MacRury (2007) notes that the micromanaging of dialogic spaces in the supervisor-student relationship curtails the natural rhythms of imagination and emphasises the outcome as opposed to process. In his pathologies of "centredness" in institutional design, he illustrates that teacher-*centred* learning, student-*centred* learning, stakeholder-*centred* research and "pure" academic research can be non-dialogic when creativity is not optimal. However, it is in academic research where creativity can be optimal, on condition that academic research finds and maintains a balance between responsiveness and independence, relevance and refinement, purity and danger. Acknowledging dialectic thinking as the crux of the creative institutional dynamics can better enable research to creatively engage with such tensions. A re-thinking of pedagogical practices to foreground dialogical relationships is essential to support the kind of transformative experience that is intrinsic to the rhythms of creative, developmental thinking: processes fundamental to creativity.

Teacher-centred dialogue, or Freire's (1971:46–47) notion of *"banking education"* can also be evident in postgraduate programmes if supervisors feel that they have power over the knowledge in their discipline and the student has to be directed because of their ignorance of the research area. The following characterisation indicates elements of the higher education system as an instrument of domination:

- The supervisor thinks and advises and suggests the way forward

- The supervisor makes decisions and enforces choices with regards to methodology, design, theories, and the students comply

- The supervisor serves as the centre of epistemological knowledge, directing the focus of the study and the student adapts to it

- The supervisor confuses the authority of knowledge with his or her own professional authority, which she/he sets in opposition to the freedom of the students.

Freire argues for a dialogic relationship in which the poles are equalised – the supervisor does not relate from a position of power because of their knowledge and the student has space and voice to contribute to knowledge. However, there is also a danger of merely reversing the polarities of the teacher-centred pedagogy and, in its place, instituting student-centred learning without it being lodged within a critical education paradigm.

Creative Capital and Scholarship

Cunningham (2006) refers to university graduates as *"creatives"*, people who focus on interactive social relationships, navigation capacity, novel challenges and the synthesising of "big picture" scenarios. Creative capital should be the core objective to ensure that students are creative thinkers who can generate ideas that can be converted into innovative products and services, where the product will be the research output (the thesis) and where the services would align with their employability. Postgraduate programmes should be the catalyst for engagement with the scholarship of discovery. Boyer (1990) identified three forms of academic scholarship: teaching, research and service. Research, in turn, can be seen to perform four functions in the academe, i.e. discovery, integration, application and dissemination.

Research for discovery includes original and fundamental research resulting in the advancement of knowledge (Boyer, 1990). Research for integration involves connecting and synthesising ideas across disciplines. Application research involves assembling knowledge to address significant societal issues and research for dissemination involves transforming knowledge in order to bridge the gap between the scholar's understanding and the knowledge consumer.

Fryer (2006b:78) notes the following notions of creativity in the academe:

+ Thinking (solving ill-structured problems in ways which show initiative)

+ Doing (developing, implementing and leading new things)

+ Thinking and doing (cerebral and practical activities)

+ The arts (artistic version of innovative)

+ Self-expression (ability to express an innate aspect of one's psyche)

+ Creativity as a continuum (great contributions to the arts, science and everyday life)

+ Context (responding to specific and challenging contextually-based problems).

It is therefore beneficial for creative capital to embrace all the functions of scholarship and not be limited to problem solving and thinking skills.

Beyond Individualism

The nature of postgraduate programmes in South African Higher Education Institutions in both coursework and the research thesis option have generally envisaged graduate attributes through an individualistic lens. The assessment criteria, thesis production and the award of degrees emphasised the achievement of the individual. Csikszentmihalyi (1999) broadens notions of creativity to include the interaction between the environment (cultural and symbolic order) the social order and the student. Essentially, creativity is the product of multiple human interactions in complex environments rather than the products of artistic individuals (McWilliam & Dawson, 2008). The challenge for higher education would be to optimise opportunities for students to engage with complexity – where simple interactions lead to complex forms of group engagement (Seel, 2006). A way of embracing complexity and ensuring that a research topic is viewed from different angles would be to work in teams. Teacher education in South Africa is an example of a complex research area and viewing studies in this area with a complexity lens would provide creative solutions to the problems. In this context, a team approach lends itself to new connections, diversity of perspectives and increased information flow into the study. According to McWilliam & Dawson (2008) the team dynamics in such studies may lead to the following:

- Connectivity with diversity – working in teams with similar interests and passions to answer research questions. The creative impact and output of such research is far more beneficial than small scale individualised studies. Divergent views force the team to view situations with different lenses and thus resulting in the outcomes having a far richer texture.

- Co-invention/co-creation with separation – a research project with a team provides more comprehensive data and addresses the complexities of the research area at a deeper level. Being informed of the complexity of the problem results in a more informed student and a better conceptualised product, albeit an individual exercise for product purposes, in this case the thesis.

- Leading and following – responsibility and leadership is shared, but students may also defer to individuals who steer because of expertise and skills. If a repertoire of methodologies is used in a research project, different students would take the lead based on their skills with regards to design, i.e. interviews, observations, questionnaires, textual analysis, etc.

- Enhancing constraints and removal of inhibitors – the team approach to a research project provides opportunities for democratic ways of working, collaborative decision making and collegiality. Bureaucratic ways of working are minimised and less emphasis is placed on commands and controls.

- Explaining less and welcoming errors – encourage making mistakes and deepening the learning as opposed to emphasis on avoiding errors by following templates.

It is therefore evident that the impact of research findings would be greater if programmes moved from an individualistic to an interactive mode where group engagement is more conducive for creativity to flourish and to solve complex problems.

Transdisciplinarity

Disciplinary silos are characteristic of the organisation of universities. It is also ironic that in a post-structuralist era, institutional discourse in South African universities is still largely stuck in the reductionist mode of disciplinary borders, in spite of the fact that this militates against the type of creative and relevant research that needs to be undertaken. McWilliam *et al.* (2008) advocate a transdisciplinary approach because it expands understandings of knowledge and encourages coexistence of a range of multidisciplinary perspectives. Max-Neef (2005) understands the concepts discipline and trans-discipline as complementary and maintains that the transit from one to the other, attaining glimpses from different levels of reality, generates reciprocal enrichment that may facilitate the understanding of complexity.

For Bernstein (2000), a crucial dynamic influencing the nature and form of pedagogic agencies, discourses and practices in higher education is the process of regionalisation: the strategic bringing together of disciplines that may previously have existed as separate units. A trans-disciplinary perspective heralds a paradigm shift in institutional discourse and introduces new complexities in terms of people management, resourcing, postgraduate programmes and structures and procedures for award of degrees. It challenges academics to re-think traditional academic habits through originality by means of original thought, vision, and modes of scholarly engagement (Koestler, 1964).

Institutional discourses are generally opposed to transdisciplinarity. The structure and control in universities, like budget allocations, workload models, time-tabling and allocation of lecture halls are entrenched and research cannot transcend this system. Supervisors who want to foster creativity by crossing borders between disciplines have to contend with traditionally-minded colleagues who fear the "washing out" or diluting of their discipline if it is not kept pure and apart. Academics claim monopoly over knowledge through controlling, selecting and organising the production of discourse within certain procedures. Such procedures comprehend external controls, internal rules and the regulation of access to knowledge. The challenge for creative students and supervisors is to enlighten the traditionalists that transdisciplinarity requires far greater epistemological and methodological flexibility than does an established disciplinary field. McWilliam *et al.* (2008) concur that crossing disciplinary borders requires the invention of new dialects and capacities for translating across bounded systems of knowledge production.

Creative Supervision of Research Projects and Theses

Essential to creative supervision would be the ability of the supervisor to foster creative spaces for postgraduate work, to connect creative capital and pedagogical approaches, to develop responsible scholars, to foreground student identity and voice as researchers, to focus on supervision as pedagogy and to encourage students to debate, question and interpret research procedures and processes.

Fostering Creative Spaces

Thesis production provides students with an excellent opportunity to be creative. As Perkins points out, it is a task that focuses on skills and understanding of factors like pattern recognition, the creation of analogies and mental models, the ability to cross domains, exploration of alternatives, knowledge of schema for problem solving, and fluency of thought as aspects of creativity (Perkins, 1981). Koestler (1964) reinforces the opportunity provided by thesis production when he describes the creative act as not creating something out of nothing; it uncovers, selects, re-shuffles, combines, synthesises already existing facts, ideas, faculties, and skills.

There are pedagogical implications for the fostering of creativity in postgraduate programmes. Discovery methods need to be favoured and students should be allowed to think in multiple modes and through the lens of different disciplines. This requires a re-think of institutional requirements for structures of student research and outputs. The challenge for universities is to reflect on the kinds of spaces that they foster for creativity among students. A prescriptive approach to theses production and examination through internal policies, higher degree regulations and national academic norms and standards may stifle innovation and the creation of unique products.

Supervisors should encourage creativity with regards to the production of theses. The nature of a study should determine decisions with regards to quantity (number of pages), structure of dissertations, style guidelines and they should be vociferous in removing constraints on creative approaches. Students should be challenged to engage with radical and unique ways to conduct their research and disseminate results. This may influence more traditional peers in the academe towards a paradigm shift with regards to postgraduate work. Supervisors not only have to employ strategies to foster creative spaces for their postgraduate students and to view creativity as a critical component of their work, but they also have to adopt innovative ways to respond to institutional realities.

Connecting Creative Capital and Pedagogical Approaches

Creative supervisors value the creative dimensions of their own scholarship and understand the connection between creative capital and pedagogical approaches. Creative supervisors are a fundamental component of creativity in higher education. A combination of the following positive dispositions towards creativity and promotion of student learning should be considered:

- Nurturing questioning and challenging students and research projects

- Encouraging students to make connections, forge relationships and use different lenses to view reality

- Envisaging what might be different and acknowledging value in the difference

- Affirming cognitive conflict, generation of ideas and keeping options opened

- Re-presenting ideas in a variety of ways

- Evaluating effects of ideas and actions

- Reflecting on the creative process.

A key factor in supervising for creativity is not only to focus on the research output (the thesis), but also to foreground the learning during the research process as an integral component of developing academic scholarship in post-graduate students.

Towards Responsible Scholars

Lin & Cranton (2005) differentiate between scholarship students and a responsible scholar. Scholarship students often mimic rather than develop, memorise rather than think, are anxious rather than confident, and are lonely and isolated rather than a part of the community of learning. The key goal of the responsible scholar is autonomy of thought and action, self-efficacy, taking full control of the process and product. Kanfer & Kanfer (1991) view self-regulation as the process by which an individual exercises control over the direction, persistence and intensity of thinking, affect and behaviour for the purpose of goal attainment. Zimmerman (1989) concurs that self-regulated students play an active participatory role in their study, especially at the metacognitive, motivational and behavioural levels. He adds that independence in these levels is essential for creativity among postgraduate students because their personal choice of strategies and methodologies and active engagement in the process leads to innovation in product formulation.

The key supervisory role in developing responsible scholars would be one of a reflective practitioner (Schön, 1983). This approach provides space and interaction with regards to the goals of the project, the strategies that have been selected, an evaluation of the outcomes and the value that the process has added to the student's learning. In this way supervisors are also engaged with a self-regulatory model since they would not limit the student to work within the confines of the traditional mould of research. They would not prevent the student from exploring new methodologies and orchestrate the thesis production exercise through their authoritative voice. This would rule out the sort of statements by supervisors that were reported by students whom I asked about their experiences of the supervision process: "It makes more sense to do it like this", "Interviews are unreliable in that context", "Questionnaires would provide visual data for the thesis", "External examiners expect deeper engagement with theories", "I would not do it like that." (Chetty, 2007)

Students' Identity and Voice as Researchers

Ownership of postgraduate research resides with the student. It is the student who should believe in its value. Supervision of theses has resulted in much trauma for students who have had their thoughts and ideas refuted by supervisors who are inexperienced, have never participated in research projects, have not read beyond their own training and who see the structure of a thesis cast in stone.

Supervisors are not experts in every area of the discipline and should concede that they learn together with the student. If the student's identity and voice emerges, supervisors should not feel intellectually insecure nor dominated by the student's independence of thought. This calls for a sensitive management of the writing process in which students are encouraged to explore their own style and voice in the research. The relationship becomes a professional partnership with sharing, collaboration and mutual benefit. An example of the latter would be journal articles and conference presentations co-authored by the student and supervisor.

Supervision as Pedagogy

Adkins (2009) asserts that the focus on postgraduate supervision as pedagogy enables the systematic inclusion of current tendencies for knowledge processes to move beyond strict boundaries of disciplines and across divisions between research and teaching, and the traditional roles of lecturer/student. Creative supervision requires academics to understand their students' research problems in terms of both a vertical (hierarchical knowledge structure) as well as a horizontal (inter-disciplinary) lens.

Restricting a study to a specific discipline may result in the findings having minimum impact on problems since the complexity of the context is influenced by more than a single discipline. For example, a study of social problems in urban classrooms would require insights into education, sociology and psychology. Similarly, engineering students should also have knowledge of the social aspects of urban design, communication and ethics. Supervisors need to integrate all these insights in order to guide the student effectively towards new domains of knowledge which would have been forbidden terrain within vertical knowledge structures.

Adkins (2009) notes that the hidden aspect of pedagogy here is that the supervisor must have sufficient understanding at a generic level of what is required for the development of knowledge through integration to provide the student with the tools to accomplish their research objectives. Supervisors should take ideas from a repertoire of disciplines, focusing on innovative ways to weaken the traditional classification of knowledge and orienting students to discovery research that enables new advances, regardless of disciplines. The key skill here is strategies for knowledge integration. By being good role models, supervisors spur students to creative heights through their own innovative ways of working with knowledge. New work across disciplines is likely to produce results that have a greater impact on research problems.

Encouraging Debate, Questioning and Interpretation

The development of critical pedagogy in postgraduate work includes interrogation of the rationale behind research procedures and processes, resistance to traditional modes of thinking and encouraging critique. What is advocated is a rethinking of the concepts "knowledge" and "ignorance" leading to a radically unconventional manner of supervision. A confrontational attitude towards students, instead of paternalism, with a critical stance towards for example, secondary sources, is mooted. When conflict is not suppressed, it forms a discursive site in which knowledge is produced. Supervisors should encourage debate and questioning of their own epistemological and methodological understandings. If knowledge is viewed as an entity that is static and fixed and absolute, no creativity is engendered because the knowledge is not open to dialogue and conversation and the role of the student is to merely master the knowledge, not create new knowledge.

Credentialism has exacerbated the situation since students are eager to tailor their theses to suit the supervisor's interpretations in order to obtain their certificates without any obstacles. Many students take advantage of this situation and do not see the need to confront the institutional discourse. Transmission education was easier and expected minimum effort while confrontation with the supervisor's interpretations demanded taking a critical position. Therefore the goal of consuming knowledge took precedence over that of production or of fostering individualism and creativity. Alternative research strategies and approaches to methodology and textual analysis are needed to promote creativity and improve student skills.

The implications for pedagogy are that discovery methods are emphasised instead of declarative supervision, students are allowed to reason and take informed decisions, space is provided for robust debates with the supervisor. This ensures that students are encouraged to construct their own meanings and that their interpretations are respected.

Conclusion

Boundary crossing and fostering opportunities for students to encounter and interrogate views that are different from their own are seen as key strategies for creativity in the academe. Institutional discourses have stymied creativity in research and innovative methodologies, designs and products by focusing on traditional academic skills that are concomitant with neo-liberal foci on marketing, funding, throughput and research outputs and products. Initiatives that promote creativity like interdisciplinary conversations, the scholarship of discovery in research, inquiry-based learning, collaboration and critical thinking need to be foregrounded. Central to creativity is the fostering of creative spaces in the university, especially at the level of the supervisor-student engagement with risk-taking, embracing conflict and debate and questioning of established notions of knowledge. The supervisors' understanding of their different roles in fostering creativity is therefore crucial to the creative process and the quality of the creative product.

About the Author

Rajendra Chetty is Professor and Head of Department of Research in the Faculty of Education, Cape Peninsula University of Technology, South Africa. He can be contacted at this e-mail: chettyr@cput.ac.za

After Image: Using Metaphoric Storytelling in the Evaluation of a Fine Art Photography Course

Brent Meistre and Dina Belluigi

Introduction

Innovations in the design of evaluation instruments and methods are often constrained by Quality Assurance (QA) requirements stipulating narrow criteria for Higher Education Institutions' (HEI) measurement of the quality of teaching and courses. In South Africa, as with the UK and Australia, the responsibility for assuring quality lies with the individual institution. The developmental nature of the evaluation policies of the university where the authors of this chapter are situated operates within a "learning model" (Boughey, 2001). This places autonomy and agency with the individual lecturer. This chapter outlines the process embarked upon by the authors, academics from fine art photography and Higher Education (HE) studies, who worked together to conceptualise, research, design, implement and then evaluate a creative approach to evaluation. The method discussed attempts to bring theory into practice with a strong focus on the student experience.

Firstly, we define the intended outcomes of the course and the purposes of the evaluation instrument. Secondly, the research and design process of the instrument itself is discussed, looking at how images have the potential to act as "triggers" of memory. A discussion of the administration of the instrument follows, with analysis of the insights it revealed into participants' experiences of learning in the course. Feedback from the participants and lecturer on their perceptions of the instrument will be analysed to determine how successful it was in terms of fulfilling the intended purposes, and its impact on the conditions for creativity. Some of the challenges of utilising such a creative approach will conclude the chapter.

This evaluation approach can be described as creative because its design involved hypothesising, synthesising, reflecting and generating ideas with divergent solutions (Biggs, 1999b) about an area of HE that is often considered mundane and bureaucratic. Consistent with the findings of The Five Colleges of Ohio (2007), the process involved intersections between creative and critical thinking, requiring careful analysis of contextual and disciplinary concerns, to link the outcomes of the course with the purposes of the instrument. Whilst this process may retrospectively be seen as "creativity in teaching", our focus has been student-centred: concerned primarily with creating conducive conditions for the development of the students' creativity.

We believe this chapter presents fresh insights and ideas for alternative methods of evaluating teaching and courses. The reader may find inspiration to be more daring with his/her own evaluation processes, or be encouraged to work collaboratively with another in the design or implementation of such innovation (Holtham, in this volume).

The Research Design Process of the Instrument

We hoped to design an instrument that would not only allow us insights into student experiences of learning, but also encourage student engagement with the conceptual criteria of the fine art photography curricula. We felt it most important that the latent and actual criteria of the course were aligned as much as possible in our design (Belluigi, 2008b). Although the espoused curricula of fine art degrees place creativity centrally, assessment processes, driven by summative pressures, often create a high-stakes environment that is not conducive for creative growth. As other authors have argued (Lange, Frick, Chetty, Belluigi, in this volume), environment has an impact on creative learning. Essentially, as evaluation is low-stakes for students, we wanted to use it as a "safe space" for them to experiment, play, reflect, and perform other aspects important to individuals' creative development. This is not the same as a "comfort zone"; here risk is explicitly enabled by separating it from the danger of failure or exposure.

Four umbrella outcomes for fine art studio practice were identified: meaning making, authentic practice, critical reflection and pluralist perspectives (Sullivan, 1993). These underpinned our design of an evaluation instrument sensitive and responsive to the fine art photography context. Informed by these umbrella outcomes and drawing on our own teaching and learning experiences, we identified three overarching and interwoven intended purposes of the evaluation instrument, which were to enable:

i.   The construction of playful visual narratives of the individual's experiences of meaning making during a course(s)

ii.   The dialectical experience of the student as both "maker" and "reader" of these visual "texts"

iii. Insights of students' experiences of and approaches to learning as meaning making.

We hoped that this process would benefit both the students (for their individual self-reflection, and for cultivating an appreciation of the diversity of learning experiences of his/her peers) and the lecturer (in terms of providing insight into their learning processes). Such affective insights would provide better understanding of how each individual's creative growth could be better facilitated in the future.

Evaluation instruments are most often used to elicit student feedback on the quality of teaching or courses. However, as this involves teacher-learner interaction, we believe that the process should do more in terms of encouraging active learning. Only when learning involves engagement with the student's being and desires can creativity flourish (Winnicot, 1971).

In this evaluation instrument, the student constructs a visual sequence of images in response to a posed statement, creating a narrative which embeds the visual in a discourse situation or context relating to his/her learning. This is also the *modus operandi* for their art making, and in this way the evaluation instrument is aligned fundamentally with the meaning making processes of their learning activities (Lange, in this volume). In contrast, more "traditional" methods such as written questionnaires are inappropriate for creative studio-based contexts (Belluigi, 2008c). Moreover, such methods rarely encourage the convergent and divergent thinking which characterises creativity.

The design was adapted from a similar instrument, *"malaise: A projective (non)test"* (Meistre & Knoetze, 2005), which was administered in 2005 to psychologists attending the International Society for Theoretical Psychology Conference, and in 2009 to viewers of the malaise exhibition from which the images in this chapter come (Meistre, 2005, 2009). Using the snapshot genre, the images are of everyday objects and scenes; any human subject is absent. Coming from fine art and psychology backgrounds respectively, Meistre & Knoetze (2005) were cognisant of the power and problematics of imagery. In education, visual imagery has mostly been relegated importance in relation to memory retention or memorialisation. However, the capacity of images to act as triggers or "punctums" – in the Barthesian sense: the detail that pierces the frozen surface of the photograph to provoke an unexpected emotional response (Barthes, 1981) – to stimulate the release of strong emotions has long been recognised by cultural theorists, artists and psychologists. Artwork can create experiences and reactions which are either implicitly or explicitly buried in the work.

The title of this chapter, After Image, alludes to the term used to describe a re-occurring image imprinted on the retina, and refers to the shift from a sensory physical encounter to its memory and representation. In the method discussed in this chapter, the student appropriates another artist's images, actively projects his/her memory of an aspect of the course on the images, and constructs a metaphoric story with those images and his/her text, which s/he uses to guide the viewer (in this case his/her peers) to interpret. This complex process involves reflection-in-action (Schön, 1983), which *"...is dialectical, engaging the student in learning-through-doing, where the reflection occurs both as work is made, and through an analysis of made work"* (Clews, 2003:10-11). In the next section, we discuss the nuts-and-bolts of how this instrument "works".

The form and administration of the instrument

Importantly, the form of the instrument is directly related to the purposes outlined above. Open-ended statements are designed to act as guiding triggers about the course (such as, *"A project, incident or experience related to your Third Year photography course, where you felt you grew the least"*), and assessment processes (such as, *"Describe as a story the emotional process of your assessments and receiving your results"*). These triggers prompt recollection by the student on his/her learning experiences and development. The decision to have three out of four of these statements be deliberately vague is informed by psychological testing where it has been found that more "open" triggers allow unstructured projections to surface.

The students' responses to these statements take the form of visual and narrative "sketches" or impressions. Choosing from the "image bank" provided, images are arranged in sequence to create a metaphoric story, captioned with key words or statements to guide interpretation. When the student finishes working individually with the instrument, group interaction allows for explanations and interpretations with the student-storyteller and his/her peers.

We were mindful of the instrument's timing and placement within the students' wider processes of reflective learning. It was administered in early 2010 to a class of final year Bachelor of Fine Art (Photography) students, on their return to campus at the beginning of the academic year. Thus reflective questions about the previous year's learning were appropriate. All six of the students present consented to participate, with the remaining student abroad. To ensure that honest disclosure was in no way constrained, the facilitator was an "outsider" to the department. A step-by-step description of the process was provided (orally and in written form), followed by a brief discussion on the importance of, on the one hand, each person feeling safe to explore and discuss any relevant aspect of their experience, and on the other, the group's role as a support structure. The value of reflection was emphasised. Students were informed that by participating in this process, the data would feed into larger course evaluation processes to inform curriculum development, in addition to research on evaluation instruments. Their participation was voluntary, and consent informed.

The students completed the instrument individually, taking about 45 minutes to respond to the four trigger statements. They then came together as a group, looking firstly at each of the image-text constructions, followed by verbal exchange of the stories within the group. The facilitator took a background role of occasionally posing probing and clarifying questions, and taking notes on each story. Refreshments were served to make the environment less formal. The image constructions were then handed in to the facilitator, scanned and returned to the students the following day, as they requested. In the immediate days following this event, students were asked to complete an on-line questionnaire established through the university's learning management system (Moodle). Specific questions, around their perception of the instrument and their experience of creating "image constructions", were posed. Space for the students to discuss any unintended outcomes of the evaluation process was provided, in addition to inviting suggestions for the instrument's improvement. Data from the students' stories, the group discussion, the on-line questionnaire and analysis of the image constructions themselves, was triangulated. Patterns emerged in terms of the instrument's efficacy in relation to:

A. how it allowed for nuanced insight into students' experiences of and approaches to learning

B. the purposes identified

C. in what ways it enabled or constrained the conditions for creativity.

The findings are discussed below.

(a) Insight into Students' Experiences of and Approaches to Learning

Mann (2001) contends that students choose to adopt surface, strategic or deep approaches to learning (Marton & Säljö, 1984) depending on whether the learning experience alienated or engaged them from their being and desire as agents. Using this framework, we analysed the stories for insight into the students' experiences of and approaches to learning.

In response to the first trigger statement: "*A project, incident or experience related to your Third Year photography course, where you learnt the most or was challenged the most*", four of the six students' stories involved obstacles, frustration, problem solving, with the eventual overcoming of difficulties, which were either self- or externally imposed.

In one student's story (Figure 1), her experience of alienation throughout her third year was upon reflection where she felt she learnt the most about herself. The flowers represented the initial expectations that she and her lecturer had had of herself; the second image was about hiding, fear, intimidation and withdrawal; with the last image of an inverted birdcage as indicating that she is "*...mentally hard on myself*". This student felt that by looking back she was able to identify that she had relinquished agency during the artmaking process, but that she would learn from that experience and adopt a different stance where, "*I refuse to stay in that position this year*".

Your words: Every Project was a hard challenge!
big expectations   fear

Figure 1: A Student's Story in Response to the Statement about Learning or Being Challenged the Most in a Course.

What is evident in this story is that, because (i) the process was described to them as helping them to reflect on past learning experiences to prepare them for the year ahead, and (ii) it required the students to verbalise their stories to their peers, many of them were able draw conclusion, identifying when and why they had made certain decisions about their learning and engagement. This is a powerful indicator of the instrument's success in encouraging deep reflection and self-evaluation.

Interestingly, only two of the stories indicated committed engagement, where the students had adopted deep approaches to learning. One of these focused on the second project of the year (Figure 2). For the student, the first image set the stage of her learning journey; the second image represented the *"...strange and unique things I experienced while doing the project"*; the last image related to how she *"...took knowledge from the process"*.

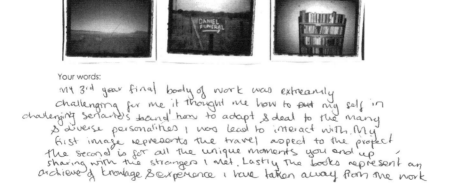

Your words:
My 3rd year final body of work was extreamly
challenging for me it thought me how to put my self in
challenging senario's band how to adapt & deal to the many
& diverse personalities I was lead to interact with. My
first image represents the travel aspect to the project
the second is for all the unique moments you and up
sharing with the strangers I met. Lastly The books represent an
archieved knowage & experience i have taken away from the work

Figure 2: A Student's Story Indicating an Engaged Experience.

Triggered by a statement requiring them to reflect on *"where you felt you grew the least"*, all of the participants told of particular instances in their learning when they were alienated from their being or desire. In one case, a student acted strategically, deciding to *"...just take the easy way out"*. In four others, they adopted surface approaches to learning. In one of these stories (Figure 3), a student told of how her fear of the consequences of exposure, particularly due to the confessional and public nature of fine art assessment practices ("the crit"), forced her withdrawal from the creative process.

Your words:

Figure 3: A Story Indicating an Experience of Alienation.

For her art project, the student chose to explore a subject that had profound personal significance. However, she avoided exposure by withholding honest disclosure during "crits" and in discussions with her lecturer, so that the project itself was left undeveloped and ultimately failed. According to Mann's (2001) perspectives, she can be seen to have chosen self preservation in the face of a potential experience of alienation. *"It was horrible"*, she explained. Her peers audibly commiserated with her. When asked by the facilitator how she thought she would deal with such a dilemma in the coming year, she said that she would need to chose topics carefully to protect herself and *"...not go too close"*. For the lecturer this confirmed concerns about how the experiences of alienation arising from the assessment practices in fine art, may constrain deep approaches to learning and ultimately creativity.

The third trigger statement was the most structured. It required students to reflect on the summative assessment experience of exhibiting their years' work and receiving their results and whether their expectations were met. As with all the stories responses varied, with four of the six students indicating some degree of disappointment at their results. One student's reflections (Figure 4) were particularly "raw", as a peer noted. This student explained that she *"... was not happy with the mark"* but that she *"...deserved it"*. The first image, of the chaos of the end of the year, has been mirrored and inverted at the end of the sequence to indicate the alignment she felt. The image of pizza with two pieces missing related to her exhibition, where she felt gaping holes were visible to the assessors and where literally *"…art pieces were missing"* and incomplete.

Exam was a mess
Your words:
                                        incomplete.
                                                                    ↑
                                                                my mark.

Figure 4: A Student's Story about Summative Assessment.

The fourth trigger was more open-ended than the others. It asked them to: "Use this space as an opportunity to express something you have not had the opportunity to 'say' about your fine art studies so far". Interestingly, the majority of students (four) constructed stories of preparation and commitment for the year to come. One of these stories was constructed with five images overlaid across the three proposed outlines (Figure 5). The first image was of *"…all the materials I had at my disposal to use"*; the second image represented the lecturer who the student felt was an additional resource at her disposal; the third image of partially eaten pizzas indicated that *"I did not take advantage of that"*; the fourth image was interpreted as a dead tree, indicating that she was *"…feeling bummed that I didn't take advantage"*. The last image of a colour field of flowers had to do with something positive resulting from *"…the terrible situation of last year"* to make the fourth year of her degree a success.

Your words:
                                        NOW ↴
                                    'I CAN DO BIG'

Figure 5: A Story about the Whole Year of Study.

Another student told of how fine art studies had taught problem-solving: that when faced with a "brick wall" other angles should be considered to find the solution. Another posed existential questions about her choice of studying fine art, with the caption *"Silly?... rewarding?"*.

Importantly, students perceived that such information would be helpful to their lecturer, assigning 4/5 to the ranked statement "My lecturer, Brent, will now have more in-depth insight of what I experienced in Third Year". However, when interviewed after these stories were retold by the facilitator and analysed, the lecturer felt that these stories confirmed what he already knew of students' experiences and self-perceptions, rather than shedding additional light. He felt that possibly if he had *"...less of a rapport with them, it would have been more revealing maybe"*. As it was a small group of students, whom he worked closely with, he had anticipated much of the responses because he knew *"...what type of people they are and the way they see the world"*. A few days later he noted that it brought him *"... on the same page with them emotionally"* and *"...that is important at this stage"*.

We realised that the greater value of the instrument lay in how it impacted on the student's sense of "self" – their developing ability to self-evaluate, and as a creative outlet for them to express and work though difficult memories. We also realised that it was important for the students to feel that the lecturer had their interests at heart, caring enough to find an alternative method to "hear" and "listen to" their stories, and the emotions attached to them. Such self-validation had the effect of creating a more positive ethos in the first week of term, with students motivated and committed to the learning processes. This was in contrast to previous classes at the same time of the year, when many students were intimidated with the proposal preparations process and often stayed away from the studio environment.

(b) The Efficacy of the Instrument in Terms of the Purposes Identified

One of the first purposes of the instrument was to encourage the students' construction of playful visual narratives. "Play" here does not mean "non-serious endeavours" but rather *"...playing with, trying out, discarding identity, purpose, shape"* (Parker 2003:541), while the student actively engages in shaping their memory into metaphor. As fine art students they were comfortable with this method, commenting to the facilitator that it was easier to construct the visual sequence than to *"...find the words"*. In this excerpt from a student's response to the questionnaire, one sees how this playful process led to in-depth reflections.

"At the end of the assessment last year I reflected in a similar way, but to present my thoughts in the form of a 'mini exhibition' was thought provoking and challenging. It required me to really dig deep into how I felt last year and what I thought was beneficial. Using the images required a lot of (abstract) creativity, and everybody's 'results' were intriguing".

Through visual metaphoric storytelling, which explicitly makes the familiar strange, students would be forced to interpret the meaning they ascribed to the images, and in so doing capture their underlying assumptions, expectations and beliefs. One student noted that, "It was also thought-provoking in the sense that afterwards one was intrigued to understand or discover the root of the surfacing emotions". In response to the questionnaire, two-thirds of the students indicated that "...telling my stories made me reflect critically on those experiences", and that "...hearing their [peers'] stories, made me rethink my own".

The written aspect of the test forced the students to integrate textual representation with the visual narrative. This, on one hand, provided their peers, as readers of their "text", another access point to the representation but, on the other, forced the students to engage with the constructedness of images when creating stories for an "other" to "read". One student observed that:

"It was quite surprising to see what images I was drawn to, the honesty due to the safety of the image as metaphor. Attraction to certain images for reasons that no other person could really fully comprehend. I found it a meaningful discovery".

Whilst the constructions involved a sense of play which contributed to creating a "safe space", this was potentially threatened by the exposure inherent to telling their stories to the group. Within this particular context, the students had worked individually throughout their degree, so that the group dynamic was a novel experience. The threat of exposure was minimised by the facilitator, who rather emphasised the importance of "hearing" pluralistic perspectives. It was hoped that such a shift in perspective would enable a dialectical experience of the student as both "maker" and "reader" of these visual "texts". This was one of the central purposes of the instrument, linked to the conceptual outcomes of the BFA. The ability of students to interpret their work from various perspectives is an important aspect of their own evaluation skills. In response to the questionnaire, one student felt the method was creative because "...it requires you to think visually and in a way that is going to reach your audience". Students assigned a value of 4.5/5 to the statement "It made me think critically about the images". The importance of utilising imagery was emphasised by this student:

"I think this a very creative method, as I feel many people are more likely to relate to an image than a body of text, an image is easier to remember, and it can raise emotions, memories, depending on how one reads them. This method allows one to react to visuals which may raise issues that the viewer might not have expected, or have encountered if it was a straightforward questionnaire".

A crucial aspect of the group discussion, from our perspective as the designers, was to create an appreciation in each individual as to the diversity of learning experiences across the class. This was confirmed by the data, as all of participants agreed that *"...having access to the stories of others, widened my understanding of their experiences".* In addition, students ranked the statement: *"It allowed diverse stories to come out"* with the score of 4.3 points out of 5. This was experienced as positive, with the statement *"...talking to my peers about my experiences was a difficult but good experience"* being assigned 4.2 points out of 5.

In addition, an unintended outcome was that students were able to draw commonalities between their experiences and *"...discover that everyone was feeling nervous and really was in the same boat that I'm in. We're all worried about this [Third] year and how it will affect the following [Fourth] year".* One student was emphatic about this point at the end of the session, telling the group that for her the greatest benefit of the process had been realising how she is *"...not the only one who struggles".* As another student wrote in the questionnaire, she discovered that *"...just knowing that the other students have felt the same way I have during the year. Sounds silly, but it always a relief to know you are not the only one".*

(c) Impact on the Conditions for Creativity

Creating an ethos or space for contemplation and freedom to play is essential when trying to establish conditions conducive for creativity to develop. Two aspects of the questionnaire related to how students characterised their experience of *"...going through the process of reflecting, constructing and telling your stories of Third Year".* Firstly, students were required to choose from a provided list of adjectives to describe their experience of engaging with the instrument. These ranged across the continuum of experiences, from "creative" to "pedestrian", "complex" to "straightforward", and so on. Four out of six of the participants chose "thought-provoking" to characterise their experience. The words "challenging", "creative", "intriguing" and "straightforward" were selected by one third of the group. Students were then asked to use the words in a paragraph, as in this excerpt below:

"It was definitely a thought provoking experience. The majority of the questions I had thought about prior to the questionnaire but it always seems a lot more real once you have ordered your thoughts and put them on paper. I found the images a great way to help verbalise my answers as well as fun, exciting method as opposed to the usual paragraphs of writing".

In ranked responses, students assigned a score of 4.3 points out of 5 to the statement that: *"I felt like this was a safe space for me to think about the year".* One student explained that *"I found it a helpful experience. It created a safe space where I was able to explore and bring closure to certain issues that worried me about last year".*

When asked if they thought this a creative method, all agreed, providing different reasons. The predominant reason was that it required them as participants to "be creative" when using images to describe their experiences. As one student put it:

"Yes for sure, due to the fact that the images provided could be read quite abstractly one had to be creative as to how they chose the image. I also felt being more able to express oneself verbally as well as creatively helped me to give a more rounded answer".

Another reason cited was that *"…it allows for another form of expression, something that you wouldn't necessarily have been able to express in words".* This aspect of "saying the unsayable" is fundamental to creative expression.

One concern that the lecturer had was that the process (of metaphoric image construction and then group discussion) may "feel" too similar to the fine art assessment method, which many of his students had experienced as negative. Concerns about the impact of Critique processes on student creativity have also surfaced repeatedly in education literature in recent years (Belluigi, Lange, in this volume). For this reason, in the questionnaire we explicitly asked students how they found this process in relation to that assessment method.

Two distinct differences emerged, which confirmed for us that this method does not replicate the high stakes environment of the assessment method, but rather encourages a more playful relationship with image-making. Firstly, student responses pointed to the different power dynamics which indicated that the environment was vastly different to the sense of judgment and scrutiny at "crits".

"Firstly, we weren't 'critted' in any form, it was not intended to be purely about our images and ideas, instead it was about how we felt, it was not to be marked,

but understood. It was for research methods and there was no better way or best way to portray something. There were also no 'lecturers' which made life a lot less nerve-racking".

"Crits often make you feel judged and 'silly'. In this space everybody's thoughts and opinions were equally important as the next".

"There was no one to judge what images you chose, how you constructed them, or your concept behind them. This image construction was accepted without anyone questioning why. There was no intimidation".

This difference in power relationships allowed the discussion to be *"…more personal, maybe because it was dealing with sensitive issues and exposure. It was intimate and safe because you knew that everyone else was working through the same personal questions".* This allowed insights *"…into things about my classmates which they usually wouldn't share so openly".*

Secondly, difference in the students' relationship with the images was cited as important, as these two excerpts indicate:

"In crits it is your own work so you are much more 'sensitive' to the comments surrounding them as they are usually more personal. The image constructions were more neutral as we didn't take the photos ourselves".

"In this method I didn't once consider the quality or the purpose of the photos, their purpose was purely to aid me in illustrating my answers. In crits it is quite the opposite I think".

Some of the Challenges of Using Such an Alternative Method

Surprisingly, from our perspective as lecturers/designers, the challenges of this method related more to the time and attention needed to make it happen effectively, than to any major conceptual concerns emerging from the implementation of the instrument itself. The research into and design of the instrument took a considerable amount of time and investment. Making multiple colour prints of the "image bank" was also expensive. However, we feel strongly that the positive impact of the instrument made these "costs" worthwhile.

Without a doubt, one of the challenges posed was to create a safe space for the students to engage with the instrument. It was important to choose a facilitator from outside of the department, who was not connected to the assessment processes. Having refreshments set an informal tone and this was re-inforced by the language used in the instrument and by the facilitator. Having the students "buy in" that this process really had their interests at heart, and that such reflection would aid them for the year, was a crucial aspect of its success.

Identified issues for improvement included increasing the range of images provided, which was confirmed by student data. Another possibility for the future, with a group comfortable with this method, would be to have the trigger statements student-devised. Data from both the lecturer and students indicated that the images should remain as an "image bank", with images they had not been introduced to in their studies, and taken by an artist(s) other than the students.

The participating students all agreed that this method was preferable to any of the others they had encountered, which included written questionnaires, group interviews and various informal methods, such as e-mails. In terms of the difficulties of engaging with this method that they identified, the most dominant related to the image-text relationship.

> "Balancing the words and images is difficult, as I wasn't sure which to put more emphasis on, or pay attention to. Working out the relation between text and image is always difficult though".

This is an important realisation for makers of art, and so this struggle with the image-text relationship in a context outside of the mainstream classroom/ studio activities is seen as a positive of the instrument.

The other difficulty related to the affective, exploratory nature of the instrument, as these three students note:

> "No difficulties, beside facing the exposed emotions".

> "Well, I didn't really want to revive what I had been thinking about concerning last year".

> "The most difficult part of this method was putting my thoughts down on the paper honestly, and revealing difficulties that I thought no one else had".

Despite this acknowledgment, the statement: *"The group discussion made me feel vulnerable in a negative way"* was ranked by the participants with the score of 4.3 points out of 5. This indicated that although the process was emotionally difficult, it was not experienced negatively. In fact, many students noted in response to the concluding question of the questionnaire: *"Did you discover anything at the end you didn't expect when you began?"* that the emotional process had positive results, increasing their intrinsic motivation. These students' comments capture the tone of the other students' responses:

> *"From something that appeared to be a straightforward and simple exercise, [it] actually turned out to be something that became intriguing and thought provoking. Through reflecting on last year, the exercise became a problem solver enabling us to do better and not make the same mistakes".*

> *"I was dreading this year's prac because of the issues I had last year – so I kind of returned to Grahamstown with a bad energy, but this method forced me to face some of my insecurities and really question some of my perceptions of last year. It helped bring closure to my Third year – which was really needed in order to start this year with confidence and enthusiasm".*

Conclusion

This chapter outlined the design, administration and evaluation of a customised evaluation instrument, where the purposes of the process undertaken were explicitly informed by both the latent and actual criteria of the course. The instrument fulfilled its objectives, by (i) allowing us access to nuanced insights into the students approaches to and experiences of learning, thereby allowing for more sensitivity towards individual learning styles and conditions for the future; (ii) enabling play and the creation of metaphors which made the familiar learning experience strange for the student, allowing underlying issues to surface; (iii) encouraging pluralistic perspectives of the individual metaphoric story and on his/her experience of learning; (iv) and most importantly, impacting positively on creating the conditions for creativity, through providing a "safe space" for students to reflect and interact.

About the Authors

Brent Meistre is a senior lecturer and section head of photography at the Department of Fine Art, Rhodes University, South Africa. He can be contacted at this e-mail: b.meistre@ru.ac.za

Dina Zoe Belluigi is a lecturer at the Centre for Higher Education Research, Teaching and Learning at Rhodes University, South Africa. She can be contacted at this e-mail: d.belluigi@ru.ac.za

Chapter Eleven
Learning through Creative Conversations

Silke Lange

Introduction

Charles Leadbeater (2007) launched the concept of "creative conversations" in his on-line draft for the book *We think: mass innovation, not mass production*. He explained: *"Creative conversations are like a shared exploration the results of which cannot be guaranteed in advance... Each participant must give something of themselves in a way that encourages the other to reciprocate"*.

Whilst writing his book, Leadbeater decided to publish his first draft on-line, set up a wiki and invite the public to contribute and comment on the document. By adopting this method of working he underlined the overall argument presented in the book, which promotes collaboration and conversation as a way of developing new ideas and products. The outcomes of Leadbeater's newly adopted approach to writing were unpredictable and open to unexpected contributions and comments, resulting in a book different from the one initially anticipated by the author.

Leadbeater used the term "creative conversations" mainly in relation to major scientific discoveries and product developments that have changed the way in which we conduct our lives. He also used the concept in relation to the ways in which societal problems might be addressed and discussed. The discussion of ideas, methods of working, issues raised through artworks and students' coursework, in particular that of a practical nature, is common practice in the learning and teaching of art and design subjects (Dineen, 2006). My own research has confirmed that these discussions are recognised as valuable contributions to students' critical and creative development and enhance students' knowledge of their subject areas. In that sense, these discussions could be described as creative conversations from which the outcomes depend on the investments made by all participants. New understanding and knowledge can be developed through active engagement with each contributor's comments and responses.

In this chapter, I explore Leadbeater's concept of creative conversations as a learning and teaching method within art and design education. I use critical review of practical coursework on a photography degree as an example of a learning environment in which creative conversations take place. This enables me, firstly, to describe how students learn through these conversations and secondly, identify what type of knowledge may be gained. The chapter concludes by summarising ways in which creative conversations can be managed for effective learning.

Research Background

The Project

The concept of creative conversations was investigated and developed as part of the research for the project *Learning through photography: Creativity as concept and process* (Lange, 2010). Particular focus was given to the role of the creative process in enabling individuals to make connections between different forms of knowledge and skills acquired, and how this process was best facilitated within an educational setting. The fieldwork was carried out between 2006 and 2008 on a photography degree at a UK university which had been a Polytechnic until 1992.

The Methodology

The case study examined the learning of photography as a complex, creative, productive and transformative act during which new thinking and ways of practicing, both personal and vocational, are developed. The study followed qualitative methods which were flexible in their design and allowed for connections to be made within and between each method (Creswell, 2007). This approach characterises the creative process as one which is constantly evolving, flexible and changing, allowing for new knowledge to emerge (Gruber & Wallace, 1999).

The research was conducted from an "insider" perspective in which the researcher's experiences influenced the design of the study. The research project was informed by the theory that photography is an active medium (Vygotsky, 1978) which opens up a world of experiences beyond mere technological knowledge. It has the potential to enable people to understand themselves and others, and supports the development of new ways of seeing through understanding connections with culture and society (Lange & Golding, 2007; Stanley, 1996). This position closely resembles the concept of constructionism in which knowledge is constructed through the interactions of human beings and their world, and is developed and transmitted within a social context (Crotty, 1998). In that sense, the research project explored the meanings of creativity in the study of photography, as constructed by students and tutors.

Research Design

During the fieldwork a total of twenty students, five alumni and six tutors participated in semi-structured discussion groups. The discussions aimed to identify participants' interpretations of creativity in the context of the course, in particular how creativity is facilitated within the learning of photography and how it is manifested in the curriculum. The format of the discussion groups reproduced a familiar mode of communication for staff and students on the course. This proved to be effective in engaging participants in meaningful discussions on the topics of the research and gaining insightful views and opinions. As part of the discussion groups, students were encouraged to bring examples of their practical coursework to describe the creative development that may have taken place during the production of the work. This approach generated a more focused discussion than had been observed with groups that did not use images as a catalyst for meaning-making. As Sarah Pink suggests in *Doing Visual Ethnography*: "*...attention to the meanings that people create when they combine images and words can create exciting new knowledge*" (Pink, 2007:86; Meistre & Belluigi, in this volume). All discussions were recorded and transcribed, and a categorical aggregation (Creswell, 2007) carried out to analyse the data.

In addition to the group discussions, four taught sessions were observed. Observations focused on the physical learning environments, the range of teaching methods, and social interactions between students and tutors, and between students and their peers, within the learning space. I recorded the data in the form of concept maps which represented visually the observations of the material that was delivered, the activities that were occurring, and any contributions that were made by students. The concept maps helped to identify what types of connections were made between all of these aspects in the learning environment. In addition, notes were taken on the delivery style of the session, interactions amongst students, interactions between the students and the lecturer, and the general atmosphere in the learning environment.

Critical Reviews

One type of session I observed was the critical review of students' practical coursework. Critical reviews are regularly practiced within art and design education and students are introduced to these types of sessions at the beginning of their course. Critical reviews provide opportunities for students to see each other's work, to test out whether their images communicate intended meanings, and to discuss their work in the wider context of historical and contemporary photographic practice. The course on which my research is based uses three different structures for critical reviews. First, the most traditional format is tutor-led. Within these, the tutor takes on a domineering position by asking most questions concerning the work presented, occasionally inviting the students to contribute. Second, the student-led reviews which a tutor facilitates. In these, students lead the critique and the tutor remains in the background, only contributing if students have difficulties in coming up with questions or comments that may generate a discussion about the work. The third and most progressive form of critical reviews is also students-led and includes peer review. Here students take complete ownership of the process by working in pairs or groups of three to five students to critique each other's work.

The session I observed followed the second format. The review was scheduled at the mid-point of the module "Documentary Photography". Within this module students choose their own subject matter and produce a body of work within the genre of documentary photography. At the outset of this module, students are introduced to the work of key historical and contemporary practitioners within the field in order to help them understand the conventions of the genre. The critical review took place in a seminar room with a large set of tables in the centre. Fifteen students were present at the session, all of whom were showing their photographic projects. Images were projected digitally on to a large screen, presented in book format, laid out on a table or pinned to the wall. The tutor explained the procedure for the critical review at the outset, clarifying the purpose and inviting all students to contribute with comments and questions. Each student was allocated fifteen minutes for their presentation, beginning with a brief introduction to the project before viewing the work. This was followed by feedback from their peers and the tutor. The aim of each review was for students to reflect on their work, engage with that of their peers, and to offer and take on board critical feedback relating to the work. As this review took place at an interim stage of the module, students had the opportunity to use any feedback given in order to develop their practice work prior to the final project submission.

The first student laid out his project on the table and everybody stood around the table to view the prints. Following the student's introduction, peers immediately started to ask questions regarding the concept of the work. They also made suggestions on how to improve the editing of the series and the tutor questioned the choice of lighting and framing used to create atmospheric images. These initial dialogues between peers, or the tutor, and the student whose work was under critique soon developed into a general debate about the issues raised. These included questions such as: *"What makes a photograph a portrait?"* and *"Do you want to be a 'fly on the wall' or intervene with your subject matter?"*.

After a more general debate on documentary photography, the tutor brought the discussion back to the student's work. The first review was concluded with a summary of visual strategies to develop and repeat advice that had been given throughout the review. The remainder of the session continued in a similar way, although the nature of the work presented varied immensely. One student had taken photographs at a recycling plant in order to represent metaphorically the effects of an illness and the notion of death. He had then posted the images on-line, inviting strangers to send him their interpretations of the images. He received comments such as: *"Are you alright?"*.

During the review the discussion focused on the use of photography as a tool for self-expression, encouraging students to relate the project critiqued to their own life experiences and how they would interpret the metaphor with which they had been presented.

The structure of the critical review encouraged the willingness of students to address issues related to their own and others' work and to express candidly their emotional responses to certain images. Students appeared to be confident and comfortable when talking about each other's work and when trying to understand the intentions of the work produced. Students' interactions were facilitated by the tutor ensuring that each student, whether strong or weak, received positive, yet critical and constructive, feedback. This approach resulted in an overwhelmingly positive and energetic atmosphere, and all participants were supportive of, and encouraging to, each student presenting (Belluigi, in this volume).

The discussions that occurred within the critical review showed parallels with Leadbeater's (2007) idea of *"shared exploration"* that takes place in creative conversations. Students had opportunities to see each other's work, assess whether their images were communicating the intended message, and to discuss their work in the wider context of historical and contemporary photographic practice. These forms of active engagement with each other's work and thought processes, such as reflecting on one's own work and that of one's peers in response to the feedback given, contribute to the creativity of the individual by *"...constructing new tools and new outcomes – new embodiments of knowledge"* (Kleiman, 2008:209).

Creative Conversations

Why Photography?

Photography is a medium that opens up a world of experiences beyond mere technological knowledge. It has the potential to enable people to grow, understand themselves and others, and supports the development of new ways of seeing through understanding connections with culture and society (Lange & Golding, 2007). The process of seeing is different for each individual as it is influenced by the photographer's (or viewer's) own knowledge, background and cultural experiences. Thus, the process of seeing is the individual's interpretation of the visual information communicated through the photograph. Students studying photography learn how to construct and control the meaning of photographs; how to communicate their ideas and concerns through the choice of subject and ways of capturing it. Students learn about photography as a visual language, understanding visual symbols and codes that create meaning in their images. The ability to construct meaning in images and decode them is referred to as being *"visually literate"* (Raney, 1999). In her extensive curriculum guide, *Focus on Photography*, Cynthia Way (2006:6) described visual literacy skills. *"When we say that students are 'seeing photographically' and have developed 'visual literacy skills', we mean that in their photographs and responses, they demonstrate that they have developed the perceptual and thinking skills to understand how the visual image communicates meaning".*

Furthermore, visual literacy is related to critical knowledge that includes *"...awareness of the intentionality of how an image is constructed in order to offer a particular response or experience"* (Abrahmov & Ronen, 2008:4). In that sense, critical knowledge refers to the context in which photographs are produced and seen, whether the photographer is making a statement or is challenging preconceptions, and whether ethical, social and political issues are raised through this process.

In the critical reviews, as described in this chapter, photographs play an important role in challenging or reinforcing individuals' perspectives, acting as catalysts for discussions and, by way of this, helping to shape ideal platforms for developing creative conversations. These types of conversations go beyond merely reflecting on a photograph or a method of working; they encourage students to discover and learn through dialogue and debate (Sawyer, 2004). Unlike the process of reflection, which could be described as an internal individual process, creative conversations are a collective, external exploration of images, processes of production and contexts within which photographs are viewed (Vygotsky, 1978). As observed by one student:

"...if I start to speak and share my idea with other people... I don't think it is about copying other people's ideas, it is kind of this interaction which enriches my way of thinking".

In other words, it is the social exchange of ideas between students and tutors during, for example, critical reviews that play a role in expanding students' minds, thus enabling them to acquire new knowledge and understandings about photography. This knowledge may comprise technical skills of the medium such as camera functions, lighting and analogue and digital processes, as well as conceptual and theoretical understandings of photographic techniques in relation to the production of images and their location in a broad cultural framework. The conceptual and theoretical understandings include visual literacy and critical knowledge – both referring to the construction of meaning in a photograph and to the context in which photographs are produced and seen – whether the photographer is making a statement or is challenging preconceptions and whether ethical, social and political issues are raised through this process. Students have confirmed the importance of engaging in these debates as a way of gaining a deeper understanding of their photographic practice:

> "*The most important thing is to discuss at the end of each lesson what people have done, just put it [the work] up and talk about it... That ongoing discussion makes you analyse and justify what you are doing*".

In that sense, talking about photographs contributes to the process of students becoming reflective practitioners (Schön, 1983), whose practice develops through a critical engagement with the creative process of image making (Adriansen, in this volume).

I would suggest that these reflections could be described as forms of social or collaborative reflection and resemble Leadbeater's idea of creative conversations. Students discuss ideas, methods of working and photographs with tutors and amongst peer groups and have the opportunities to reflect on the development of their ideas as well as processes related to the production of their photographic work and that of their peers. This is the space where, according to Leadbeater (2007), "*...each participant must give something of themselves in a way that encourages the other to reciprocate*". In relation to my own research, this space is where students develop new knowledge collaboratively – through asking questions, analysing and explaining their creative practice – and begin to give and receive constructive criticism. Students' contributions in these conversations may be experiential, factual, emotional or personal in nature, adding several dimensions to the knowledge shared and gained from each other. All of this knowledge may assist students in developing different aspects of their creative practice, nurturing their learning and their ideas, thus enabling them to acquire further knowledge relevant to their field of study. This knowledge is not taken solely from textbooks, but partially developed from students' experiences and the exchange of these experiences with their peers.

Making Connections

Creative conversations foster students' abilities to make connections between the technical and conceptual sides of photography: technically, connections can simply be made between camera settings and light intensity; conceptually, connections can allude to symbols and signifiers within a photograph, and how these relate to one's own culture or life experiences. Once students are technically confident they can focus on developing visual strategies which address, for example, conceptual and ethical challenges of photographic work. One such challenge was described by a student who had been working with an asylum seeker on the photographic project *Silent Voices* (Figure 1 and 2) which deals with themes of exile, displacement, cultural difference and human rights. Such themes pose ethical challenges of representation and protection of the subjects' identity, requiring the photographer to carefully consider the visual approach to the subject matter.

Figure 1 and 2: Images of the Series "Silent Voices" © Amelia Shepherd. Printed by permission.

> *"Using the subject's narratives as a starting point I began to visually interpret the emotions and events I was being told about… In each shot I attempted to convey a sense of this essence – or 'emotion' – by combining place, atmosphere, lighting, framing and sometimes symbolism and representation. Although the shots were my interpretations of what I was being told they were also highly informed by my conversations with my subject. In this way I intended the work to place the audience in to the position of what it actually feels like – on a day-to-day level – to be an asylum seeker in the UK".*

This student's account of developing the story they wished to communicate highlights how connections between prior knowledge and new knowledge were made, how meaning was constructed through applying visual literacy skills and how somebody else's story was told through the eyes of a photographer.

During the critical review of this work the peer group and the tutor took on the role of the audience. Therefore, in this case, the audience was placed in the position of *"what it actually feels like – on a day-to-day level – to be an asylum seeker in the UK"*. This positioning provided several starting points for a creative conversation during which the ethical and societal meaning of the work could be discussed, including how the work may be perceived by different audiences. In this case an exploration of the photographer's choice of the visual strategies to interpret and represent the experiences of the subject was worthwhile, and the work contributed an insightful critical comment on current affairs in regard to seeking asylum in the UK.

The Learning Environment

Supportive Structures

Creative conversations do not just happen in any learning environment. My earlier description of the critical review illustrated that students need encouragement and facilitation to build up their confidence and feel comfortable in their environment. Only when supportive structures are set up and tutors assume the role of facilitator do discussions take place; students are more likely to be open to new ideas and thought processes and are prepared to take risks and make mistakes (Belluigi, in this volume). As described by one alumnus:

> "What I think it [the critical review] also taught people was not only accepting criticism, but how to give criticism, but in a nice way. In a way that is kind, and is constructive rather than obstructive so that you don't actually lambaste their pictures and hurt their feelings, but you make them grow, you don't make them shrivel up".

This description of the critical review highlights how these sessions assist students in the advancement of their photographic work, as well as their self-development. Furthermore, the comment echoes Amabile's (1996:17) claim that: "Whatever an individual's talents, domain expertise and creative thinking skills, that individual's social environment — the conditions under which he or she works — can significantly increase or decrease the level of creativity produced".

During the critical review described in this chapter, students felt comfortable enough to participate and engage at a personal level of conversation which requires them to "…give something of themselves in the way that encourages the other to reciprocate" (Leadbeater, 2007). One of the influencing factors for this participation to occur is the size of a group. My research has shown that a group size of between 15 and 24 students is more suited to learning collectively. This finding echoes those of other scholars who claim that a medium-sized group offers more opportunities for students to contribute and share their ideas through various arrangements of the group, such as working in pairs or a small group of the entire group (Jaques, 1984; Wolf, 2003). Such an environment provides opportunities for students to question the material presented, including comments offered by peers and tutors, and students are more likely to be open to taking risks and to making mistakes in regard to contributions made and issues raised. These forms of engagement enhance students' ability to think critically as well as playing with their ideas, both of which are attributes that encourage creative conversations.

My own research confirmed that a supportive and student-centred learning environment as described in this chapter creates a safe foundation for students to present work, share their ideas and offer constructive criticism to each other. This was reflected in the ways in which the students and the tutor interacted with each other, the depth of discussions individuals were involved in and the amount of personal information, (relating to the work produced) students revealed. Students took risks by opening up to each other and, by way of this, hoped to gain valuable feedback for their work. As one alumnus participating in the research commented:

"Crits [jargon for critical reviews] were one of the things that I found most valuable, ...without that input from other people, and without that kind of encouragement, or without other people's eye and just saying 'I don't understand that, I think that is too obvious, I don't think that picture works...'".

This former student describes the critical review as an environment within which students and tutors offer their honest views and opinions about a piece of work. This honesty grows out of trust and confidence, the latter being a key factor for students to develop their role as informed practitioners and critical commentators on society, using photography as their tool to do so. In addition to obtaining feedback on their own photographic practice, students gained new knowledge about photography, discovered new ways of working within the medium, and expanded upon their understandings of photography as a visual language. Another alumnus remarked:

"...also I found with the crits it sometimes sparked off another idea, another way, it sort of fed you, it fed your creativity. And you know, when we were in our groups with people from all walks of life and we would see things in a very different way and have different experiences".

This statement confirms my earlier observation that the process of seeing is different for each individual as it is influenced by the photographer's (or viewer's) own knowledge, background and cultural experiences. These differences are not only evident in the actual process of seeing, but also in the production and interpretation of images, therefore providing a basis upon which to challenge and reinforce individual's perspectives and perceptions in creative conversations (Meistre & Belluigi, this volume).

These comments by students are also worth considering in the light of Blair's (2006) study on the traditional format of studio critiques (another term used for critical reviews) in which she concluded that *"the crit was not perceived by any student as a particularly important 'learning environment'"*. My own research of critical reviews seems to suggest the opposite view, which is that critical reviews are generally perceived as a crucial part of students learning. Moreover, it was suggested by students that critical reviews provide a learning environment which facilitates their creative development through encouraging imagination and broadening their horizons.

Images as Catalysts

The diversity of knowledge, background and cultural experiences that is implicit in the learning environment of the course on which my research is based is evident in the work that students produce, and ultimately contributes to expanding students' knowledge bases during creative conversations. One student, for example, created spoof images of couples considering civil partnership (Figure 3: "Civil Partners") in response to a brief which was set as part of a digital imaging module. The campaign challenges assumptions and stereotypes of relationships through exploring and playing on representations of same sex couples preparing for their "wedding".

Work of this nature uses photography and digital imaging as creative tools to rethink societal issues and to raise awareness amongst audiences. For students to produce work of such sophisticated quality they have to be competent in using appropriate technical devices of the media and understand photography's role in offering critical commentary on society, thus using images as a catalyst for initiating dialogue and debate. In the campaign described here, this understanding is informed, for example, by knowledge of recent developments in the construction of advertising campaigns which employ photographic and digital techniques specifically to construct meaning. Campaigns include the much debated Benetton advertising from the early 1990's (Ramamurthy, 2000) or the recently *"deemed too shocking"* campaigns by charities such as Barnardo's and the National Society for the Prevention of Cruelty to Children (NSPCC) (Blackburn, 2006; Wnek, 2003).

Figure 3: "Civil Partners" Ó Caroline Ellis. Printed by permission.

In the case of Benetton, well-known documentary images of, for example, David Kirby dying of AIDS (Ramamurthy, 2000:211) were used to promote the company's products. By crossing the boundaries of using real life in the imagined world of advertising, ethical and moral questions were raised and many consumers expressed their views by boycotting the label. Barnardo's challenged assumptions through exploring and playing on stereotypical representations of real life issues such as substance abuse or homelessness, questioning society's prejudice towards marginalised members of the community.

Students are introduced to these kinds of conventions and image making practices throughout their course of study and constantly engage in discussions of images and their meaning in specific contexts. These discussions help to increase students' awareness of using photography and image making as tools to assist in communicating their views and concerns, to recognise the constraints of image making, and ultimately to enable them to develop their role as critical commentators on society. In that sense, the practice students embark upon on this photography course acts as a vehicle through which creative conversations can be initiated and knowledge can be acquired.

Creative Conversations Beyond Photography

Transferring the Concept

This chapter has highlighted that a supportive and student-centred learning environment, combined with photographs as catalysts and prior knowledge of the subject, can enable creative conversations in critical reviews on a photography degree. This leads to the challenge: "how can creative conversations be initiated in disciplines other than those producing photographs or any other artifacts; can creative conversation start by presenting abstract ideas, theories or formulas?"

In order to explore these questions, it was necessary to try some of the findings of my research, those related to the concept of creative conversations, in a non-specialist environment. Such an opportunity arose during the workshop "The University in the Knowledge Society" (held at a Chinese university, in 2009), where I was invited to work with students and professors from non-art and design disciplines. The focus of the workshop was still on photography but no images were presented, only recalled from memory. Photography is a universally understood visual medium which is immediate and accessible. Most people will have had some encounter with photography, either through family albums, snap shots from holidays or friends, or images presented in the press and advertising. Considering this, the aforementioned questions were addressed with participants, firstly by engaging in a creative conversation and secondly, by reflecting as a group on their experiences during these conversations. I asked participants to think about a photograph with personal significance to them and, without showing the actual photograph, to exchange this photograph "verbally" with the person next to them. During this exchange, the emphasis was on finding out how much we can discover about an object unknown to us, in dialogue with the person who knows the object. Participants were encouraged to ask open questions that led to answers other than a simple "yes" or "no". After five minutes of conversations in pairs, participants shared with the rest of the group the knowledge they had gained. Participants agreed that they had learnt particular aspects about the objects discussed, including information such as when and where the photograph was taken, the relationship between the people captured in the photograph, and the historical, personal or social relevance of the photograph discussed. In summary, the knowledge gained was mainly of emotional, factual and personal nature.

On reflection, participants felt that to have a meaningful creative conversation it was important to have some prior knowledge about the object/subject under discussion. If this were not possible, it would help to have, in the case of photography, some basic understanding of how the medium could be applied as a tool for communicating ideas and meaning. The creative conversation provided participants with a base from which to begin gaining deeper understanding. Participants' opinions were divided about whether a creative conversation requires a tangible object such as a photograph as a starting point, or whether the conversation could also be initiated through an abstract idea or theory.

Conclusion

My research highlights that the format of a student-led critical review, as discussed in this chapter, provides an effective framework for encouraging creative conversations as a teaching and learning method in art and design education. Unlike with the traditional format of critiquing students' photographic work, this student-centred, supportive approach engages students in insightful discussions about photographs that enable them to develop a better understanding of how to construct and control the meaning of their photographs; how to communicate their ideas and concerns through the choice of subject and ways of capturing it, thus becoming more creative and critically informed practitioners. Because this format of critical reviews has proved a successful method for engaging students in meaningful discussions about their work, other course teams within the department are now also using it.

About the Author

Silke Lange is Director of Learning and Teaching in the School of Media, Arts and Design at the University of Westminster, London, United Kingdom, where she also teaches photography. She can be contacted at this e-mail: langes@ wmin.ac.uk

From Disorder to New Order: the Complexity of Creating a New Educational Culture

Matti Rautiainen, Tiina Nikkola, Pekka Räihä, Sakari Saukkonen and Pentti Moilanen

Creativity and Educational Change

In this article we examine creativity as a characteristic of community in the context of educational change. Communal creativity means a community's ability to renew its actions and processes in order to meet the challenges of a transformative environment. Nowadays it seems that flourishing organisations and communities are able to execute self-directive and internally led transformations (Ståhle & Kuosa, 2009). Creativity is a normal part of the life of human beings, because we need creativity for the optimal management of all the things we face in our work or in our daily routines. The need for creativity in the community varies in time but the basic need for creativity is always the same: the aim to improve an individual's own life and the conditions in the community (Toivola, 1984). Our aim is to enhance the quality of teacher education and the conditions of learning and schooling.

Creative work and process take time, usually many years, even many decades. We believe that three elements are needed: a culture containing symbolic domain rules, a person or a group which brings novelty to this domain, and experts who validate the new intervention. From this point of view creativity is systemic rather than an individual phenomenon. The results of this process are changes in the culture, not just the demolishing of the old structures and routines, but also creating new ones (Csikszentmihalyi, 1997). Educational change contains the same elements, because change always requires a new idea to challenge the symbolic domain. This state of confusion and disorder – entropy – is a prerequisite for bifurcation and for "the new order". We will analyse our creative educational process using the concepts of entropy and bifurcation. Before this analysis, we briefly describe the basic ideas of the Critical Integrative Teacher Education project (CITE).

An Attempt at Change

The CITE is an attempt to improve Higher Education (HE) and also to gain better understanding of teacher profession's and school's complexity. After several years as teacher educators we have become convinced that student teachers (on a 5 year master's program) had not achieved conceptual understanding of the discipline. They can memorise concepts, theoretical models and pedagogical practices, but because they do not deeply understand the meanings and rationalities behind the theories, they can not apply them in practice. Students' transition from epistemological orientation towards ontological orientation has not succeeded well enough (Reid & Petocz, 2008; Dall'Alba & Barnacle, 2007).

The CITE aimed at solving the problem of superficial understanding of learning in teacher education. In addition, the curriculum is very fragmented and gives a poor basis for generating and integral understanding of schooling. Teachers are also facing an increasing number of changes in their job context (Ballet & Kelchtermans, 2008).

A major re-shaping of curriculum as well as teaching and learning practices was needed. We started from the idea that the world is not structured according to school subjects. Accordingly, the school itself should not be based on such an artificial division. In addition the preconditions of learning should be taken into account. These premises led us to define the general conditions of learning and the specific conditions of learning (for a more detailed description, see Nikkola *et al.* 2008)

The general conditions include the contexts of learning, e.g. group dynamics, and the individual conditions of learning. Learning within an educational institution often occurs in groups. These learning groups are meaningful, because the processes of learning are connected to group dynamics and interactions. Yet the group is quite often treated superficially only as an organisational entity without understanding the group dynamics, which are very important for both individual and collective learning.

The specific conditions of learning are the content-specific features of learning. Traditionally the HE curriculum splits the phenomenon of learning into distinct parts that are loosely connected to the individuals' everyday experience or, in other words, their life-world. Learning takes place in everyday experiences but these experiences are infrequently encountered during studies. Knowledge can be perceived as a product or process. Educational tradition has prioritised the former. Knowledge has been interpreted as something you can find in a textbook. This perspective ignores knowledge construction as a collaborative, social endeavor.

In sum, the traditional curriculum is unintegrated. Everyday experience is often devalued. Knowledge is seen mostly as a product, not as a process.

Knowledge construction should be seen both as a personal and a social process. Therefore we approach knowledge construction through three domains of knowing: 1) factual knowledge, 2) contractual/conventional knowledge, and 3) aesthetic knowledge.

Factual knowledge can be considered as true or false. It is justified to ask at what temperature water boils. Contractual/conventional knowledge is not true or false in the same sense. It is a matter of cultural meaning-making, a matter of interpretations. You cannot give a precise answer to the question of whether the war in Iraq is about freedom or an expression of colonial power. The answer depends on the interpreter's cultural perspective. Aesthetic knowledge is a way of understanding one's own experiences. By the same token, a work of art expresses and structures individual experience. Aesthetic knowledge can be perceived through a combination of intellectual, emotional and physical activity.

After several years of involvement in the project it has become possible to analyse where we might have succeeded. Yet the more important aspects in terms of the development of the project are the problems we have faced in creating a new educational culture.

In the context of teacher education our aim has been to educate prospective teachers who are able to understand the restraints of school subjects from the perspective of knowledge construction processes. We do not ignore the subjects, yet we try to educate prospective teachers to understand school's intellectual aims from the viewpoint of these processes. During the first two years in the project the student teachers went through a similar process themselves. First, they reflected on their own experiences from school. Then they faced the challenge of understanding the knowledge construction processes by carrying out research themselves. Finally they went out to schools to do their practical training period.

During the practical training period the student teachers tried to adopt knowledge construction processes in their own teaching practices. They also had to decide what is worth learning and teaching in school. Both of these tasks have proved to be very difficult. Our student teachers seem to know – i.e. they have "learned" – what we mean by knowledge construction processes, but they have limited ability to demonstrate that knowledge in practice. They also had difficulties in deciding what is worth teaching in school. This leads to our basic question: have teacher students really understood the value of life-world and knowledge processes in teaching? Why is it so difficult to assimilate a new way of thinking and action? This question is a problem not only in teacher education. Similar difficulties have been reported in other academic fields such as mathematics and music (Reid & Petocz, 2008).

At the Heart of Change

Research Data and Analysis

We have interlinked teacher education and research in the CITE project. The development of CITE is based on on-going research carried out both by teacher educators and student teachers. The approach can be labelled as action research, where research focuses on the intervention with the purpose of changing reality (Cohen *et al.*, 2003). In our analysis we combine different data gathered since the evolving of the CITE project in 2003. Our own experiences form one important data source. Over the years we have written down memos and event logs and exchanged ideas on a regular basis to keep a permanent record of these experiences. For evaluative purposes we have interviewed student teachers. They have also written plans and reports related to their practical teaching periods, which constitute a rich data source. For the purposes of this article we refer to two explicit datasets: the interviews with 14 students and practice period reports of 13 students who started the two-year CITE education in autumn 2005 and 2007 respectively.

Student teachers were interviewed in three separate groups of three to six participants with interviews lasting 55 to 65 minutes. The interviews were recorded and transcribed. Each interview produced 23 to 29 pages of textual material. Practice period reports varied in length from three pages to twelve pages. All this text was collaboratively read and analysed using content analysis (Flick, 2006). The findings were structured in line with the theoretical notions of entropy and bifurcation – notions which are explained below.

Entropy and Bifurcation

Radical changes in an educational culture rarely begin from the mainstream, but more likely from the margin, where an individual or a group creates new ideas and action. This process is communal, because new ideas cannot live without living space given by the community. If the community is defensive, adventurists run the risk of arousing strong resistance against the change.

There has been a lively discussion among pedagogical theorists of the relevance of Ilya Prigogine's theory of self-organising structures (Doll, 2001; Gilstrap, 2007; Ståhle & Kuosa, 2009; Mennin, 2010). Prigogine's thinking is grounded in natural sciences and it has been shown to be applicable in human and social sciences. It is this latter path we will follow in our article the social science applications of Prigogine's thinking in the field of pedagogy. According to Doll (2001), Gilstrap (2007) and Mennin (2010), Prigogine's main concepts – equilibrium, entropy, self-organisation, self-referring and bifurcation – give a powerful insight into the process of creative change in human systems.

At the heart of Prigogine's thinking is the process of becoming self-organising systems – how order is created out of chaos (Prigogine & Stengers, 1990). Prigogine found that external or internal tensions in the natural world can create system fluctuations and lead to instabilities of a chaotic nature (Gilstrap, 2007). These instabilities can provoke a new self-organisation of the system. Prigogine stated this to be a common feature of systems (Ståhle & Kuosa, 2009).

According to Prigogine, self-organisation occurs only in systems with increased disorder; that is, systems far away from equilibrium (Ståhle & Kuosa, 2009; Doll, 2001). Transformations and qualitative developments go through a process of equilibrium – disequilibrium – re-equilibrium. In open systems there is a dialectic of equilibrium and chaos which is known as entropy.

Entropy is the measure of unavailable energy in relation to random disorder in a system. In a state of entropy, energy (or information) produced by a system is not exploitable by that system. Out of entropy new qualitative transformations emerge. External or internal tensions create system fluctuations leading to instabilities. In western culture, disorder is usually something we want to avoid. Therefore in social systems entropy is usually restricted. However, a certain amount of disequilibrium is necessary for productive bifurcation and change (Ståhle & Kuosa, 2009; Doll, 2001; Gilstrap, 2007).

Systems need information to adequately interact with their environment and to keep internal processes going. Rich feedback loops are predominant for self-organising systems. Both positive and negative feedback allows systems to develop in an iterative manner. Iterative development is the basis of system re-organisation (Ståhle & Kuosa, 2009).

When entropy increases, old structures eventually give way to new ones as the system re-organises. A moment of sudden and unexpected change is called bifurcation (Ståhle & Kuosa, 2009). At this point the system finds new equilibrium in a state of higher developmental level. When systems go through bifurcation they rely on their history in order to arrive at their final composition: a process of self-referring (Gilstrap, 2007). In other words a certain amount of past knowledge is needed for bifurcation to achieve re-equilibrium from disorder. Bifurcation constitutes a split from the original system when tension increases in a system moving away from equilibrium. At some point the system bifurcates and sometimes that involves transformative change in which the end result is different from the original (Gilstrap, 2007).

Applying the notions of order out of chaos and of bifurcation leading to essential qualitative change to the human world, it can be argued that system bifurcation is a chance for radical renewal. Through bifurcation, systems and individuals create differences and make choices. People have to act in a creative manner in order to give up old restrictive habits and replace them with new, more effective ones. For an individual this is a process of identity-building in a space between freedom and necessity (Hyyppä, 2009).

Real change – new order – is action; it is not only criticism and speeches. The theoretical backgrounds and actions used in CITE created a new and strong entropy in our community. Because entropy is a natural part of communities we have created a space where this natural process can evolve. Creativity is promoted by giving enough time and space for learning. This always leads to a certain amount of entropy but we have tried to tolerate this.

The beginning of our program in 2003 was actually a bifurcation in one process, because it started a new educational culture which was radically different from the mainstream education in our teacher education tradition.

In the following analysis we shall focus on the student teachers to ascertain whether or not they can create new action and culture in their own group and in the school where they carry out their teacher practice.

Uncertainty of Being a Student Teacher

Teacher practice is an intensive six-week period that student teachers spend in school after studies in the CITE program. They familiarise themselves with the class one to two months before they start their own teaching. They begin to make plans for teaching even earlier – four months before their own teaching period. The practice is evaluated in line with the aims of CITE, especially on how well they can apply the three forms of knowledge (factual, contractual, aesthetic). The overall period lasts from September to March, when the practice is evaluated by the whole group. The student teachers' experiences of this process are mentally demanding, not only for individuals but also for the group, because the practice is the touchstone for the whole CITE education: a new way of thinking must be transmitted to the culture where it does not exist.

Student teachers find this situation contradictory. They are struggling between a new and an old culture of schooling, especially in the teacher practice. Firstly, the start of planning in September was like a return to the start of CITE. During their first year students had studied inductive teaching, forms of knowledge and subjective relationships towards different phenomena. At the beginning of the second year both teacher educators and student teachers felt that all the processes, which should now have been implemented in practice, had been lost.

> "Before the practice I thought it impossible to put into practice the idea that you are flexible in your teaching according to the needs of the class and the situation".

> "I remember that before the practice I was sometimes annoyed when people were afraid and complained about how this kind of 'new way of teaching' could be taken into the school, whose culture is so strong, in the minds of both the pupils and the teachers".

The same uncertainty, lack of faith, helplessness and even angst returned before the practice period in school. In both cases student teachers had lost faith in the principles of CITE education, especially towards forms of knowledge and inductive teaching. There were strong contradictions between the following pairs of concepts: learning as a learner process/learning as a teacher process; situational flexibility/predestined; open/enclosed.

The fulcrum of creativity is the capacity for change in theory and in practice. Both in teaching and learning we understand this process more from the viewpoint of group dynamics than individual dynamics. Education is typically a communal process because our activities and ideas obtain their meanings in the interaction with the other members of a group and community.

We stress the basis of creativity as the capacity of individuals to give space to all the members of the group. A group or community cannot be an instrument or an object for one individual's creativity restricting other members' creativity. Without this idea being realised in practice a new way of thinking and acting is not possible. The transition from the safe and familiar CITE group to schools was difficult. Uncertainty and loss of faith returned, feelings which were partly resolved by adapting the routine school culture.

> "I wrote already earlier that I got frightened of the culture of discipline and obedience prevailing in the school. I noticed that I implemented it myself sometimes".

> "When the struggle between the traditional and the inductive way of teaching was strongest, you started in a way to combine the different teaching styles, a sprinkling of the old and a sprinkling of the new, which more likely made the pupils even more confused".

> "During the practice I encountered learnt structures that were difficult to break".

The practice period simulates the transition to a teacher's real work. Students are still teacher trainees but the culture they face during the practice is the same. A new culture is possible if school teachers have the capacity to tolerate criticism and the requisite competences to implement the new ideas and activities. Some of our student teachers managed to do this, but in the school context the attraction of clear routines was very strong, particularly because of incapability, structures and timidity. In contrast, successful teaching was based on the understanding of the forms of knowledge, a belief in one's own capacity and a conviction that school can be changed.

> "Not a feeling that I was teaching something useless, but that I can justify things to the children, and this has a quite clear effect on the child's motivation, too".

> "I noticed how I myself however had stopped thinking about the projects from the point of view of the subject. For example, in the friendship project I was quite appalled to notice how detached from the subjects [I was]. I was rushing ahead".

It was noticeable that student teachers evaluated their actions conceptually. For example, they were highly conscious of the difference between emotionally orientated versus professionally orientated teaching. If a teacher is emotionally orientated, their solutions in a given situation are based on a desire to fulfill their own prevailing needs, instead of which a professionally orientated teacher tries logically to adapt theory to practice.

The student teachers also made critical observations on everyday school life. An interesting finding is a pupil behavior labelled "diversionary learning". In a classroom, pupils tend to behave as if they were acting according to the school teacher's instructions. Closer observation reveals that pupils are mostly like actors: fulfilling their expected roles but not going into the assignments in any depth. This leads to superficial and ritual learning behavior. The student teachers also devote discussion to the nature and overall meaning of school institution. Their interpretations are mainly critical and say that there is lack of creativity in everyday school life.

Complexity of Belonging to Communities

A certain indication of bifurcation is seen in the ways student teachers in the CITE group see themselves in relation to other student teachers and teacher educators at the Department of Teacher Education.

> "In some way I thought it was great that there was a place that was like your own, a place that others didn't have – that others were like scattered all over the place. And then we still had like a classroom of our own in principle, the one where we have our group sessions and others".

> "I mean, what you like normally do here, you don't because sometimes there seems to be quite a big, big difference in the way you do things, like what you do as a group and what you do here. So probably you subconsciously did something while you were coming here".

A feeling of distance from others did not develop only because of the physical location of CITE but also because of the organisational arrangements. The CITE group studied together every Monday and Tuesday. Studies were so intensive that there was no time for other studies during those days. It was only from Wednesday to Friday that student teachers could take other study modules forming part of their training. As the other student teachers had usually already taken these study modules at the beginning of week, the CITE students had no choice but to go on studying together for the whole week. This meant the CITE students only rarely integrated with other student teachers and this led to a certain degree of freedom in relation to the standard education program. On the other hand it made the bonds among CITE students even stonger. Paradoxically, this double mechanism was simultaneously liberating and restricting.

Although the CITE students themselves felt special, something also recognised by the other student teachers, they were not free of feelings of uncertainty and doubt. This created a need for discussion in the wider student teachers community. However the CITE studies were not widely discussed among different student teachers' groups. The CITE students preferred to discuss their studies with their own family members. The rationale for this may be the fact the phenomena discussed and the conceptual language used in CITE was unfamiliar to the standard education students. A collision of paradigms was evident (see Kuhn, 1962).

> "I probably became suspicious at the point when I was talking to my mum and then she asked 'what is it, what do you do and what is the purpose of it?' And then I could not, I couldn't explain, but I was very strongly of the opinion that this is a really good thing. But, then my mum was a bit like 'what, you don't even know what it's about?', or something like that. So, then I maybe started to question it a bit more myself, about what if I don't know anything about this or something I cannot quite explain, what is happening here in a way. Or in a way that's just it, maybe I have to think a bit more about it".

> "Yes, and then somehow, what I think is contradictory, is that if on the one hand you would like to talk to somebody about these experiences and share them, then there would be a homeroom teacher or pupils who do the same work, but those are the very ones you don't talk to. I talked to my friends; to my family I have talked a lot about everything. But not to other students who could in some way, I can't say benefit from it, but they could, you know, it would interest them. But somehow they are the last group that…".

There also emerged clashes between different views among the teacher educators. In CITE various courses were combined into larger units and it included courses taught by colleagues not participating in CITE. Consequently CITE teacher educators started to teach these courses to their own group of student teachers. Some colleagues took offence at this. They felt that their professional skills were not being acknowledged or they questioned the professional skills of the CITE teacher educators in teaching their courses.

We have come up against the same phenomenon among the teacher educators, even if in a more hidden and complex form. It is a kind of ideological conflict. Questions about how to teach and what to teach are activated. In addition there are disparities among the teacher educators with regard to the theoretical underpinnings of CITE, the individual motives for participating in the project. Furthermore, involvement in the development of CITE studies also differs.

In addition there have been some complaints from the Department of Teacher Education about the secrecy surrounding CITE. For example, complaints have been made about the concealment of information about arrangements. Staff have complained about not knowing what CITE is like and what is happening in it. These complaints are interesting because the information given about CITE was no less than other information provided about teaching. Yet CITE teacher educators have experienced some kind of threat from some of their colleagues.

Indications of a New Order (Bifurcation)

There are some indications of a new order. There were signs of autonomous learning, where the student teachers took responsibility for their learning. Signs of a new order are present in the student's spontaneous studies. For instance, one group of student teachers refused to study species in the traditional way but wanted instead to study forest ecology on a two-day field trip. The lecturer welcomed this initiative and considered it valuable; student teachers even got some financial support for their field trip.

> "...when we were thinking about the animal and plant exams, which at least seemed stupid, we were thinking... that maybe they could be replaced by something else that we think would make more sense".

There are also examples of self-organised learning projects without teacher educators. For instance, a group of student teachers studied the history of Finnish school education by themselves because they felt there was a lack of teacher education curriculum in this area.

> "...first we decided on the common research question and then everybody decided on a related topic of their own and studied and made presentations and such like... And then in a way through history we tried to understand the reality of the present-day school. People studied different topics and then we got together and talked about them".

There is also a student teachers' discussion circle with two school teachers participating. Student teachers said that they wanted an opportunity to have discussions about school education with experienced teachers. Therefore they asked the two school teachers to join the circle.

The nature of bifurcation is that it is sudden and unexpected. In the first autumn the students had a lot of freedom in organising their learning. They were given various projects to complete and just before Christmas they had to report on what they had accomplished. Unfortunately, the student teachers had not taken responsibility for their learning and had lived under the illusion of successful learning. When teacher educators made this reality apparent to student teachers, they experienced a crisis as a group. They got very angry and disappointed at themselves and also at the teacher educators. A student teacher doing research in the group called this incident a "sign-event". It was an incident that led the student teachers to see their learning in a totally new way. Until this moment they did not understand what freedom combined with responsibility means in their learning.

Difficulties in Creating Change

For people in organisations it is more common to oppose than to allow and support change. This conclusion is consistent with our own experience and the student teacher data. The most important element in the process of change has been to create a goal or idea that the educators' community shares, and thus co-operates to achieve.

There are two ways how the creativity aspect emerges in the teaching of CITE. Firstly the teacher educators have voluntarily challenged their traditional teaching models without being given a clear alternative model. As a result the teacher educator's group created new, sometimes revolutionary, ways of teaching. For the student teachers the integrative model has been also challenging. They have gone through quite a demanding process to first forget how they have studied earlier and then to learn totally differently. Both teacher educators and teacher students have dealt with these challenges in a creative manner. At its best this may lead to an improvement of study culture.

In the CITE project there also seem to be difficulties in learning the new study culture. Student teachers are required to be autonomous researchers of learning processes but they would like to remain in the role of student at school. The student teachers use different strategies (e.g., pretended helplessness) to prevent change. These strategies are difficult to observe. Staff members have their own strategies to prevent change. Co-operation with teacher educators can actually turn out to be superficial. If somebody ignores jointly-agreed aims, principles and methods, other teacher educators are helpless. It is not unusual that one member continually forgets to attend meetings or that the teacher educator is recurrently occupied with other duties.

It is our experience that in such an extensive and all-embracing project all parties encounter problems. Gaining a deep understanding of educational practices and theories is difficult for the student teachers. By the same token we have had to admit that the implementation of a new logic of thinking, teaching and organisation is a huge challenge for us as the teacher educators. It takes a lot of courage, creativity and stamina to put forth arguments that challenge the current teaching paradigm. Our project, and also our work as teacher educators, has been questioned, derided and undermined. As we struggle forward, we have adopted the assumption that a really creative project cannot avoid clashes of opinions with those in power.

We have been forced to ask a painful question: how can we not accept the student teachers' poor understanding of educational theory and practice, when we as teacher educators are undoubtedly in a very similar situation? We seem to know how the project should be implemented and we have quite a substantial theoretical knowledge in support of our arguments, but from time to time we have to face our inability to translate theory into practice.

Time is essential for individual change and growth. Development and understanding are not instantaneous and direct but happen in unpredictable spurts; i.e. bifurcations. Therefore time is a key factor. Individuals must have time to reflect and an opportunity to disagree (Doll, 2001; Ståhle & Kuosa, 2009). Furthermore, space and time are essential for creativity. They represent structural possibilities and impossibilities which enable to link studies and the handling of emotions, such as fear and courage. Educational institutions are usually inflexible and do not allow different solutions concerning time and space. In CITE all Mondays and Tuesdays are reserved for studies in CITE during the whole of the semester. In university culture, where lectures and small-group sessions tend to underpin the teaching culture, these kinds of educational solutions are very rare.

Space and time are essential also for communal creativity in CITE. Concessions in terms of time and space have given freedom and power, but also the responsibility for the CITE group to decide its own activities and culture. This power, together with long-term education, has made it possible for both student teachers and teacher educators to make a safe transition through a chaotic phase to a new order. As a result development of CITE education has become reality. Throughout this transition we have considered the teacher's work from a different theoretical viewpoint, which has required new structures.

We have allowed more space for chaos through freedom. At the same time our university institution tries to control chaos by means of bureaucracy and has also tried to define in advance the terms of reference for teaching to make it predictable. This mode of action seems to be typical of all institutional education systems. Although CITE's size in our Department of Education is quite small, its significance is much greater. Both the education provided by CITE and its research are ranked at a high level, not only in our department but also in our university. This means that anomaly, in the sense used by Kuhn's (1970), is spreading from CITE to the whole community and the community cannot continue to remain unresponsive. Renewal starting at the edges can lead from the margin to the centre (Hyyppä, 2009).

About the Authors

Matti Rautiainen is Lecturer at Department of Teacher Education, University of Jyväskylä, Finland. He can be contacted at this e-mail: matti.rautiainen@jyu.fi

Tiina Nikkola is Researcher and Teacher Educator at Department of Teacher Education, University of Jyväskylä, Finland. She can be contacted at this e-mail: tiina.nikkola@jyu.fi

Pekka Räihä is Researcher and Teacher Educator at Department of Teacher Education, University of Jyväskylä, Finland. He can be contacted at this e-mail: pekka.raiha@edu.jyu.fi

Sakari Saukkonen is Research Coordinator at Finnish Institute for Educational Research, University of Jyväskylä, Finland. He can be contacted at this e-mail: sakari.saukkonen@jyu.fi

Pentti Moilanen is Professor at Department of Teacher Education, University of Jyväskylä, Finland. He can be contacted at this e-mail: pentti.moilanen@jyu.fi

Chapter Thirteen

Inaugurating a Creativity Initiative in Higher Education

Clive Holtham

Introduction

This paper is set in the context of an institution-wide initiative on creativity across disciplinary and professional boundaries, and then focuses in on an early initiative which typifies this approach, linking fine arts to improving professional practice.

City University London is named after the City of London, the financial and commercial district, and is strategically positioned as "the University for Business and the Professions". In 2008 its Vice-Chancellor (President) initiated an internal competition for cross-disciplinary centres to be created whose remit covered teaching and learning, research and knowledge transfer. Six centres were funded for a two year period, and this paper reports on the Centre for Creativity in Professional Practice (C2P2).

The University already has a School of Arts which is active in relation to the creative industries, but that is not the central thrust of the new centre. By contrast and more unusually, the particular focus of this centre is creativity within and across the wider professions such as law, engineering, health, education, and business.

Certainly in the UK, it is unusual to create inter-disciplinary centres which are not either exclusively research or exclusively teaching/learning based. Secondly, the aim of all six City University centres is not simply to focus on a topic in a "single-loop learning" fashion (Argyris, 1977). This concerns the transmission of well-understood concepts. They are also explicitly geared to "double-loop learning", of developing new learning in the process, and hence to promoting change in educational and research practices and behaviours within the institution.

British Context

The current strategic importance of creativity has been acknowledged by many commentators, both:

- at the international level – the Nomura Institute's proposition is that "Creativity will be the next economic activity, replacing the current focus on information" (Murakumi, 2000)

- within the UK, where the Cox review commissioned by the then Chancellor Gordon Brown in 2005 saw exploitation of the nation's creative skills as *"vital to the UK's long-term economic success"* (HM Treasury (2005)). The Cox review concluded that "the success of the creative industries notwithstanding, there is evidence that UK business is not realising the full potential of applying creativity more widely, and emphasised the need for interdisciplinary teaching in universities." Brown added that the challenge is: *"…not just to encourage creative industries, our priority is to encourage all industries to be creative"*. Creativity and design, used effectively, are important competitive tools for firms and the formal education system, enhancing the supply of creativity and design skills, and management and business skills more generally (DTI, 2005).

C2P2: Creativity in Professional Practice

The first step involved developing a University-wide understanding of creativity that built cross-discipline communication and collaboration, including two sub-objectives:

- Developing new high–engagement, experience-based approaches with which to learn about creativity good practices, techniques and tools, drawn from science, business and the arts

+ Researching and developing new activities, tools, techniques and resources that enhance and support creative problem solving in a range of professional practices that draw on City's unique disciplinary mix.

The Centre was set up with a brief to undertake five main activities:

1. Creation of a core team (director and researcher) to stimulate and orchestrate interdisciplinary working, to secure funding and to disseminate outcomes

2. Creation of a national research seminar series network running up to 6 seminars in 2009-2010

3. Creation of small innovative projects in each main school involved

4. Creation of a university, rather than school-based, masters degree in innovation, creativity and leadership

5. Promotion of a university-wide approach to creativity at undergraduate level within schools and disciplines.

C2P2 in London

The Centre's director was appointed in May 2009 marking the effective start of the project. This highlighted the need to progress several of the activities in parallel, in particular the research seminar series.

One of the key aims of the Centre is to draw on the creative potential of London as a geographical place. Of crucial importance here is the clustering of museums and art galleries of almost ever conceivable type – from narrow niche museums, to world-class art collections. Another early action has been to develop a group of associates from different backgrounds in a range of professions, specifically including artists. This group has been involved in field-testing innovative approaches to creativity including the specific example addressed here.

This paper is focused specifically on work at the Whitechapel Gallery, which is in the East End of London and immediately adjacent to the City. The Gallery was reopened in April 2009 after a major refurbishment incorporating the former Victorian public library next door. At the opening one exhibition held in the Gallery drew explicitly on the heritage of the building. This was the Bloomberg Commission by Polish artist Goshka Macuga, "The Nature of the Beast" (Whitechapel Gallery, 2009). It included the display of a full size tapestry reproduction of Picasso's Guernica on loan from its normal location in the United Nations, New York. The original version of Guernica was displayed in the Whitechapel Gallery in 1939 to raise awareness of, and funds for, the Republicans in Spain. Macuga's project *"...draws connections across historic and contemporary world affairs, their protagonists and the cultural ripple effects they have triggered. The room has been designed to accommodate meetings, discussions and debates around a central table, with Guernica once again as a backdrop"*.

What was highly unusual about this exhibition was an announcement by the gallery that meetings could be arranged around the table. There were two main conditions, namely that visitors would still be in the gallery uninterrupted, and that the photos, videos and write ups of every meeting would be made available to the artist and Gallery archive.

Three Events

The Whitechapel Gallery announcement in April 2009 came at exactly the time that C2P2 was keen to make rapid progress, and as a result three bookings were made to utilise the unique features of the exhibition to support the inaugural activities of C2P2. The general objectives for all three events started from the utilisation of this highly unusual location for events that would add cachet to, and attract interest, in those events. This was an almost unique opportunity for participants to work physically within an art gallery. This aspect was augmented by working in an environment that was fully open to the public. The use of a very large round table is itself quite a rare event. What turned out to be crucial was that the events were supported by a strong administrative and logistical infrastructure on behalf of the Whitechapel Gallery, which was essential for exploratory events of this nature.

The three meetings can be summarised as below, using the naming convention W1, W2, W3.

	Participants	Purpose	Duration
W1	Associates	Pilot event	2hrs
W2	MBA Elective Session	Class including arte-fact production	1hr + 2hrs in educa-tion studio
W3	Multi-university network	Inaugural Meeting	2hrs

Table 1: Overview of Events

The C2P2 team set up the three events as experiments into whether creative activities of knowledge workers could be enhanced by being held in this unusual, indeed unique, iconic space. This enhancement could either be directly, e.g. by use of the space or artefacts, or indirectly, e.g. by attracting interest in attending the meeting. There was however an aim shared for all of the meetings to be more effective or productive as a result of being in this specific physical location. Effective or productive in the context of knowledge work means that there is improved sharing of experience, creation of knowledge, and commitment to action.

In reality, the experiments cannot be treated as situated in a laboratory, closely controlled only for the variable of physical place. Most significantly, the facilitation method and meeting processes were highly customised in all three cases to the specific place, purpose, and people. So really place and facilitation need to be considered conjointly.

Analytical Framework

Our analytical framework for creativity in general is based on the long-standing model developed by Rhodes (1961) also discussed by Scritchfield (1999). This is the four "P" model of process, product, people and press. Isaksen *et al.* (1994) enhanced the 4P model by showing that although the themes overlapped, they operated together and that in all cases, the context plays a major role.

In this paper, we have however in line with some others, changed the fourth P of "press" into "place". Slightly unusually, but addressing at once two of the 4 Ps, we are here treating the creation of our own centre as itself the **product** of a creativity **process**. Central to that are the various **people** involved, and in this paper the **place** dimension is of particularly great significance. We also concur with Fritz (1993), who strongly emphasises how much creativity, problem solving and innovation are themselves essentially change management processes.

The key relationships, just discussed, are represented in diagrammatic form in Figure 1.

Scharmer & Käufer (2000) proposed seven theses to re-orientate the 21st Century university, and their thesis number 7 saw *"universities as birthplaces and hubs for communities of creation"*, which *"…do not strive for a type of science which merely reflects the world, but for a science capable of grasping reality by contemplating the underlying forces of its genesis. In such a university, learners and researchers shift from being distant observers to creative co-designers of a praxis in progress – to midwives assisting in the birth of innovation*". Organising these events would be very much this midwife role for a university.

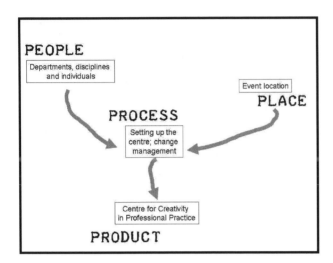

Figure 1: The Overall Approach Under Review

Event Details

W1 was a small pilot event held with six associates or members of C2P2 who had all been closely involved in some direct way with creativity processes. This was regarded as a very high risk venture, and was also arranged at short notice. This meant there was very little time to choreograph the event, so it had a highly improvisational quality. It was the first "live" meeting held in the Gallery in front of the public (as opposed to events at private views) and is shown in Figure 2.

Figure 2: Event "W1" with Six Participants at the Table (others in the picture are members of the public visiting the gallery on that day)

This was a creativity workshop, with associates of C2P2 demonstrating creativity tools they used in their own professional practice. The participants sat at the large round table, which was glass-topped to show off documents and other artefacts about life in the East End of London around the late 1930s.

Event W2, seen in Figure 3, involved a half-day session of a Cass Business School MBA elective called "Business Mystery: The Art of Management" being held in the Gallery with 19 participants in total.

Figure 3: Event "W2"

This too was regarded as risky, as this type of fine-art based activity had not been attempted on the elective in its previous four years of operation. Compared with W1, more time was available for planning, and this was needed to create just the right balance of challenge and business focus for the student activities.

The overt aim of the session was to produce an optych, an eight piece painted artwork made up of eight segments of a circle, mirroring the eight segments of the table. One hour was spent at the table, including in break out groups, on the concept and overall design. The group then went to the Gallery's Clore Studio, where they spent two hours on the more detailed planning of each segment, the design of the segment, and finally its actual painting on foamboard, shown in Figure 4.

Event W3 was the inaugural meeting of the Research Series Seminar Network, with 20 participants. In order to moderate the inherent risk, this event had even more significant amounts of prior planning and facilitation. Participants first introduced themselves by walking with one or two others around the gallery, with groups reporting back on their experience. The same groups then brainstormed proposals for the operation of the network on a triangular

Figure 4:
The Optych: Flow
Tide and Rapids

Figure 5:
W3. The Larger
Group Work
Synthesis

pre-printed sheet. New and larger groups then formed at one side of the gallery (Figure 5) to synthesise by theme the proposals of the individual teams.

The penultimate stage involved a promenade with all participants being presented with the three syntheses laid out on the floor of the gallery. The final plenary session was feedback on the whole event.

The round table itself was an artwork, and for W3 and especially W2, participants did not work at the table for the majority of the time, nor use the table artefacts to any great extent. All meetings and especially W2 and W3 had objectives that were largely independent of the gallery location. In particular, the organisers had very limited time. It was decided not to have a computer, projector and powerpoint, and at no time was that a problem, not least as the whole event was predicated on not needing these facilities, so choreographed accordingly. Use was made of small group activity (W1 had consisted only of one small group), break out groups and use of other areas, namely the education studio for W2 and the large empty floor space for W3.

A method called the "Twitter Telegram" (140 characters on a stylised telegram form) was introduced as a method of getting feedback very quickly and worked extraordinarily well.

Event Lessons

One thing that was very clear was that there was a noticeable learning curve between the events. A key lesson from W1 was that the impact of working in a public place had been underestimated by both facilitators and participants; so this was emphasised a lot more for W2 and W3. There was a concern with the security of personal items left around the table. This was also covered in W2 and W3 briefings. There was a distinct issue with the noise levels when there were many visitors in the gallery, but no real way of amplifying audio by participants. The most important lesson of all from W1 was that the use of the room was feasible even for high-stakes events. And one member of the public had actually joined in the exercises.

There was a quite different lesson from W2: there was little doubt that having 19 people seated round the table acted as a deterrent to the public. In W3, despite being a Friday afternoon, the Gallery was very quiet and once again the presence of a table full of people, viewed through the glass door to the gallery, even seemed to deter some public from coming into the gallery at all.

Working in Public

The differing aspects of working in public are summarised in Table 2 below:

Public Involvement	W1	W2	W3
Watching	Quite high	Minimal	1 person closely
Participation	One person	None	None
Visitor numbers	High	Medium	Low

Table 2: Interactions with public

The question of working in public is not a unique situation. Retail and customer services staff do it all the time, though for them linking with the public is an integral part of their job. It is much rarer for knowledge workers, though it happens in the public sector, for example in central and local government, where meetings including formal advice and cross-examination are often open to the public. Artistic performances are explicitly put on for the public and some hybrids, arguably courts of law, are a combination of several of the above.

Working in public can be associated with deep symbolic values such as promoting openness and transparency. Yet at the very same time it could have negative connotations – a privileged group, or a set of people self-consciously performing in public. It was also noticeable that the experience was very different even for different participants in the same meeting. It is not just a shared, but potentially also a contested space. The meeting participants clearly could affect the visitor's enjoyment of the gallery, firstly just by physical presence, secondly via noise, and thirdly through preventing access to the exhibits, particularly at the round table.

Working across Disciplines

Our specific concerns are with collaboration across what we call *"wide boundaries"*, also using the term *"extreme collaboration"* (Holtham *et al.*, 2006). Contemporary academia is heavily focussed around academic disciplines. But going back into the deep traditions of the academy, at various points in history there has been little or not role for disciplines and hence of disciplinary boundaries. This was certainly true for Ancient Greeks such as Aristotle; it was true again during the Renaissance, and it was maintained through most of the enlightenment. It was the coming of the industrial revolution, the parallel explosion in scientific discovery and in the creation of professions, together with the creation of the modern university in the second half of the 20th century, that accelerated the creation of disciplines.

The generic limitations of over-focus on single discipline-based work are well enough understood. Indeed, it is one of the very pillars of the logic of a knowledge-based society that increasing amounts of research will be carried out by collaboration across disciplines, for example the concepts of Mode 2 research and inter-disciplinarity. Hammersley (1999) provides an excellent summary of Mode 2 research, which is worth quoting at length:

> "Mode 1 research is based primarily in universities, is focused on disciplines, and is concerned simply with contributing to a cumulating body of knowledge; so that any 'application' of the knowledge is a secondary matter, and one that is seen as beyond the responsibility of researchers. /.../ Mode 2 research contrasts with Mode 1 in several respects:

> First, it is focused on solving problems that arise in particular practical contexts. The aim is to generate some solution or product, rather than simply to contribute to a body of knowledge.

> Secondly, it takes place via team work, involving researchers from diverse disciplinary backgrounds. And these teams are seen as 'non-hierarchical, heterogeneously organised forms which are essentially transient' (Gibbons et al 1994:vii).

> Thirdly, Mode 2 research is transdisciplinary in orientation. In other words, while disciplinary knowledge is drawn on, even more important are the knowledge, understanding and techniques that those engaged in Mode 2 research accumulate in the course of doing it.

> Finally, accountability is practical in character, involving users as well as researchers. Indeed, there is no permanent body of researchers that could play the kind of role in accountability that the discipline plays in Mode 1 research".

Louis & Bartunek (1992) suggested that research teams in which one or more members are relative insiders to a setting, and one or more members are relative outsiders, offer distinct advantages for integrating diverse perspectives on organizational activities. The approach taken builds on insights about insider and outsider collaboration presented by Evered & Meryl (1981).

Typical Channels for Connections across "Wide Boundaries"

Physical proximity can be of significance. The Oxbridge College/Senior Common Room model did permit and still does permit social interactions across wide disciplinary boundaries. But this does not necessarily translate itself into inter-disciplinary research or interdisciplinary teaching and learning. But more generally, the scope for interdisciplinary collaboration has been reduced as universities have grown in size and specialisation. It is perfectly feasible for many academics to spend all their time on research and teaching working only with other academics in the same discipline or from closely related disciplines. This is not simply confined to lack of contact between faculties such as engineering and management. The discipline of management is itself made up of six to ten academic groupings with perhaps relatively little academic contact between them.

Our concern here is not per se with disrupting this typical behaviour. It is rather about asking what may be lost through such intense focus, and in particular with examining vehicles which positively stimulate the possibility of making connections across disciplinary boundaries.

Important Factors which Emerged

One aspect which was very clear in W1 and also in W3 was that working across disciplines enhances the possibilities of drawing on associates from outside one's own discipline. Also, because no single school, department or discipline can "own" the topic of creativity, there are attractions in events which bring many disciplines together on neutral ground.

In business strategy one of the key findings relating to innovation is that it is more likely to occur when there are "weak ties" between potential collaborators (Granovetter, 1973), compared to the formalised "strong ties" found within organisational structures and hierarchies. This underlies the importance when creating a cross disciplinary network, of sustaining weak ties, even at the risk of some loss of focus.

Building a community or network may be said to have at least two speeds. One is slow – and a good example here has been the UK National Teaching Fellowship scheme, several members of which contributed to the W3 event. Fellows are appointed for life and most typically meet physically at an annual Fellows symposium. So relationships evolve slowly over quite long periods of time. By contrast, other teams or collaborations are driven by quite short-term instrumental goals, such as winning or implementing a grant application. Here immediacy, novelty and getting things done tend to dominate.

All three Whitechapel events were unconventional, and as such carry extra risks as outlined above. But they also extended the potential opportunities, not least the advantages of holding the events in an iconic location.

Revisiting the 4 Ps

	People	Process	Place	Product
W1	Ad Hoc; weak ties	Improvis-ational	Gallery	Proof of concept of place and process
W2	Well-estab-lished team; strong ties	Highly structured	Gallery and art education room	A collabora-tive artwork; optych
W3	Inaugural meeting of network; strong, medium and weak ties	Semi-structured	Gallery	Team building and action planning

Table 3: Summary Relative to the 4 Ps

Product: Each event had a purpose. Also, the events cumulatively formed an explicit part of the setting up and evolution of C2P2. Interestingly, as a result of the double-loop learning dimension, the process itself was also a product.

People: This is one of the most intriguing aspects of the experience. The three sets of participants were quite different from each other, though there was some minor overlap of facilitators and participants across the three events. As a result there was very little process similarity between the three events, which had to be highly customised to reduce the risks involved.

Process: Firstly, there was and is an overall change management process, namely trying to shift attention from an approach wholly based on school/department/ discipline. Secondly, there was the actual process used in the events themselves. This involved some form of facilitation, which differed significantly across the three events.

Place: This is relatively unusual in that there were different types of event held in that one physical place. In fact even then, there were quite different types of use of the spaces in the Gallery on each occasion. Jeffrey (2003) identified a number of tools that characterize and support the collaboration process, including story-lines and metaphor, choice of vocabulary, the nature of dialogue and the role of mediating agents. In this context, physical place is very much a mediating agent, which can impact on dialogue and also enable metaphor to be very directly drawn upon.

Discussion

The lessons learnt from this experience fall into three groups:

The Importance of Place

It was clear from feedback at all three events that participants were very much affected by working in an iconic and unusual space. There were expected indirect benefits from building on the ambience of the art gallery to create different types of dialogue. Billoni (2002) has identified the general potential of using an art experience as a stimulus to wider knowledge and insight.

It was also expected that in forming and storming, the artefacts gave people something interesting to catch their joint eyes. As it turned out, almost everyone mentioned the war crimes video exhibit as "*disturbing*", "*dislocating*". Surprisingly, Guernica itself was less often mentioned, perhaps because it is such a familiar image.

Working in Public

What was striking about the workshop was firstly the almost completely unexpected nature of the relationship between the public and the participants of the workshop. There were no groundrules; all those involved had to adjust their behaviour. Perhaps most strikingly, the workshop participants became part of an art installation, themselves being observed at work by the gallery visitors. In the next level, visitors asked if they could participate. This had been anticipated and in fact it was agreed in advance that participation would be encouraged.

Designing Events for a Creativity Network

We benefitted greatly from the diversity of colleagues attracted to the external events W1 and W3. We also benefitted from the rather radical experiences of the MBA students, who had not been expecting to produce an artwork at the gallery. There is every indication from participant feedback that weak ties are of some considerable significance in building an ongoing creativity network, and hence unusual events providing a *"neutral ground"* may be often more appropriate than more formal events concerned with e.g. knowledge exchange between academia and business.

Wider Implications

According to the feedback, it certainly proved to be a valuable event for the participants (and hence for C2P2), and allowed deeper learning about how the creative process is affected by location and novel stimuli. It is also unlikely that this event would have been initiated without the new Centre providing a climate for innovation in creativity methods across disciplinary boundaries.

This approach of holding a real meeting in a public art space surrounded by ordinary visitors could be replicated in almost any art space in the world, given some degree of courage and support by the gallery itself, as well as some willingness on the part of both meeting attendees and the visitors to take risks.

Conclusion

From the viewpoint of creativity a number of key messages could be derived from this initiative:

+ There was a strong opportunistic element in the design. Given constraints of time and resources, it was necessary to some extent to improvise an approach, rather than to wait for the ideal circumstances to arise

+ There was a very strong disposition to experiment particularly in order to reduce risk, and also because in an unusual context there was simply no easy precedents which could be drawn upon. Two pilot events were run, with many lessons learnt. The nature of the event also made it essential to be constantly awaiting the unexpected

+ The question of the physical place for the creativity event took on and became of very great significance

+ There was a huge investment of effort in the planning, operations and documentation of the event; both divergent and convergent creativity phases were essential. This continually needed a team approach, as any one individual may not be equally competent in both phases

+ The experiences reinforced the idea that creativity initiatives much themselves "practice what they preach" and explicitly set out to include original but risky approaches in their own high-profile activities.

Special Thanks

The Whitechapel Gallery were exceptionally helpful:

1. They accepted the artist's conditions to make the room available free of charge for meetings

2. They put up with strange and unusual requests in the context of a gallery

3. They were extremely helpful in fixing up electricity supplies and extension cables

4. They tolerated risks in terms of using the glass topped table

5. Nicky Sim was involved throughout, with intern Sara Guerrero being heavily involved in W2 in particular. The Gallery Assistants were uniformly helpful, particularly in W3 where we felt the public was being deterred, and the assistants told people lurking at the doors that they were welcome to come in.

About the Author

Clive Holtham is Professor of Information Management and Director of the Learning Laboratory at Cass Business School, City University London. He can be contacted at this e-mail: c.w.holtham@city.ac.uk

Bibliography

Abinun, J. (1981). Creativity and Education: Some Critical Remarks. *Journal of Aesthetic Education*, Vol. 15, No. 1, pp. 17–29.

Abrahmov, S. L. & M. Ronen (2008). Double blending: online theory with on-campus practice in photography instruction. *Innovations in Education and Teaching International*, Vol. 45, No. 1, pp. 3–14.

Adkins, B. (2009). PhD pedagogy and the changing knowledge landscapes of universities. *Higher Education Research & Development*, Vol. 28, No. 2, pp. 165–177.

Ahmad, Y. & M. Broussine (2003). The UK Public Sector Modernization Agenda. Reconciliation and renewal? *Public Management Review*, Vol. 5, No. 1, pp. 45–62.

Alexander, R. R. (1981). The Ghost of Creativity in Art Education. *Art Education*, Vol. 34, No. 4, pp. 28–30.

Almeida, P.; H. Pedrosa de Jesus & M. Watts (2008). Developing a mini-project: students' questions and learning styles. *The Psychology of Education Review*, Vol. 32, No. 1, pp. 6–17.

Amabile, R. C.; H. Coon; J. Lazenby & M. Herron (1996). Assessing the Work Environment for Creativity. *The Academy of Management Journal*, Vol. 39, No. 5, pp. 1154–1184.

Amabile, T. M. (1983). The social psychology of creativity: A componential conceptualization. *Journal of Personality and Social Psychology*, Vol. 45, pp. 357–376.

Amabile, T. M. (1988). A model of organisational innovation. In B. M. Staw & L.L. Cummings (Eds.), *Research in Organizational Behaviour, Vol. 10*, pp. 123–167. Greenwich, CT: JAI Press.

Amabile, T. M. (1996). *Creativity in Context. Update to the Social Psychology of Creativity*. New York: Springer-Verlag.

Amabile, T. M. (2008). *Getting down to the business of creativity*. Harvard Business School. http://hbswk.edu/item/5902.html [accessed July 15, 2010].

Amabile, T. M.; K. G. Hill; B. A. Hennessey & E. Tighe (1994). The Work Preference Inventory: Assessing intrinsic and extrinsic motivation orientations. *Journal of Personality and Social Psychology*, Vol. 66, pp. 950–967.

Argyris, C. (1977). Double-loop learning in organizations. *Harvard Business Review*, January–February, pp.115–124.

Arrowsmith, W. (1970). The creative university. In J. D. Roslansky (Ed.), (1990), *Creativity*, pp. 53–78, Amsterdam: North-Holland.

Atlay, M. T. (2008). *Education Strategy (2008–2011): Transformational Education*. Luton: University of Bedfordshire.

Austin, A. E. & M. McDaniels (2006). Preparing the professorate of the future: Graduate student socialization for faculty roles. In J. C. Smart (Ed.), *Higher education: Handbook of theory and research*, pp. 397–455. Dordrecht: Springer.

Austin, A. E. (2002). Preparing the next generation of faculty: Graduate education as socialization to the academic career. *The Journal of Higher Education*, Vol. 73, No. 2, pp. 94–122.

Austin, A. E. (2009). Cognitive apprenticeship theory and its implications for doctoral education: A case example from a doctoral program in higher and adult education. *International Journal for Academic Development*, Vol. 14, No. 3, pp. 173–183.

Australasian Qualifications Framework Advisory Board (2007). *Australasian Qualifications Framework implementation handbook*. Fourth Edition. Carlton: Impact Printing.

Bailin, S. (1987). Critical and creative thinking. *Informal Logic*, Vol. IX, No. 1, pp.23–30.

Bailin, S.; R. Case; J. R. Coombs & L. B. Daniels (1999). Conceptualizing critical thinking. *Journal of Curriculum Studies*, Vol. 31, No. 3, pp. 285–302.

Bakewell, C. & V. Mitchell (2003). Generation Y female consumer decision-making styles. *International Journal of Retail and Distribution Management*, Vol. 31, No. 2, pp. 95–106.

Ball, C. (1986). *Transferable Personal Skills in Employment: The Contribution of Higher Education*, National Advisory Board for Public Sector Higher Education and University Grants Council, London.

Ballard, B. & J. Clanchy (1997). *Teaching international students: A brief guide for lecturers and supervisors*. Deakin ACT, IDP Education Australia.

Ballet, K. & G. Kelchterman (2008). Workload and Willingness to Change: Disentangling the Experience of Intensification. *Journal of Curriculum Studies*, Vol. 40, No. 1, pp. 47–67.

Baltzer, S. (1988). A validation study of a measure of musical creativity. *Journal of Research in Music Education*, Vol. 36, No. 4, pp. 232–249.

Bargar, R. R. & J. K. Duncan (1982). Cultivating creative endeavour in doctoral research. *Journal of Higher Education*, Vol. 52, No. 1, pp. 1–31.

Barnacle, R. (2005). Research education ontologies: Exploring doctoral becoming. *Higher Education Research and Development*, Vol. 24, No. 2, pp. 179–188.

Barnard-Brak, L. & W. Lan (2009). Epistemological beliefs across faculty experts and student non-experts. *Journal of Further and Higher Education*, Vol. 33, No. 3, pp. 289–306.

Barnett, R (2005). *A Will to Learn: being a student in an age of uncertainty*. Buckingham: Open University Press, McGraw-Hill Education.

Barnett, R. (2000). *Realising the University in an age of supercomplexity*. Buckingham: The Society for Research into Higher Education and Open University Press.

Barnett, R. (2010). Lifewide education: A new and transformative concept for higher education? In Jackson, N. J. and R. K. Law (Eds.), *Enabling A More Complete Education: encouraging, recognizing and valuing lifewide learning in Higher Education*. http://lifewidelearningconference.pbworks.com/E-proceedings [accessed July 15, 2010].

Barron, F. (1988). Putting creativity to work. In R. J. Sternberg (Ed.), *The nature of creativity: contemporary psychological perspectives*. Cambridge: Cambridge University Press.

Barron, F. (1995). *No rootless flower: An ecology of creativity*. Cresskill: Hampton.

Barthes, R. (1981). *Camera Lucida: Reflections on Photography*. New York: Hill and Wang.

Bartlett, M. (2004). Understanding what shapes generation can help the Analyst. *Credit Union Journal*, Vol. 8, No. 2, pp. 14–17.

Beatty, L.; G. Gibbs & A. Morgan (1997). Learning orientations and study contracts. In F. Marton; D. Hounsell & N. Entwistle (Eds.), *The experience of learning: Implications for teaching and studying in higher education*. Edinburgh: Scottish Academic Press.

Beauchamp, C.; M. Jazvac-Martek & L. McAlpine (2009). Studying doctoral education: Using activity theory to shape methodological tools. *Innovations in Education and Teaching International*, Vol. 46, No. 3, pp. 265–279.

Becher, T. (1989). *Academic Tribes and Territories: intellectual inquiry and the culture of disciplines*. Buckingham: Society for Research into Higher Education/Open University Press.

Belluigi, D. Z. (2008a). *Excavating the 'Critique': An investigation into disjunctions between the espoused and the practiced within a Fine Art Studio Practice curriculum*. Masters in Education (Higher Education) thesis, Rhodes University. http://eprints.ru.ac.za/972/01/BelluigiMEd2008.pdf [accessed July 15, 2010].

Belluigi, D. Z. (2008b). Making allowance for doubt: Arguing for validity in evaluation processes. In C. Nygaard & C. Holtham (Eds.), *Understanding Learning-Centred Higher Education*. Frederiksberg: Copenhagen Business School Press.

Belluigi, D. Z. (2008c). Making the Student Feedback Questionnaire a contextual, reflective tool for teacher and student alike. In A. Boddington & D. Clews (Eds.), *ELIA Teachers' Academy Papers*. Nottingham: Nottingham Trent University.

Belluigi, D. Z. (2009). Exploring the discourses around 'creativity' and 'critical thinking' in a South African creative arts curriculum. *Studies in Higher Education*, Vol. 34, No. 6, pp. 699–717.

Benfari, R. C. (1999). *Understanding and changing your management style*. San Francisco, Jossey-Bass.

Bennett, R. (2002). Employers' Demands for Personal Transferable Skills in Graduates: a content analysis of 1000 job advertisements and an associated empirical study. *Journal of Vocational Education and Training*, Vol. 54, No. 4, pp. 457–476.

Bernstein, B. (2000). *Pedagogy, symbolic control and identity*. New York, Rowan & Littlefield.

Best, D. (1991). Creativity: Education in the Spirit of Enquiry. *British Journal of Educational Studies*, Vol. 39, No. 3, Aug., pp. 260–278.

Biggs, J. & C. Tang (2007). *Teaching for Quality Learning at University*. Berkshire: The Society for Research into Higher Education and Open University Press.

Biggs, J. & K. Collis (1982). *Evaluating the Quality of Learning: the SOLO taxonomy*. New York: Academic Press.

Biggs, J. (1994). Asian learners through western eyes: An astigmatic paradox. *Australian and New Zealand Journal of Vocational Education Research*, Vol. 2, No. 2, pp. 40–63.

Biggs, J. (1999a). *Teaching for quality learning at university*. Buckingham: Society for Research in Higher Education & Open University Press.

Biggs, J. (1999b). What the Students Does: teaching for enhanced learning. *Higher Education Research & Development*,Vol. 18 No. 1, pp. 57–75.

Billoni, A. G. (2002). *The art gallery excursion as a bridge to idea generation and a heightened aesthetic experience*. Masters Thesis, International Centre for Studies in Creativity, Buffalo State College, Buffalo, NY. http://www.buffalostate.edu/orgs/cbir/readingroom/theses/Billotgt.pdf [accessed July 15, 2010].

Blackburn, J. (2006). Wit and imagination deliver the biggest shock of all. *The Guardian*. 08 November. http://www.guardian.co.uk/society/2006/nov/08/voluntarysector10 [accessed July 15, 2010].

Blair, B. (2006). *Perception, interpretation, impact; an examination of the learning value of formative feedback to students through the design studio critique*. Unpublished doctoral thesis. London: University of London Institute of Education.

Bleakley, A. (2004). 'Your creativity or mine?': a typology of creativities in higher education and the value of a pluralistic approach. *Teaching in Higher Education*, Vol. 9, No. 4, pp. 463–475.

Boden, M. A. (2000). Computer models of creativity. *The Psychologist*, Vol 13, No 2, pp. 72–6.

Bohm, D. (1996). On dialogue. In L. Nichol (Ed.), *Bohm: On dialogue*, pp. 6–54. London: Routledge.

Bohm, D. (1998). *On creativity*. London: Routledge.

Boud, D. (2006). Foreword. In C. Bryan & K. Clegg (Eds.), *Innovative assessment in higher education*, pp. xvii–xix. Wiltshire: Routledge.

Boughey, C. (2001). Evaluation as a means of assuring quality in teaching and learning: Policing or development? In B. Otaala & F. Opali (Eds.), *Teach your very Best: Selected Proceedings of a Regional Conference for Staff from Tertiary Institutions from SADC Countries*. Windhoek, Namibia.

Boyer, E. L. (1990). *Scholarship reconsidered: priorities of the professoriate*. Princeton, NJ: Carnegie Foundation.

Brenner, M.; J. Brown & D. Canter (Eds.) (1985). *The Research Interview. Uses and Approaches*. London: Academic Press.

Bridges, D. (1993). Transferable Skills: A Philosophical Perspective. *Studies in Higher Education*, Vol. 18, No. 1, pp. 43–51.

Bronowski, J. (1970). The creative process. In J. D. Roslansky (Ed.), *Creativity*, pp. 1–16. Amsterdam: North-Holland.

Brown, K. L. (2003). From teacher-centered to learner-centered curriculum: Improving learning in diverse classroom. *Education*, Vol. 124, No. 1, pp. 49–54.

Bruner, J. S. (1960). *The Process of Education*. Harvard: Harvard University Press.

Bruner, J. S. (1964). The Conditions of Creativity. In H. E. Gruber (Ed.), *Contemporary Approaches to Creativity*. New York: Atherton Press.

Bruner, J. S. (1965). *The Process of Education*. New York: Random House, Inc.

Bruner, J. S. (1986). *Actual Minds, Possible Worlds*. Cambridge, MA: Harvard University Press.

Buehl, M. M. & P. A. Alexander (2005). Motivation and performance differences in students' domain-specific epistemological belief profiles. *American Educational research Journal*, Vol. 42, No. 4, pp. 697–726.

Burgart, H. J. (1961). Art in Higher Education: The Relationship of Art Experience to Personality, General Creativity, and Aesthetic Performance. *Studies in Art Education*, Vol. 2, No. 2, pp. 14–35.

Burningham, C. & M. A. West (1995). Individual, climate, and group interaction processes as predictors of work team innovation. *Small Group Research*, Vol. 26, No. , pp. 106–117.

Busch, P.; K. Venkitachalam & D. Richards (2008). Generational differences in soft knowledge situations: Status, need for recognition, workplace commitment and idealism. *Knowledge and Process Management*, Vol. 1, No. 1, pp. 45–58.

Canfield, T. (1961). Creativity in Music Education. *Music Educators Journal*, Vol. 48, No. 2, pp. 51–56.

Carin, A. A. & R. B. Sund (1985). *Teaching modern science*. Columbus, Ohio: Charles E. Merrill Publishing Co.

Case, J. & R. Gunstone (2003). Going deeper than deep and surface approaches: A study of students' perceptions of time. *Teaching in Higher Education*, Vol. 8, No. 1, pp. 55–69.

Central Advisory Council for Education (England) (1967). *Children and their Primary Schools*. London: Her Majesty's Stationery Office.

Chehore, T. & Z. Scholtz (2008). Exploring a Pedagogy that Supports Problem-Based Learning in Higher Education. In C. Nygaard & C. Holtham (Eds.), *Understanding Learning-Centred Higher Education*, pp.145–160, Frederiksberg: Copenhagen Business School Press.

Chetty, R. (2007). *A paradigm shift in teacher education: Towards normative management principles*. Unpublished MBA thesis. University of Cape Town.

Cheung, H. Y. & A. W. H. Chan (2009). *Education and competitive economy: How do cultural dimensions fit in?* Higher Education online first.

Chin, C. & J. Osborne (2008). Students' questions: a potential resource for teaching and learning science. *Studies in Science Education*, Vol. 44, pp. 1–39.

Choi, H. & L. Thompson (2005). Old wine in a new bottle: Impact of membership change on group creativity. *Organizational Behavior and Human Decision Processes*, No. 98, pp. 121–132.

Clark, C. M.; D. J. Veldman, & J. S. Thorpe (1965). Convergent and Divergent Thinking Abilities of Talented Adolescents. *Journal of Educational Psychology*. Vol. 56, June, pp.157–163.

Claxton, G., Edwards, L. & V. Scale-Constantinou, (2006). Cultivating creative mentalities: a framework for education. *Thinking Skills and Creativity*, Vol. 1, No. 1, pp. 57–61.

Clements, D. H. (1995). Teaching Creativity with Computers. *Educational Psychology Review*, Vol. 7., No. 2., pp. 141–161.

Clews, D. (2003). Imaging in Education: Imaging in preliminary-level studio design technology projects. *Art, Design & Communication in Higher Education*, Vol. 2 No. 1, pp. 7–28.

Cohen, L.; L. Manion & K. Morrison (2003). *Research Methods in Education*. 5th edition. Padstow: Routledge-Falmer.

Conti, R.; H. Coon & T. M. Amabile (1996). Evidence to support the componential model of creativity: Secondary analysis of three studies. *Creativity Research Journal*, Vol. 9, pp. 385–389.

Coppieters, P. (2005). Turning schools into learning organizations, *European Journal of Teacher Education*, Vol. 28, No. 2, pp. 129–139.

Corner, F. (2005). Identifying the core in the subject of Fine Art. *International Journal of Art & Design Education*, Vol. 24, No.3, pp. 334–342.

Court, A. W. (1998). Improving Creativity in Engineering Design Education. *European Journal of Engineering Education*. Vol. 23, No. 2, pp. 141–154.

Covey, S. (2004). *The 8th Habit: from Effectiveness to Greatness*. London and New York: Simon and Schuster.

Covington, M. V. (1967). Teaching for Creativity: Some Implications for Art Education. *Studies in Art Education*, Vol. 9, No. 1, pp. 18–32.

Cowdroy, R. & E. de Graaf. (2005). Assessing highly-creative ability. *Assessment & Evaluation in Higher Education*, Vol. 30, No. 5, pp. 507–518.

Cowdroy, R. (2000). Contract assessment: self-evaluation and empowerment for excellence. In P. Michialino & M. Voyatzaki (Eds.), *Les Cahiers de l'enseignement de l'architecture*. Louvaine-La Neuve: European Association for Architectural Education.

Craft, A. (2003). The Limits to Creativity in Education: Dilemmas for the Educator. *British Journal of Educational Studies*, Vol. 51, No. 2, Jun., pp. 113–127.

Craft, A. (2005). *Creativity in Schools: Tensions and Dilemmas*. London: Routledge.

Craft, A. (2006). Creativity in Schools. In N. Jackson; M. Oliver; M. Shaw & J. Wisdom (Eds.), *Developing creativity in higher education: An imaginative curriculum*, pp. 19–28. Chippenham: Routledge.

Creativity in Education. (2003). *Creativity in Education*. http//www.ltscotland.org.uk/creativity/section2c.asp [accessed July 15, 2010].

Creswell, J. W. (2007). *Qualitative Enquiry & Research Design: Choosing among five approaches*. London: Sage Publications.

Crockenberg, S. B. (1972). Creativity Tests: A Boon or Boondoggle for Education? *Review of Educational Research*, Vol. 42, No. 1, pp. 27–45.

Cropley, D. H. & A. J. Cropley (2000). Fostering Creativity in Engineering Undergraduates. *High Ability Studies*, Vol. 11, No. 2, pp. 207–219.

Crotty, M. (1998). *The Foundations of Social Research: Meaning and Perspective in the Research Process*. London: Sage Publications.

Csikszentmihalyi, M. (1990). The domain of creativity. In M. Runco & R. Albert (Eds.), *Theories of Creativity*, pp. 190–212, Sage Publications.

Csikszentmihalyi, M. (1997). *Creativity. Flow and the Psychology of Discovery and Invention*. New York: Harper Perennial.

Csikszentmihalyi, M. (1999). Implications of s systems perspective for the study of creativity. In R. J. Sternberg (Ed.), *Handbook of Creativity*, pp. 325–339. Cambridge: Cambridge University Press.

Cunningham, S. (2006). What price a creative economy? *Platform Papers: Quarterly Essay on the Performing Arts*, 9, July.

Dall'Alba, G. & R. Barnacle. (2007). An ontological turn for higher education. *Studies in Higher Education*, Vol. 32, No. 6, pp. 679–691.

Dallow, P. (2003). Representing creativeness: practice-based approaches to research in creative arts. *Art, Design and Communication in Higher Education*, Vol. 2, pp. 49–66.

Dalton, J. (1995). *Adventures in thinking*. South Melbourne, Nelson.

Darsø, L. (2001). *Innovation in the making*. Gylling: Samfundslitteratur.

Darsø, L. (2008). Leadership through artful learning design. Paper presented at the 4th *Art of Management and Organisation Conference*, The Banff Centre, Canada September 9–12, 2008.

Davis, G. A. (1967). Teaching Creativity. *The Clearing House*, Vol. 42, No. 3, pp. 162–166.

Davis, G. A. (1992). *Creativity is forever*. Dubuque: Kendall/Hunt.

de Bono, E. (1967). *The Five Day Course in Thinking*. New York: Basic Books.

de Bono, E. (1977). *The mechanism of mind*. Aylesbury: Penguin Books.

Deleuze, G. & F. Guattari (1991). *What is philosophy?* London: Verso.

Deleuze, G. (1995). *Negotiations, 1972–1990*. New York: Columbia University Press.

Department for Education and Employment (1999). *All Our Futures: Creativity, Culture & Education*. Sudbury: Department for Education and Employment Publications.

Derell, G. R. (1963). Creativity in Education. *The Clearing House*, Vol. 38, No. 2, pp. 67–69.

Dewett, T.; S. J. Shin; S. M. Toh & M. Semadeni (2005). Doctoral student research as a creative endeavour. *College Quarterly*, Vol. 8, No. 1, pp. 1–20.

Dewey, J. (1933). *How we think: a restatement of the relation of reflective thinking to the educative process*. Boston: D.C. Heath.

Dewey, J. (1938). *Experience and education*. USA: Kappa Delta Pi.

Dewulf, S. & C. Baillie (1999). *CASE Creativity in Art, Science and Engineering: how to foster creativity*. Department for Education and Employment.

Diakidoy, I. N. & E. Kanari (1999). Student teachers' beliefs about creativity. *British Educational Research Journal*, Vol. 25, pp. 225–243.

Dillon, J. T. (1988). The remedial status of student questioning. *Journal of Curriculum Studies*, Vol. 20, pp. 197–210.

Dineen, R. (2006). Views from the chalk face: Lecturers' and students' perspectives on the development of creativity in art and design. In Jackson, N., M. Oliver, M. Shaw & J. Wisdom (Eds.), *Developing Creativity in Higher Education: An imaginative curriculum*. pp. 109–117. London: Routledge.

Dineen, R.; E. Samuel & K. Livesey (2005). The promotion of creativity in learners: theory and practice. *Art, Design & Communication in Higher Education*, Vol. 4, No. 3, pp. 155–172.

Doll, W. E. (2001). Prigogine: A new sense of order, a new curriculum. *Theory Into Practice*, Vol. 25, No. 1, pp. 10–16.

Donelly, R. (2004). Fostering of creativity within an imaginative curriculum in higher education. *The Curriculum Journal*, Vol. 15, No. 2, pp. 155–166.

DTI (2005). *Creativity, Design and Business Performance*. UK Department of Trade & Industry TI Economics Paper No.15, November.

Eckel, P. D. (2007). Redefining Competition Constructively: The Challenges of Privatisation, Competition and Market-based State Policy in the United States. *Higher Education Management and Policy*, Vol. 19, pp. 66–83.

Edwards, M.; C. McGoldrick & M. Oliver (2006). Creativity and curricula in higher education: academics' perspectives. In Jackson, N., M. Oliver, M. Shaw & J. Wisdom (Eds.), *Developing creativity in higher education: An imaginative curriculum*, pp. 59–73, Routledge.

Eisner, E. W. (1993). Forms of understanding and the future of educational research. *Educational Researcher*, Vol. 22, No. 7, pp. 5–11.

Eraut, M. (2009). How Professionals Learn through Work. In N. Jackson (Ed.), *Learning to be Professional through a Higher Education*. http://learningtobeprofessional.pbworks.com/How-professionals-learn-through-work [accessed July 15, 2010].

EUA (2007). *Creativity in Higher Education – report on the EUA creativity project 2006–2007*. Brussels: European University Association.

Evans, P. & G. Deehan (1988). *The keys to creativity*. London: Grafton.

Evered, R. & R. L. Meryl, (1981). Alternative Perspectives in the Organizational Sciences: Inquiry from the Inside and Inquiry from the Outside. *Academy of Management Review*; 1981 Vol. 6 Issue 3, p385–395.

Facione, P. A. (1990). *Critical Thinking: A Statement of Expert Consensus for Purposes of Educational Assessment and Instruction. Executive Summary "The Delphi Report"*. California: California Academic Press.

Feist, G. J. (1999). The influence of personality on artistic and scientific creativity. In R. J. Sternberg (Ed.), *Handbook of creativity*, Cambridge, Cambridge University Press.

Feldhusen, J. & B. E. Goh (1995). Assessing and accessing creativity: an integrative review of theory, research, and development. *Creativity Research Journal*, Vol. 8, No. 3, pp. 231–247.

Feldman, D. H. (1994). *Beyond universals in cognitive development*. Second edition. Norwood: Ablex.

Feyerabend, P. (1975). *Against method: Outline of anarchistic theory of knowledge*. New York: Humanities Press.

Flick, U (2006). *An introduction to qualitative research*. London: Sage.

Florida, R. (2005). *Cities and the Creative Class*. Routledge, London.

Force, J. (2000). Creative Questioning: the art of asking dumb questions. *Leadership Compass*, Winter/Spring, pp. 28–29.

Ford, C. M. (1996). A theory of individual creative action in multiple social domains. *Academy of Management Review*, 21(4), pp. 1112–1142.

Forman, J. & L. Markus (2005). Research on Collaboration, Business Communication and Technology: Reflections On An Interdisciplinary Academic Collaboration. *Journal of Business Communication*, Volume 42, Number 1, January 2005, 78–102.

Foucault, M. (1972). *The order of things: An archaeology of the human sciences*. Translated by A. Sheridan-Smith. London: Tavistock.

Freeman, J. (2006). First insights: Fostering creativity in university performance. *Arts and Humanities in Higher Education*, Vol. 5, No. 1, pp. 91–103.

Freire, P. (1971). *Pedagogy of the oppressed*. New York, Continuum.

Frick, L. (2009). Improving students' learning outcomes: What about doctoral learning outcomes? In C. Nygaard; C. Holtham & N. Courtney (Eds.), *Improving students' learning outcomes*, Frederiksberg: Copenhagen Business School Press.

Frick, L. (2010). The Mystery of the Original Contribution:Solving the Creativity Conundrum in Doctoral Education. *International Doctoral Education Research Network Seminar Series*, 21–23 April, University of Putra Malaysia, Kuala Lumpur, Malaysia.

Fritz, R. (1993). *Creating: A practical guide to the creative process and how to use it to create anything – a work of art, a relationship, a career or a better life*. Ballantine Books.

Fryer, M. (2006). Facilitating creativity in higher education: A brief account of National Teaching Fellows' views. In N. Jackson; M. Oliver; M. Shaw & J. Wisdom (Eds.), *Developing creativity in higher education: An imaginative curriculum*. London: Routledge.

Fryer, M. (2006). Making a difference: a tribute to E. Paul Torrance from the United Kingdom. *Creativity Research Journal*, Vol. 18, No. 1, pp. 121–128.

Gardner, H. (1984). *Art, mind, and brain: a cognitive approach to creativity*. New York: Basic Books.

Gardner, H. (1988). Creative lives and creative works: a synthetic scientific approach. In R. J. Sternberg (Ed.), *The nature of creativity: Contemporary psychological perspectives*, pp. 298–321, Cambridge University Press.

Gardner, H. (1993). *Creating minds: An anatomy of creativity seen through the lives of Freud, Einstein, Picasso, Stravinsky, Eliot, Graham, and Ghandi*. New York: Basic.

Gengerelli, J. A. (1964). The Education of Future Scientists: Is Technical Expertise Stifling Scientific Creativity? *The Journal of Higher Education*, Vol. 35, No. 2, Feb., pp. 61–70.

Gibbons, M.; C. Limoges; H. Nowotny; S. Schwartzman; P. Scott & M. Trow (1994). *The New Production of Knowledge: The Dynamics of Science and Research in Contemporary Societies*. London: Sage.

Gibbons, M.;. C. Limoges; H. Nowotny; S. Schwartzman; P. Scott & M. Trow

(1994). *The New Production of Knowledge: The Dynamics of Science and Research in Contemporary Societies*. London: Sage.

Gibson, H. (2005). What Creativity Isn't: The Presumptions of Instrumental and Individual Justifications for Creativity in Education. *British Journal of Educational Studies*, Vol. 53, No. 2, Jun., pp. 148–167.

Gillham, B. (2000). *Case study research methods*. London: Continuum.

Gilstrap, D. L. (2007). Dissipative structures in educational change: Prigogine and the academy. *International Journal of Leadership in Education*, Vol. 10, No. 1, pp. 49–69.

Gino, F.; L. Argote; E. Miron-Spektor; G. Todorova (2010). First, get your feet wet: The effects of learning from direct and indirect experience on team creativity. *Organizational Behavior and Human Decision Processes*, Vol. 111, Iss. 2, pp. 102–115.

Goodson, I. (2005). *Learning, Curriculum and Life Politics. The selected works of Ivor. F Goodson*. London: Routledge.

Gordon, J. (2004). The 'wow' factors: the assessment of practical media and creative arts subjects. *Art, Design and Communication in Higher Education*, Vol. 3, No. 1, pp. 61–72.

Gow, G. (2000). Understanding and teaching creativity. *Tech Directions*, January, pp. 32–34.

Graesser, A. C. & B. A. Olde (2003). How Does One Know Whether a Person Understands a Device? The Quality of the Questions the Person Asks When the Device Breaks Down. *Journal of Educational Psychology*, Vol. 95, No. 3, pp. 524–536.

Granovetter, M. S. (1973). The Strength of Weak Ties. *American Journal of Sociology*; Vol. 78, No. 6, pp. 1360–1380.

Gray, J. (1960). Music Education and Creativity. *Music Educators Journal*, Vol. 46, No. 4 Feb–Mar, pp. 58+62.

Greene, T. R. (2004). *32 capabilities of highly effective people in any field*. http://www.scribd.com/doc/2162334/32-Capabilities-of-Highly-Effective-Persons [accessed July 15, 2010].

Griffin, M. D.; B. A. P. Jones & M. S. Spann (2008). Knowledge vs. Certification: Which is the premier emphasis for Gen Y business students? *International Journal of Business Research*, Vol. 8, No. 4, pp. 61–69.

Gross, M. U.; B. MacLeod; D. Drummond & C. Merrick (2001). *Gifted students in primary schools – differentiating the curriculum*. Sydney: Gifted Education Research, Resource and Information Centre, The University of NSW.

Gruber, H. E. & D. B. Wallace (1999). The case study method and evolving systems approach for understanding creative people at work. In R. J. Sternberg (Ed.), (1999). *The Handbook of Creativity*. pp. 93–115. Cambridge: Cambridge University Press.

Hall, E. T. & M. R. Hall (1990). *Understanding cultural differences*. Yarmouth, MA, Intercultural Press.

Hammersley, M. (1999). Report – Interactive Social Science: A conference on the production and consumption of social science research. *Research Intelligence*, No 68 April 1999.

Hampden-Turner, C. (1994). Getting wiser about the Asians. *Director*, Vol. 47, No. 11, pp. 44–47.

Hancock, D. R.; M. Bray & S. A. Nason (2002). Influencing university students' achievement and motivation in a technology course. *Journal of Educational Research*, Vol. 95, No. 6, pp. 365–372.

Hardy, T. (2003). The trouble with Ruskin… *International Journal of Art & Design Education*, Vol. 22, No. 3, pp. 335–341.

Harrison, M. E. & W. B. Whalley (2006). *Combining student independent learning and peer advice to improve the quality of undergraduate dissertations*. http://www.gees.ac.uk/planet/p16/mh.pdf [accessed July 15, 2010].

Harvey L. & P. T. Knight (1996). *Transforming Higher Education*. Buckingham: Open University Press.

Hassall, T. & J. Joyce (2001). Approaches to learning of management accounting students. *Education and Training*, Vol. 43, No. 3, pp. 145–153.

Heaney, J. (2007). Generations X and Y's internet banking usage in Australia. *Journal of Financial Services Marketing*, Vol. 11, No. 3, pp. 196–210.

Helgøy, I. & A. Homme, A. (2006). Policy Tools and Institutional Change: Comparing education policies in Norway, Sweden and England. *Journal of Public Policy*, Vol. 26, No. 2, pp. 141–165.

Hennesey, B. A. & T. M. Amabile (1988). The conditions of creativity. In R. J. Sternberg (Ed.), *The nature of creativity*, pp. 11–4, Cambridge: Cambridge University Press.

Higher Education Academy (2009). *Personal Development Planning*. http://www.heacademy.ac.uk/ourwork/learning/pdp [accessed July 15, 2010].

HM Treasury (2005). *Cox Review of Creativity in Business: building on the UK's strengths*. London: HM Treasury.

Hofstede, G. & G. J. Hofstede (2005). *Cultures and organizations software of the mind: Intercultural cooperation and its importance for survival*. Sydney: McGraw-Hill.

Hofstede, G. (1980). *Culture's consequences: International differences in work-related values*. London: Sage Publications.

Hofstede, G. (1991). *Cultures and organisations: Software of the mind*. New York: McGraw-Hill.

Hofstede, G. (2001). *Culture's consequences: Comparing values, behaviours, institutions, and organisations across nations*. London: Sage Publications.

Holtham, C.; C. Harrington; A. Owens & N. Duncan (2006). Extreme Collaboration: Working across Wide Disciplinary Divides in University Teaching and

Learning. In proceedings of the *International Society of the Scholarship of Teaching and Learning* (ISSOTL), Washington DC, 9th–12th November.

Honey, P. & A. Mumford (1992). *The manual of learning styles.* Berkshire: Peter Honey.

Honey, P. & A. Mumford (1995). *Using your learning styles.* Berkshire: Peter Honey.

House, R. J. & M. Javidan (2004). Overview of GLOBE. Culture, leadership, and organisations. In R. J. House; P. J. Hanges; M. Javidan; P. Dorfman & V. Gupta (Eds.), *The GLOBE study of 62 societies.* pp. 9–28, London: Sage Publications.

Hughes, A. (1999). Art and intention in schools: Towards a new paradigm. *Journal of Art & Design Education, Vol.* 18, No. 1, pp. 129–134.

Hyyppä, H. (2009). Kytkeytymisen ihme. Uni ja muuttuva yhteisöajattelu. In T. Heikkilä; H. Hyyppä H. & R. Puutio (Eds.), *Yhteisön lumo. Systeemisiä kytkeytymisiä,* pp. 31–49. Oulu: Metanoia instituutti.

Isaksen, S. G.; K. B. Dorval, & D. J. Treffinger (1994). *Creative approaches to problem solving.* Dubuque, IA: Kendall-Hunt.

Jackson, N. J. & M. Shaw (2006). Developing subject perspectives on creativity in Higher Education. In Jackson, N., M. Oliver, M. Shaw & J. Wisdom (Eds.), *Developing Creativity in Higher Education: An imaginative curriculum,* pp. 89–108. Abingdon: Routledge.

Jackson, N. J. (2002). *A guide for busy academics: Nurturing creativity.* York, UK: LTSN Generic Centre.

Jackson, N. J. (2004). *Creativity: Can it be Taught and Caught?* http://learning.londonmet.ac.uk/TLTC/learnhigher/Resources/resources/Creativity/Staff/Creativity+can+it+be+taught+and+caught.doc [accessed July 15, 2010].

Jackson, N. J. (2005). *Assessing Students' Creativity: Synthesis of Higher Education Teachers' Views.* www.heacademy.ac.uk/2841.htm [accessed July 15, 2010].

Jackson, N. J. (2006). Imagining a different world. In Jackson, N., M. Oliver, M. Shaw & J. Wisdom (Eds.), *Developing creativity in higher education: An imaginative curriculum,* pp. 1–9. Chippenham: Routledge.

Jackson, N. J. (2008). Tackling the wicked problem of creativity in higher education. Background paper for a presentation at the ARC Centre for the *Creative Industries and Innovation, International Conference* Brisbane June 2008 Creating Value: Between Commerce and Commons Available on-line http://imaginativecurriculumnetwork.pbworks.com.

Jackson, N. J. (2010). Developing Creativity through Lifewide Education. http://imaginativecurriculumnetwork.pbworks.com/ [accessed July 15, 2010].

Jackson, N. J.; M. Oliver; M. Shaw & J. Wisdom (Eds.) (2006). *Developing creativity in higher education: An imaginative curriculum.* Chippenham: Routledge.

Jaques, D. (1984). *Learning in Groups.* London: Kogan Page.

Jasvac-Martek, M. (2009). Oscilating role identities: The academic experiences of education doctoral students. *Innovations in Education and Teaching International,* Vol. 46, No. 3, pp. 253–264.

Jeffrey, P. (2003). Smoothing the Waters: Observations on the Process of Cross-Disciplinary Research Collaboration. *Social Studies of Science* (Sage); August 2003, Vol. 33 Issue 4, pp539–563.

Johnson-Laird, P. N. (1988). Freedom and constraint in creativity. In R. J. Sternberg (Ed.), *The nature of creativity*. pp. 202–219. Cambridge: Cambridge University Press.

Joio, N. D.; M. Mailman; H. Halgedahl; G. Fletcher; G. Beglarian & L. G. Wersen (1968). The Contemporary Music Project for Creativity in Music Education. *Music Educators Journal*, Vol. 54, No. 7, pp. 41–72.

Jones, T. P. (1972). *Creative learning in perspective*. London: University of London Press.

Juwah, C.; D. Macfarlane-Dick; B. Matthew; D. Nicol; D. Ross & B, Smith. (2004). *Enhancing Student Learning through Effective Formative Feedback*. The Higher Education Academy Generic Centre, UK: http://www.ltsn.ac.uk/genericcentre/senlef [accessed July 15, 2010].

Kanfer, R & E. H. Kanfer (1991). Goals and self-regulation: applications of theory to work settings. In M. L. Maehr & P. R. Pintrich (Eds.), *Advances in Motivation and Achievement, Vol. 7*. pp. 287–326. Greenwich, CT: JAI Press.

Kao, J. (1996). *Jamming: The Art and Discipline of Business Creativity*. HarperCollins.

Kaufman, J. C. & R. J. Sternberg (2007). Creativity. *Change: The Magazine of Higher Learning*, Vol. 39, No. 4, pp. 55–60.

Kaufman, J.; J. Lee; J. Baer & S. Lee (2007). Captions, consistency, creativity, and the consensual assessment technique: new evidence of reliability. *Thinking Skills and Creativity*, Vol. 2, No. 2, pp. 96–106.

Kiley, M. (2009). Identifying threshold concepts and proposing strategies to support doctoral candidates. *Innovations in Education and Teaching International*, Vol. 46, No. 3, pp. 293–304.

Kilgore, D. (2001). Critical and postmodern perspectives on adult learning. *New Directions for Adult and Continuing Education*, Vol. 89, pp. 53–61.

Kirton, M. J. (1989). A theory of cognitive style. In M. J. Kirton (Ed.). *Adaptors and innovators. Styles of creativity and problem-solving*. pp. 1–36. London: Routledge.

Kleiman, P. (2008). Towards transformation: conceptions of creativity in higher education. *Innovations in Education and Teaching International*. Vol. 45, No. 3, pp. 209–217.

Knight, P. T. (2001). *A briefing on key concepts – formative and summative, criterion & normreferenced assessment*. Learning and Teaching Support Network Generic Centre: 30.

Knight, P. T. (2002a). *Notes on a creative curriculum*. Learning and Teaching Support Network Generic Centre. http://www.palantine.ac.za/files/1039.pdf

Knight, P. T. (2002b). The idea of a creative curriculum. *Imaginative Curriculum Network*, http://www.palatine.ac.uk/files [Retrieved 4/02/2010]

Knight, P. T. (2005). Grading, classifying and future learning. In D. Boud & N. Falchikov (Eds.) (2006). *Rethinking Assessment for Future Learning*. Maidenhead: The Society for Research in Higher Education and the Open University Press.

Knowles, M. S.; E. Holton & R. A. Swanson (1998). *The adult learner: The definitive classic in adult education and human resource development*. Houston, TX: Gulf Pub. Co.

Koestler, A. (1964). *The Act of Creation*. New York: Macmillan.

Koestler, A. (1981). *The four stages of creativity*. Kaleidoscope, London: Hutchinson.

Kolb, A. Y. & D. A. Kolb (2005). Learning styles and learning spaces: Enhancing experiential learning in higher education. *Academy of Management Learning and Education*, Vol. 4, No. 2, pp. 193–212.

Kolb, D. A. (1976). *The learning styles inventory*. Boston: McBer and Co.

Kolb, D. A.; R. E. Boyatzis & C. Mainemelis (2002). Experiential learning theory: Previous research and new directions. In R. J. Sternberg & L. F. Zhang (Eds.), *Perspectives on cognitive, learning, and thinking styles*. Mahwah, NJ: Lawrence Erlbaum.

Kraiger, K. (2008). Transforming our models of learning and development: Web-based instruction as enabler of third-generation instruction. *Industrial and Organisational Psychology*, Vol. 1, No. 4, pp. 454–467.

Kristensen, P. H. & J. Zeitlin (2001). The Making of a Global Firm: Local Pathways to Multinational Enterprise. In G. Morgan; P. H. Kristensen & R. D. Whitley (Eds.), *The Multinational Firm. Organizing Across Institutional and National Divides*. pp. 172–195. Oxford: Oxford University Press.

Kristensen, P. H. (1997). National Systems of Governance and Managerial Prerogatives in the Evolution of Work Systems. England, Germany, and Denmark compared. In R. Whitley & P. H. Kristensen (Eds.), *Governance at Work. The Social Regulation of Economic Relations*. pp. 3–46. Oxford: Oxford University Press.

Kuhn, T. (1962). *The structure of scientific revolutions*. Chicago: Chicago University Press.

LAICS, (2010). *Learning approach*. http://www.laics.net/LLD_everest/Publications/LAICS/20050906151900/CurrentVersion/LAICS%20Learning%20Approaches%20WEB.pdf [accessed July 15, 2010].

Lane, Christel (1997). The Governance of Interfirm Relations in Britain and Germany. Societal or Dominance Effects? In R. Whitley & P. H. Kristensen (Eds.), *Governance at Work. The Social Regulation of Economic Relations*. pp. 62–85. Oxford: Oxford University Press.

Lange, S. & A. Golding (2007). The Interactive Photograph: Photography's role in the acquisition of creative skills. *International Journal of Art and Society*, Vol. 1, No. 4, pp. 133–140.

Lange, S. (2010). *Learning through Photography: Creativity as concept and process*.

Unpublished doctoral thesis London: University of London Institute of Education.

Lather, P. (1998). Critical pedagogy and its complicities: a praxis of stuck places. *Educational Theory*, Vol. 48, No. 4, pp. 487–498.

Laurell, A. C. & O. L. Arellano (1996). Market commodities and poor relief: The World Bank proposal for health. *International Journal of Health Services*, Vol. 26, No. 1, pp. 1–18.

Law No. 115/97. D.R. No. 109, I Series A of 19.9.97. Framework Law on the Education System. Assembly of the Portuguese Republic.

Law no. 46/86. D.R. No. 237, I Series of 14.10.86. Framework Law on the Education System. Assembly of the Portuguese Republic.

Law no. 49/2005. D.R. No. 166, I Series A of 30.8.05. Second amendment to the Basic Education System Act and first amendment to the Basic Higher Education Financing Act. Assembly of the Portuguese Republic.

Leadbeater, C. (2007). We Think: why mass creativity is the next big thing. http://www.wethinkthebook.net/cms/site/docs/charles%20full%20draft.pdf [accessed July 15, 2010].

Leavitt, H. J. (1962). Unhuman organizations. *Harvard Business Review*, pp. 90–98.

Lehman, R. A. (1972). The effects of creativity and intelligence on pupils' questions in science. *Science Education*, Vol. 56, No. 1, pp. 103–121.

Lewis, A. & D. Smith (1993). Defining Higher Order Thinking. *Theory into Practice*, Vol. 32, No. 3, pp. 131–137.

Lewis, T. M. (2004). Creativity on the teaching agenda. *European Journal of Engineering Education*, Vol. 29, No. 3, pp. 415–428.

Libby, W. F. (1970). Creativity in science. In J. D. Roslansky (Ed.), *Creativity*, pp. 33–52. Amsterdam: North-Holland.

Lilja, K. (1997). Bargaining for the Future. The Changing Habitus of the Shop Steward System in the Pulp and Paper Mills of Finland. In R. Whitley & P. H. Kristensen (Eds.), *Governance at Work. The Social Regulation of Economic Relations*. pp. 123–136. Oxford: Oxford University Press.

Lin, L. & P. Cranton (2005). From scholarship student to responsible scholar: a transformative process. *Teaching in Higher Education*, Vol. 10, No. 4, pp. 447–459.

Lindström, L. (2006). Creativity: What is it? Can you assess it? Can it be taught? *JADE*, Vol. 25, No.1, pp. 53–66.

Livingston, L. (2010). Teaching Creativity in Higher Education. *Arts Education Policy Review*, No. 111, pp. 59–62.

Lizzio, A. & K. Wilson (2004). Action learning in higher education: An investigation of its potential to develop professional capability. *Studies in Higher Education*, Vol. 29, No. 4, pp. 469–488.

London Metropolitan University (2010). *Graduate attributes*. https://intranet.

londonmet.ac.uk/prog-plan/higher-line/graduate-attributes.cfm [accessed July 15, 2010].

Louis, M. & J. Bartunek (1992). Insider/Outsider Research Teams: Collaboration Across Diverse Perspectives. *Journal of Management Inquiry*, Vol. 1 Iss. 2, pp. 101–110.

Lovitts, B. E. (2005). Being a good course-taker is not enough: A theoretical perspective on the transition to independent research. *Studies in Higher Education*, Vol. 30, No. 2, pp. 137–154.

Lovitts, B. E. (2007). *Making the implicit explicit*. Stirling: Stylus.

Lubart, T. I. (1994). Creativity. In R. J. Sternberg (Ed.), *Thinking and problem solving*. pp. 290–332. USA: Academic Press.

Lubit, R. (2004). The tyranny of toxic managers: Applying emotional intelligence to deal with difficult personalities. *Ivey Business Journal*, March/April 2004, pp. 1–8.

Luckett, K. & L. Sutherland. (2000). Assessment practices that improve teaching and learning. In S. Makoni (Ed.), *Teaching and learning in higher education: A handbook for South Africa*. Johannesburg: Witwatersrand University press.

MacKinnon, D. (1970). Creativity: A multi-faceted phenomenon. In J. D. Roslansky (Ed.), *Creativity*, pp. 17–32, Amsterdam: North-Holland.

MacRury, I. (2007). Institutional creativity and pathologies of potential space: The modern university. *Psychodynamic Practice*, Vol. 13, No. 2, pp. 119–140.

Manathunga, C.; P. Lant & G. Mellick (2006). Imagining an interdisciplinary doctoral pedagogy. *Teaching in Higher Education*, Vol. 11, No. 3, pp. 365–379.

Mann, S. (2001). Alternative Perspectives on the Student Experience: alienation and Engagement, *Studies in Higher Education*, Vol. 26 No. 1, pp. 8–19.

Marton, F. & R. Säljö. (1984). Approaches to learning. In F. Martin; D. Hounsell & N. Entwistle. (Eds.), (1997). *The Experience of Learning*. Edinburgh: Scottish Academic Press.

Maslow, A. H. (1959). Creativity in self-actualising people. In H. H. Anderson (Ed.), *Creativity and its cultivation*. East Lansig: Harper.

Massey, A. (2006). Developing creativity for the world of work: a case study. *Art, Design & Communication in Higher Education*, Vol. 4, No.1, pp. 17–30.

Matare, J. (2009). Creativity or musical intelligence? A comparative study of improvisation/ improvisation performance by European and African musicians. *Thinking Skills and Creativity*, Vol. 4, pp. 194–203.

Max-Neef, M. A. (2005). Foundations of trandisciplinarity. *Ecological Economics*, Vol. 53, pp. 5–16.

Maxwell, J. (1996). *Qualitative research design: An interactive approach*. Thousand Oaks: Sage.

Mayer, R. E. (1999). Fifty years of creativity research. In: R.J. Sternberg (Ed.), *Handbook of creativity*. Cambridge: Cambridge University Press.

McPherson, J. H. (1964). Environment and training for creativity. In C. W. Taylor

(Ed.), *Creativity: Power and potential*, pp. 130–153, New York: McGraw-Hill.

McWilliam, E. & S. Dawson (2008). Teaching for creativity: towards sustainable and replicable pedagogical practice. *High Education*, Vol. 56, pp. 633–643.

McWilliam, E.; G. Hearn & B. Haseman, (2008). Transdisciplinarity for creative futures: what barriers and opportunities? *Innovations in Education and Teaching International*. Vol. 45, No. 3, pp. 247–253.

Mednick, S. A. (1962). The Associative Basis of the Creative Process. *Psychological Review*. Vol. 69, No. 3, pp. 220–232.

Meier, F. & C. Nygaard (2008). Problem Oriented Project Work in Higher Education. In C. Nygaard & C. Holtham (Eds.), *Understanding Learning-Centred Higher Education*, pp.131–144, Frederiksberg: Copenhagen Business School Press.

Meistre, B. & J. Knoetze (2005). malaise: a projective (non-test) for the *International Society for Theoretical Psychology Conference*, UCT Business School, Cape Town, South Africa 20–24 June 2005.

Meistre, B. (2005). malaise (solo exhibition) for the *International Society for Theoretical Psychology Conference*, UCT Business School, Cape Town, South Africa. 20–24 June 2005.

Meistre, B. (2009). malaise (solo exhibition). *Albany History Museum, Grahamstown*, South Africa. 18 March–9 April 2009.

Melby, E. O. (1952). Education, Freedom and Creativity. *Music Educators Journal*, Vol. 38, No. 6, pp. 14–17.

Mennin, S. (2010). Self-organisation, integration and curriculum in the complex world of medical education. *Medical Education*, Vol. 44, No. 1, pp. 20–30.

Merton, R.; G. Reader & P. Kendall (1957). *The student physician*. Cambridge: Harvard University Press.

Metzner, S. & V. F. Sharp (1973). Education in China and the Death of Creativity. *The Phi Delta Kappan*, Vol. 55, No. 4, pp. 265–266.

Meyer, J. H. F. & R. Land (2005). Threshold concepts and troublesome knowledge (2): Epistemological considerations and a conceptual framework for teaching and learning. *Higher Education*, Vol. 49, No. 3, pp. 373–388.

Meyer, J. H. F. & R. Land (2006). *Overcoming Barriers to Student Understanding: Threshold concepts and troublesome knowledge*. Abingdon: Routledge.

Mezirow, J. (1991). *Transformative Dimensions of Adult Learning*. San Francisco: Jossey-Bass.

Miller, B. C., & D. Gerard (1979). Family Influences on the Development of Creativity in Children: An Integrative Review. *The Family Coordinator*, Vol. 28, No. 3, pp. 295–312.

Moger, S. & R. Rickards (2000). Team Development Revisited: preliminary evidence supporting a two-barrier model. *Global Business Review*, Vol. 1, No. 1, pp. 49–65.

Mohrman, S.; S. Cohen & A. Mohrman (1995). *Designing team based organizations: New forum for knowledge work*. San Francisco: Jossey-Bass.

Moon, J. A. (2004). *A Handbook of Reflective and Experiential Learning: Theory and Practice*. New York: Routledge.

Morgan, G. (1997). Financial Security, Welfare Regimes, and the Governance of Work Systems. In R. Whitley & P. H. Kristensen (Eds.), *Governance at Work. The Social Regulation of Economic Relations*. pp. 104–122. Oxford: Oxford University Press.

Murakumi, T. (2000). *Encouraging the emergent evolution of new industries*. Nomura Research Institute, NRI Paper 1.

Nahavandi, A. (2006). *The art and science of leadership*. Upper Saddle River, NJ: Pearson/Prentice Hall.

New Zealand Qualifications Authority (2001). *National Qualifications Framework*. Wellington: New Zealand Qualifications Authority.

Nickerson, R. S. (1999). Enhancing creativity. In R. J. Sternberg (Ed.), *Handbook of creativity*, pp. 395–430. Cambridge: Cambridge University Press.

Nickerson, R. S.; D. N. Perkins, & E. E. Smith. (1985). *The Teaching of Thinking*. London: Lawrence Erlbaum.

Nikkola, T.; P. Räihä; P. Moilanen; M. Rautiainen & S. Saukkonen (2008). Towards a deeper understanding of learning in teacher education. In C. Nygaard & C. Holtham (Eds.), *Understanding Learning-Centred Higher Education*, pp. 251–263. Frederiksberg: Copenhagen Business School Press.

Nygaard, C. & C. Holtham (Eds.), (2008). *Understanding Learning-Centred Higher Education*. Frederiksberg: Copenhagen Business School Press.

Nygaard, C. & I. Andersen (2005). Contextual Learning in Higher Education. In R. G. Milter; V. S. Perotti & M. S. R. Segers (Eds.), *Educational Innovation in Economics and Business IX. Breaking Boundaries for Global Learning*. Springer Verlag.

Nygaard, C. & P. Bramming (2008). Learning-centred public management education. *International Journal of Public Sector Management*, Vol. 21, No. 4, pp. 400–417.

Nygaard, C.; C. Holtham & N. Courtney (Eds.) (2009). *Improving Students' Learning Outcomes*. Frederiksberg: Copenhagen Business School Press.

Nygaard, C.; T. Højlt & M. Hermansen (2008). Learning-based Curriculum Development. *Higher Education*, Vol. 55, No. 1, pp. 33–50.

Oldham, G. R. & A. Cummings (1996). Employee Creativity: Personal and Contextual Factors at Work. *Academy of Management Journal*, Vol. 39, No. 3, pp. 607–634.

Oliver, M.; B. Shah; C. McGoldrick & M. Edwards (2006). Students' experiences of creativity. In N. Jackson; M. Oliver; M. Shaw & J. Wisdom (Eds.), *Developing creativity in higher education: An imaginative curriculum*, pp. 43–58, London: Routledge.

Osche, R. (1990). *Before the gates of excellence: the determinants of creative genius*. Cambridge: Cambridge University Press.

Parker, I. (1992). *Discourse dynamics: Critical analysis for social and individual psychology*. London: Routledge.

Parker, J. (2003). Reconceptualising the Curriculum: from commodification to transformation. *Teaching in Higher Education*, Vol. 8 No. 4, pp. 529–543.

Parks, G. (1970). Creativity to me. In J. D. Roslansky (Ed.), *Creativity*, pp. 79–90. Amsterdam: North-Holland.

Paul, J. L. & K. Marfu (2001). Preparation of educational researchers in philosophical foundations of inquiry. *Review of Educational Research*, Vol. 71, No. 4, pp. 525–547.

Paulus, P. B. (2000). Groups, teams and creativity: The creative potential of idea generating groups. *Applied Psychology: An International Review*, Vol. 49, pp. 237–262.

Pedrosa de Jesus, M. H.; J. J. C. Teixeira-Dias & M. Watts (2003). Questions of chemistry. *International Journal of Science Education*, Vol. 25, pp. 1015–1034.

Pedrosa de Jesus, M. H.; P. Almeida & M. Watts (2007). Learners' questions meet modes of teaching: a study of cases. *Research Education*, Vol. 78, pp. 1–20.

Perkins, D. N. (1981). *The mind's best work*. Cambridge, MA: Harvard University Press.

Perkins, D. N. (1999). How Cheetah Writes "Hamlet". *Psychological Inquiry*, Vol. 10, No. 4, pp. 348–350.

Perkins, D. N. (1999). The many faces of constructivism, *Educational Leadership*, Vol.57, No. 3, pp. 126–137.

Petocz, P. & A. Reid (2010). On becoming a statistician: a qualitative view. *International Statistical Review*, Vol. 72, No. 2.

Petocz, P.; A. Reid, & P. Taylor (2009). Thinking outside the square: business students' conceptions of creativity. *Creativity Research Journal*, Vol. 21, No. 4, pp. 1–8.

Phillips, V. & C. Bond (2004). Undergraduates' experiences of critical thinking. *Higher Education Research & Development*, Vol. 33, No. 3, pp. 277–294.

Piaget, J. (1956). *The Origins of Intelligence in Children* (M. Cook trans.). New York: International University Press.

Piaget, J. (1971). The theory of stages in cognitive development. In D. Freen; M. Ford & G. Flamer (Eds.), *Measurement and Piaget*. pp. 1–11, New York: McGraw-Hill.

Pink, D. H. (2005). *A Whole New Mind: Moving from the Information Age to the Conceptual Age*. New York: Penguin.

Pink, S. (2007). *Doing Visual Ethnography*. London: Sage.

Pithers, R. T. & R. Soden (2000). Critical thinking in education: a review. *Educational Research*, Vol. 42, No. 3, pp. 237–249.

Pizzini, E. & D. P. Shepardson (1991). Student questioning in the presence of the teacher during problem solving in science. *School and Mathematics*, Vol. 91, pp. 348–352.

Pope, R. (2005). *Creativity: Theory, history, practice*. London: Routledge.

Prigogine, I. & I. Stengers (1990). *Order out of Chaos. Man's New Dialogue with Nature*. London: Flamingo.

Raiker, A. (2009a). Transformational learning and e-portfolios: a pedagogy for improving student experience and achievement. *The International Journal of Learning*, Vol.16, No 8. http://www.Learning-Journal.com, ISSN 1447–9494.

Raiker, A. (2009b). A Personalised Approach to Improving Students' Learning Outcomes. In C. Nygaard, C. Holtham & N. Courtney (Eds.), *Improving Students' Learning Outcomes*. Frederiksberg: Copenhagen Business School Press.

Raleigh, H. P. (1966). Creativity, Intelligence, and Art Education. *Art Education*, Vol. 19, No. 8, pp. 14–17.

Ramamurthy, A. (2000). Constructions of illusion: photography and commodity culture. In L. Wells (Ed.), (2000). *Photography: A Critical Introduction* (second ed., pp. 165–214). London: Routledge.

Ramsden, P. (1992). *Learning to teach in higher education*. London: Routledge.

Raney, K. (1999). Visual literacy in the art curriculum. *International Journal of Art & Design Education*. Vol. 18, No. 1, pp. 41–47.

Reid, A. & I. Solomonides. (2007). Design students' experience of engagement and creativity. *Art, Design & Communication in Higher Education*, Vol. 6, No. 1, pp. 27–39.

Reid, A. & P. Petocz (2003). Completing the circle: researchers of practice in statistics education. *Mathematics Education Research Journal*, Vol. 15, No. 3, pp. 288–300.

Reid, A. & P. Petocz (2004). Learning domains and the process of creativity. *Australian Educational Researcher*, Vol. 31, No. 2, pp. 45–62.

Reid, A. & P. Petocz (2008). A Tertiary Curriculum for Future Professionals. In C. Nygaard & C. Holtham (Eds.), *Understanding Learning-Centred Higher Education*, pp. 31–49. Frederiksberg: Copenhagen Business School Press.

Reid, A.; L. O. Dahlgren; P. Petocz, & M. A. Dahlgren (2008). Identity and engagement for professional formation. *Studies in Higher Education*, Vol. 33, No. 6, pp. 729–742.

Rhodes, M. (1961). *An analysis of creativity. Phi Delta Kappan*, 42, pp 205–210.

Rickett, C. (2010). Co-Curricular and Extra-Curricular Awards: a new phenomenon in Higher Education for recognizing and valuing lifewide learning. InN. J. Jackson & R. K. Law (Eds.), *Enabling a More Complete Education: Encouraging, recognizing and valuing lifewide learning in Higher Education*. http://lifewidelearningconference.pbworks.com/Eproceedings [accessed July 15, 2010].

Rittel, H. & M. Webber (1973). *Dilemmas in a General Theory of Planning*, Policy Sciences 4. Amsterdam: Elsevier Scientific Publishing, pp. 155–159.

Roberts, L. (2003). Creativity. *Tech Directions*, October 2003, p. 12.

Robertson, C. J. & J. J. Hoffman (2000). How different are we? An investigation of

Confucian values in the United States. *Journal of Managerial Issues*, Vol. 12, No. 1, pp. 34–47

Runco, M. A. (2004). Creativity. *Annual Review of Psychology*, Vol. 55, pp. 657–687.

Rusaw, A. C. (2007). Changing Public Organizations: Four Approaches, *International Journal of Public Administration*, Vol. 30, No. 3, pp. 347–361.

Ruscio, J.; D. M. Whitney & T. M. Amabile (1998). The fishbowl of creativity. *Creativity Research Journal*, Vol. 11, pp. 243–263.

Russell, C. L. (1979). Modifying Creative Behaviors. *Art Education*, Vol. 32, No. 6, pp. 20–21.

Russell, C. L. (1981). Mediational Modification of Creative Behaviors. *Studies in Art Education*, Vol. 22, No. 3, pp. 42–48

Sawyer, R. K. & S. DeZutter (2009). Distributed Creativity: How collective creations emerge from collaborations. *Psychology and Aesthetics, Creativity and the Arts*, Vol. 3, No. 2, pp. 81–92.

Sawyer, R. K. (2004). Creative Teaching: collaborative discussion as disciplined improvisation. *Educational Researcher*, Vol. 33, pp. 12–20.

Scharmer, C. & K. Käufer (2000). *Universities as the Birthplace for the Entrepreneuring Human Being*. http://www.ottoscharmer.com/docs/articles/2000_Uni21us.pdf [accessed July 15, 2010].

Scharmer, O. (2007). *Theory U: leading from the future as it emerges. The social technology of presencing*. Cambridge, Massachusetts: SOL.

Schmidt, D. T. (1955). Creativity Is an Attitude: An Approach to Elementary Music Education. *Music Educators Journal*, Vol. 41, No. 3, Jan., pp. 23–25.

Schön, D. A. (1983). *The Reflective Practitioner: how professionals think in action*. New York: Basic Books.

Schön, D. A. (1987). *Educating the Reflective Practitioner*. San Francisco: Jossey-Bass.

Scritchfield, M. (1999). *The creative person, product, process and press: The 4Ps*. Buffalo, NY: International Center for Studies in Creativity. http://www.buffalostate.edu/orgs/cbir/readingroom/html/Scritchfield-99.html [accessed July 15, 2010].

Seel, R. (2006). *Emergence in organisations*. [Retrieved 5/02/2010.] http://www.theoliedmeier.nl/EmergenceinOrganisations

Seltzer, K. & T. Bentley (1999). *The creative age: Knowledge and skills for the new economy*. Buckingham: Demos.

Sfard, A. (2001). There is more to discourse than meets the ears. Learning from mathematical things we have not known before. *Education Studies in Mathematics*. Vol. 46, No. 1, pp. 13–57.

Shackelford, J. (1992). Feminist Pedagogy: A Means for Bringing Critical Thinking and Creativity to the Economics Classroom. *The American Economic Review*, Vol. 82, No. 2, pp. 570–576.

Shuman, R. B., & H. Marriner (1979). Speaking Out: Creativity and Education for the Future. *The Clearing House*, Vol. 52, No. 8, p. 354.

Siegel, S. M. & W. F. Kaemmerer. (1978). Measuring the Perceived Support for Innovation in Organisations. *Journal of Applied Psychology*, Vol. 63, No. 5, pp. 553–562.

Silva, P.; C. Martin & E. Nusbaum (2009). A snapshot of creativity: evaluating a quick and simple method for assessing divergent thinking. *Thinking Skills and Creativity*, Vol. 4, pp. 79–85.

Simonton, D. K. (2000). Creativity: cognitive, personal, developmental, and social aspects. *American Psychologist*, Vol. 55, No. 1, pp.151–158.

Sloane, K. & L. Nathan. (2005). Art transforms education. *Journal of the New England Board of Higher Education*, Vol. 20, No. 1, pp.18–20.

Smith, M. K. (2001). *Evaluation*. INFED (National Grid for Learning): http://www.infed.org/biblio/b-eval.htm. [accessed July 15, 2010].

Smith, N. R. (1980). Development and Creativity in American Art Education: A Critique. *The High School Journal*, Vol. 63, No. 8, pp. 348–352.

Smith-Bingham, R. (2006). Public policy, innovation and the need for creativity. In N. Jackson; M. Oliver; M. Shaw & J. Wisdom (Eds.), *Developing creativity in higher education: An imaginative curriculum*. pp. 10–18. Chippenham: Routledge.

Snyder, E. E. (1961). The Concept of Polarity in Creativity: A Theoretical Orientation Applicable to Education. *Journal of Educational Sociology*, Vol. 35, No. 4, pp. 178–180.

South East England Consortium for Credit Accumulation & Transfer (2003). *Credit Level Descriptors and FE/HE Partnerships* http://www.seec.org.uk/docs/viewpublications.htm [accessed July 15, 2010].

Ståhle, P. & T. Kuosa (2009). Systeemien itseuudistuminen – uutta ymmärrystä kollektiivien kehittymiseen. *Aikuiskasvatus* Vol. 29, No. 2, pp. 104–114.

Stanley, N. (1996). Photography and the Politics of Engagement. *Journal of Art & Design Education*. Vol. 15, No. 1, pp. 95–100.

Stein, M. I. (1984). *Stimulating Creativity, Vol. 1: Individual Procedures*. New York: Academic Press.

Stephani, L.; R. Mason & C. Pegler (2007). *The Educational Potential of e-Portfolios: Supporting personal development and reflective writing*. London: Routledge.

Sternberg, R. J. & E. L. Grigorenko (2008). *Teaching for successful intelligence to increase student learning and achievement*. Thousand Oaks, CA: Corwin Press.

Sternberg, R. J. & T. I. Lubart (1991). Creating creative minds. Phi Delta Kappan, Vol. 71, No. 1, pp. 608–14.

Sternberg, R. J. & T. I. Lubart (1999). The concept of creativity: Prospects and paradigms. In R. J. Sternberg (Ed.), *Handbook of creativity*, pp. 3–15, Cambridge: Cambridge University Press.

Sternberg, R. J. (1985). *Beyond IQ: A triarchic theory of human intelligence*. Cambridge: Cambridge University Press.

Sternberg, R. J. (1988). Wisdom and its relation to intelligence and creativity. In R. J.

Sternberg (Ed.), *Wisdom*, pp. 142–159, Cambridge: Cambridge University Press.

Sternberg, R. J. (1990). *The triarchic mind: A new theory of human intelligence*. New York: Viking.

Sternberg, R. J. (1997). *Thinking styles*. Cambridge: Cambridge University Press.

Sternberg, R. J. (2002). *The creativity conundrum*. London: Psychology Press.

Sternberg, R. J. (2006). The nature of creativity. *Creativity Research Journal*, Vol. 18, No. 1, pp. 87–98.

Sternberg, R. J. (Ed.) (1988). *The Nature of Creativity: Contemporary psychological perspectives*. New York: Cambridge University Press.

Sternberg, R. J.; L. Jarvin & E. L. Grigorenko (2009). *Teaching for wisdom, intelligence, creativity, and success*. Thousand Oaks, CA: Corwin Press.

Sternberg, R. J.; M. Ferrari; P. Clinkenbeard & E. L. Grigorenko (1996). Identification, instruction, and assessment of gifted children: A construct validation of a triarchic model. *Gifted Child Quarterly*, Vol. 40, pp. 129–137.

Stes, A.; D. Gijbels & P. Van Petegem (2008). Student-focused approaches to teaching in relation to context and teacher characteristics. *Higher Education*, Vol. 55, pp. 255–267.

Sullivan, G. (1993). Art-Based Art Education: Learning that is Meaningful, Authentic, Critical and Pluralist. *Studies in Art Education*, Vol. 35, No.1, pp. 5–21.

Swede, G. (1993). *Creativity: A new psychology*. Toronto: Wall & Emerson.

Talbot, P. (1998). In praise of art schools. *Journal of Art & Design Education*, Vol. 17, No. 2, pp. 139–144.

Taylor, C. W. (1988). Various approaches to and definitions of creativity. In R. J. Sternberg (Ed.), *The nature of creativity*. pp. 99–124, Cambridge: Cambridge University Press.

Taylor, M. & C. McCormack (2005). Effective verbal feedback for project-based assessment: a case study of the graphic design critique. Paper presented at the first *International Conference on Enhancing Teaching and Learning through Assessment*, 15th June, 2005, Hong Kong.

Teixeira-Dias, J. J. C.; H. Pedrosa de Jesus; F. Neri de Souza & M. Watts (2005). Teaching for quality learning in chemistry. *International Journal of Science Education*, Vol. 27, pp. 1123–1137.

Ten Dam G. & M. Volman (2004). Critical thinking as a citizenship competence: teaching strategies, *Learning and Instruction*, Vol. 14, pp. 359–379.

The Five Colleges of Ohio (2007). *Creative and Critical Thinking: Assessing the Foundations of a Liberal Arts Education*. The College of Wooster. http://www3.wooster.edu/teagle/default.php [accessed July 15, 2010].

The Quality Assurance Agency for Higher Education (2007). *Subject benchmark statements: academic standards – Biosciences*. http://www.qaa.ac.uk/academicinfrastructure/benchmark/statements/Biosciences07.pdf [accessed July 15, 2010].

Thompson, R. (2009). Creativity, Knowledge and Curriculum in Further Education: A Bernsteinian Perspective. *British Journal of Educational Studies*, Vol. 57, No. 1, pp. 37–54.

Toivola, Y. (1984). Luova toiminta organisaatiossa. In Haavikko & Ruth (Eds.), *Luovuuden ulottuvuudet*, pp. 189–206. Espoo: Weilin+Göös.

Tom, A. (1997). The deliberate relationship: a frame for talking about faculty-student relationships. *Alberta Journal of Educational Research*, Vol. 63, pp. 3–21.

Toohey, S. (1999). *Designing courses for higher education*. Buckingham: SRHE and Open University Press.

Torrance, E. P. (1964). Education and creativity. In C. W. Taylor (Ed.), *Creativity: Power and potential*. pp. 50–128, New York: McGraw-Hill.

Torrance, E. P. (1988). The nature of creativity as manifest in its testing. In R. J. Sternberg (Ed.), *The nature of creativity*. pp. 43–75. Cambridge: Cambridge University Press.

Torrance, E. P. (1993). Understanding and recognizing creativity. In S. G. Isakeson; M. C. Murdoch; R. L. Firestien & D. J. Treffinger (Eds.), *The emergence of a discipline*. Norwood, NJ: Ablex Publishing Corporation.

Tosey, P. (1993). Interfering with the interference. *Management Education and Development*, Vol. 24, No. 3, 187–204.

Tosey, P. (2006). Interfering with the interference: an emergent perspective on creativity in higher education. In N. Jackson; M. Oliver; M. Shaw & J. Wisdom (Eds.), *Developing creativity in higher education: An imaginative curriculum*, pp. 29–42. Chippenham: Routledge.

Trafford, V. & S. Leshem (2009). Doctorateness as a threshold concept. *Innovations in Education and Teaching International*, Vol. 46, No. 3, pp. 305–316.

Trompenaars, F. (1994). *Riding the waves of culture*. New York, Irwin.

Umans, S. (1967). Projects to Create Creativity in Education. *Journal of Reading*, Vol. 10, No. 8, May, pp. 542–545.

United Kingdom Quality Assurance Agency for Higher Education (2008). *The framework for higher education qualifications in England, Wales and Northern Ireland*. Mansfield: Linney Direct.

United States of America Council of Graduate Schools (1995). *Research student and supervisor: An approach to good supervisory practice*. Washington D.C.: Council of Graduate Schools.

University of Queensland (2010). *Statement of graduate attributes*. http://www.uq.edu.au/hupp/?page=25095&pid=25075 [accessed July 15, 2010].

Vermunt, J. D. & N. Verloop (1999). Congruence and friction between learning and teaching. *Learning and Instruction*, Vol. 9, pp. 257–280.

Vygotsky, L. S. (1978). *Mind in Society: The Development of Higher Psychological Processes*. Cambridge MA: Harvard University Press.

Vygotsky, L. S. (1986). *Thought and Language*. Cambridge, MA: Massachusetts Institute of Technology.

Walker, G. E.; C. M. Golde; L. Jones; A. C. Bueschel & P. Hutchings (2008). *The formation of scholars: Rethinking doctoral education for the twenty-first century*. The Carnegie Foundation for the Advancement of Teaching. San Francisco: Jossey-Bass.

Wallas, G. (1926). *The art of thought*. New York: Harcourt Brace.

Way, C. (2006). *Focus on Photography: A Curriculum Guide*. New York: International Center of Photography.

Webster, H. (2005). The architectural review: a study of ritual, acculturation and reproduction in architectural education. *Arts and Humanities in Higher Education*, Vol. 4, No. 3, pp. 265–282.

Wenger, E. (1999). *Communities of Practice: Learning, Meaning, and Identity*. Cambridge: Cambridge University Press.

Wheeler, S.; S. J. Waite & C. Bromfield (2002). Promoting creative thinking through the use of ICT. *Journal of Computer Assisted Learning*, Vol. 18, No. 3, pp. 367–378.

White, J. P. (1968). Creativity and Education: A Philosophical Analysis. *British Journal of Educational Studies*, Vol. 16, No. 2, Jun., pp. 123–137

Whitechapel Gallery (2009). *Goshka Macuga: The Nature of the Beast*. Bloomberg Commission. http://www.whitechapelgallery.org/exhibitions/the-bloomberg-commission-goshka-macuga-the-nature-of-the-beast [accessed July 15, 2010].

Whitley, R. D. (1994). Dominant Forms of Economic Organization in Market Economies. *Organization Studies*, Vol. 15, No.2, pp. 153–182.

Whitley, R. D. (2001). How and Why are International Firms Different? The Consequences of Cross-Border Managerial Coordination for Firm Characteristics and Behaviour. In G. Morgan; P. H. Kristensen & R. Whitley (Eds.): *The Multinational Firm. Organizing Across Institutional and National Divides*. pp. 27–68. Oxford: Oxford University Press.

Winnicott, D. W. (1971). *Playing and Reality*. London: Tavistock.

Wisker, G. & G. Robinson (2009). Encouraging postgraduate students of literature and art to cross conceptual thresholds. *Innovations in Education and Teaching International*, Vol. 46, No. 3, pp. 317–330.

Wnek, M. (2003). Why Barnardo's got it wrong. *The Guardian*, 15 December p. 8.

Wolburg, J. M. & J. Pokrywczynski (2001). A psychographic analysis of Generation Y college students. *Journal of Advertising Research*, Vol. 41, No. 5, pp. 33–53.

Wolf, P. (2003). Interview with Etienne Wenger on Communities of Practice. Communities and Collaboration. http://www.knowledgeboard.com/cgi-bin/item.cgi?id=458 [accessed July 15, 2010].

Wolfe, S. & R. J. Alexander (2008). *Argumentation and Dialogic Teaching: Alternative Pedagogies for a Changing World*. London: Futurelab.

Woodman, R. W.; J. E. Sawyer & R. W. Griffin (1993). Toward a Theory of Organizational Creativity. *The Academy of Management Review*, Vol. 18, No. 2, pp. 293–321.

Wright, J. (2005). The Artist, the Art Teacher, and Misplaced Faith: Creativity and Art Education. *Art Education*, Vol. 43, No. 6, pp. 50–57.

Yamamoto, K. (1975). Creativity and Higher Education: A Review. *Higher Education*, Vol. 4, No. 2, pp. 213–225.

Yang, H. & H. Cheng (2010). Creativity of student information system projects: From the perspective of network embeddedness. *Computers & Education*, Vol. 54, Iss. 1, pp. 209–221.

Yorke, M. (2006). Employability in higher education: What it is, what it is not. In M. Yorke (Ed.), *Learning and employability, Series 1*. New York: Learning and Teaching Support Network.

Yukl, G. (2006). *Leadership in Organizations*. Upper Saddle River, NJ: Prentice Hall.

Zimmerman, B. J. (1989). Models of self-regulated learning and academic achievement: an overview. *Educational Psychologist*, Vol. 25, No. 1, pp. 3–17.

Zoller, U. & D. Pushkin (2007). Matching Higher-Order Cognitive Skills (HOCS) promotion goals with problem-based laboratory practice in a freshman organic chemistry course. *Chemistry Education Research and Practice*, Vol. 8, pp. 153–171.

Zoller, U.; G. Tsaparlis; M. Fatsow & A. Lubezky (1997). Student self-assessment of higher-order cognitive skills in college science teaching. *Journal of College Science Teaching*, Vol. 27, pp. 99–101.